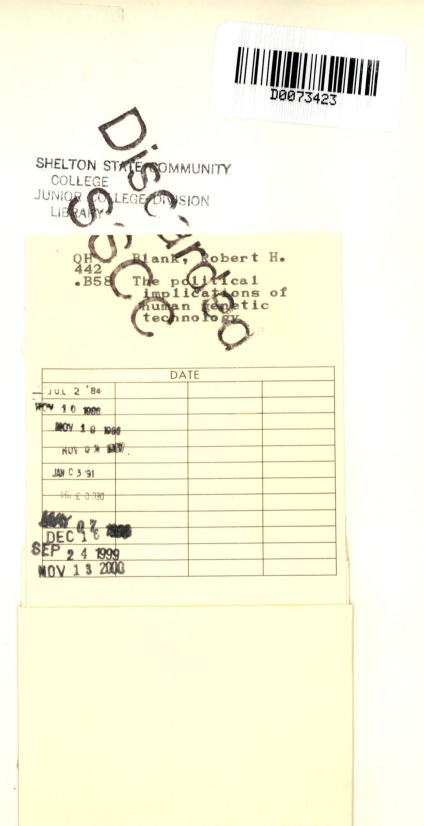

The Political Implications of
Human Genetic Technology

Also of Interest

* Available in hardcover and paperback

Westview Special Studies in Science, Technology, and Public Policy

The Political Implications of Human Genetic Technology
Robert H. Blank

Human genetic technology has advanced rapidly in recent years to the point where amniocentesis is commonplace and in vitro fertilization has been successful. On the horizon looms the specter of human cloning and genetic engineering, raising a storm of new moral and ethical questions.

These questions, asserts the author, are not the only ones to be considered; the impact and role of public policy are equally critical. What part should the state play in human genetic intervention? To what extent does a democratic society have the duty to take steps to reduce genetic disease and improve the quality of life through genetic engineering? If society has such responsibility, at what stage does societal good preempt individual rights? What is society's obligation toward future generations and is genetic manipulation justifiable on these grounds? After surveying the state of the art, the author grapples with these questions, contending that decisions ultimately will not be based on ethical and moral grounds — they will be fought out in the political arena.

Robert H. Blank is professor and chairman of the Department of Political Science at the University of Idaho.

TO JEREMY

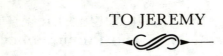

The Political Implications of Human Genetic Technology

Robert H. Blank

Westview Press / Boulder, Colorado

Westview Special Studies in Science, Technology, and Public Policy

Copyright © 1981 by Westview Press, Inc.

Published in 1981 in the United States of America by
  Westview Press, Inc.
  5500 Central Avenue
  Boulder, Colorado 80301
  Frederick A. Praeger, Publisher

Library of Congress Cataloging in Publication Data
Blank, Robert H
  The political implications of human genetic technology.
  (Westview special studies in science, technology, and public policy)
  Bibliography: p.
  Includes index.
  1. Genetic engineering—Government policy. 2. Human genetics—Government policy. I. Title. II. Series.
QH442.B58   362.1'96042   80-25114
ISBN 0-89158-975-9

Printed and bound in the United States of America

Contents

Figures and Tables

Figures

Tables

Preface

The primary goal of this book is to explicate and analyze the political aspects of human genetic technology. Although the complexity of social reality requires consideration of the technical and ethical dimensions as well, the emphasis here is not on discussion of bioethics, nor on private moral decisions, but rather on public policy. What role should a state play in human genetic intervention? To what extent does a democratic society have the duty to take steps necessary to reduce genetic disease and improve the quality of life through genetic intervention? If it has such a responsibility, at what stage does societal good preempt individual rights to procreation, privacy, and self-actualization? What responsibility does society have toward future generations, and is human genetic intervention justifiable on these grounds? These questions obviously have no simple or absolute solutions, but they are questions that must be examined in detail when discussing any attempts to intervene in the genetic composition of the population.

The contention here is that whatever the technical possibilities are, and despite the ethical frameworks available to evaluate these techniques, decisions ultimately will be made in the political arena. Until now the government has avoided these issues. The sensitive nature of genetic intervention and its perceived threat to strongly held values present substantial problems for the political system. This book argues that in the long run it is more reasonable to face up to these problems now than to delay discussion of them. Although the process of bargaining and compromise breaks down on these highly charged issues, and traditional institutions appear to be incapable of handling them, the crucial nature of the issues requires immediate attention.

The focus of this book is on human genetic technology, but the issues raised here are common to all areas of biomedical technology. The possibilities of indefinite artificial maintenance of life, drug therapy, more sophisticated applications of psychosurgery, and organ transplants are but a few related areas of research that, while offering new hope for many, also create difficult ethical dilemmas and force us into serious moral binds.

These areas have in common their promises of more control over our destiny and that of our offspring, but not without costs. The decision to include only genetic technology here, then, was made not because the questions it raises are easily distinguishable, but simply to allow for more adequate and detailed coverage.

It is only within recent decades that we have come to have a basic understanding of the nature and extent of genetically related health problems. Knowledge of many multifactorial diseases such as cystic fibrosis, diabetes, and rheumatoid arthritis remains limited, and the causes of many diseases continue to be unknown; however, understanding of many single-gene and chromosomal disorders and an increasing number of metabolic disorders is advancing rapidly. Along with this understanding have come techniques designed to identify and in several cases treat genetically related disorders. Increasingly accurate and inclusive prenatal testing has been matched by more precise neonatal and adult screening techniques. Many of the techniques for human genetic intervention such as gene therapy and surgery remain only theoretical possibilities, but advances are being made in genetic counseling and screening, prenatal diagnosis, eugenic techniques such as sterilization and artificial insemination, and research on the mutagenic effects of various environmental factors.

Along with these technological advances, value changes have taken place in American society that tend to facilitate the acceptance and application of techniques that until very recently might have been rejected by most people. For example, although it is still highly controversial, abortion of diagnosed defective fetuses appears to be viewed as justified by a substantial majority. In many sectors a more realistic view of genetic disease is held than ever in the past. Guilt might still trouble families with genetically affected offspring, but society as a whole appears to be more understanding. These perceived attitude shifts have reinforced the acceptance of technologies such as amniocentesis and certain screening procedures and have created an atmosphere conducive to genetic counseling services. In spite of the opposition of certain groups, the government and a majority of the citizens appear to accept innovations in these areas.

In the past, genetic disease has been considered a fact of life with little human intervention possible in its reduction, and negative eugenic attempts such as compulsory sterilization, laws against certain types of consanguineous marriages, and premarital blood tests for syphilis have had little overall impact on the population. Today, however, in light of new diagnostic and screening techniques, genetic disorders or even carrier status can be identified with a high degree of accuracy. What in the past was considered unavoidable—children with genetic disabilities—now is avoidable in many instances. The presence and promise of these advances in genetic technology necessitate analysis of the extent to which particular genetic disorders must be considered within a public-health context, i.e., the extent to which reasonable public policies must be deliberated and implemented. This book attempts to support a case for public concern.

Chapter 1 points out the aspects of genetic technology that make it unique and describes the interrelations between the values, structures, and processes of society and the technology itself. Although much emphasis has been placed on the technical, economic, and ethical aspects of such research, only marginal attention has been directed toward the political realm. This chapter summarizes the major ethical orientations utilized in discussions of genetic intervention and emphasizes the need for similar political applications. It concludes by suggesting that despite much opposition to direct genetic intervention in humans by means of gene manipulation, the social and political climate appears to offer a favorable context for programs based on available technology such as genetic screening or prenatal diagnosis. Before widespread application of any technique, however, it must be thoroughly evaluated in terms of its social and political as well as economic and technical impact.

Chapter 2 provides a review of the current state of human genetic technology and describes the features and premises common to the many specific techniques. It also distinguishes between the two major incentives for the application of these techniques: the individually oriented health-care rationale and the population-oriented eugenic rationale. The first emphasizes reduction of the human suffering produced by genetic disease and the second focuses on improvement of the gene pool of the population. The implications of each of these approaches are discussed in relation to the state of the art. The chapter concludes by summarizing the technological dimensions of human genetic intervention and illustrating the scope and nature of the problems raised by them.

Chapter 3 begins by presenting several theoretical frameworks for examining the role of the government in human genetic intervention. It contrasts the assumptions and implications of theories emphasizing individual prerogatives with approaches directed toward some societal good. This chapter also analyzes the concept of rights in a democracy, demonstrating the conflicts among the rights of various individuals as well as the stress between individual rights and the collective good. Finally, the chapter examines political issues raised by genetic intervention relating to individual rights and obligations to protect public health and maintain order.

The issues raised by genetic technology most likely will be intensified in the next decade, and the government will be forced to face these difficult questions, many of which are "no win" from a political standpoint. Chapter 4 summarizes the potential involvement of Congress, the courts, government bureaucracy, and other political institutions in decision making relating to human genetic intervention. It also discusses current public opinion on these issues, the lack of information accessible to the public, and interest-group alignments on genetic issues. Finally, the chapter reviews governmental responses to genetic technology and presents proposed alternative public decision-making mechanisms.

Chapter 5 continues the examination of the political context and focuses on the methods of policymaking commonly applied to problems raised by technology. Specifically, it describes technology-assessment techniques and cost-benefit analysis, applying them to several genetic intervention methods, and demonstrates the limitations of the application of such evaluative techniques to the complex questions raised by human genetic intervention, especially the question of determining nonmonetary costs and benefits and their ultimate distribution to various elements in society. This chapter also discusses the stages of the public-policy process and indicates at which stages immediate concern should be directed.

The final chapter summarizes the problems and concerns raised by human genetic technology and reaffirms the urgent need to assess and analyze the political implications of each potential application. It argues that a democratic society does have a responsibility to reduce genetic disease and educate the public on human genetics. That responsibility, however, must be exercised with full concern for the rights of individuals and a clear understanding of the political, social, and technical ramifications of each innovation prior to its widespread application. At present, there is no need for exaggerated or unrestrained decisions in either direction, but now is the time to conscientiously review the implications of each action or inaction and to establish new public-policy mechanisms that are responsive to the kinds of issues raised by biomedical technology and that result in fair and rational decisions.

Acknowledgments

This project could not have been completed without the support of Thomas Wiegele and the facilities of the Center for Biopolitical Research in DeKalb, Illinois, which Dr. Wiegele graciously made available while I was scholar in residence during 1979-1980. Thanks also go to the University of Idaho for giving me a sabbatical leave in order to complete my research for this book.

Donna Day Baird, Joseph Losco, and April Rubin, M.D., provided crucial insights from the viewpoints of a biologist, a political philosopher, and a clinician, respectively, and each read all or part of the preliminary draft. Joan Flaherty provided an invaluable service by editing the manuscript and giving stylistic advice. Various persons worked on typing the manuscript, but Linda Phipps deserves special thanks for her dedication in typing the final manuscript in record time. Although their contributions strengthened the final product, any remaining errors are solely my responsibility.

Finally, I thank Mallory, who put up with still another major move and resulting family disruptions so that I might complete the project, and Jeremy, Mai-Ling, and Maigin for their patience and cooperation.

1
Genetic Technology and Society

Technology alternately has been praised by those who extol its benefits and condemned by those who view it as a harmful influence on society. Technology, however, does not exist independently; it has always interacted with the social and cultural context within which it functions. The values and institutions of a society in large part define the boundaries of the scope as well as the speed by which technological applications are accepted and used. According to Kieffer (1979: 416), science [1] reflects the "social forces which surround it" and society may well write the rules to be followed in technological pursuits. Although subject to pressure for change by technology, the value system, passed from one generation to the next largely intact, is resistant to major alterations. Established social institutions, too, resist change and attempt to minimize alterations in the status quo. Societal priorities, therefore, always reflect existing social values and structures. Not surprisingly, technologies that challenge the most strongly held values and threaten existing social structures are less likely to be readily accepted.

Just as values shape the development of technology and set limits on it, so each technological application affects society. Technology reinforces and promotes certain values and patterns of social relationships and weakens or undercuts others. Despite the persistence of social values and structures, any innovation leads to some degree of change in life-style, causing priorities to shift and thereby making some values easier to attain and others more difficult. Although these changes are normally subtle and incremental, such as the gradual breakdown of the family in recent decades, the cumulative impact of technology is profound. All aspects of twentieth-century America reflect this pervasive influence of technology on values and institutions. The more salient and intrusive the technology (for instance, the automobile, television, and the contraceptive pill), the greater its potential impact on society.

It is difficult to demonstrate a cause-and-effect relationship between technology and society, however, because the relationship is interactive and dynamic. The question of whether changes in social structures and values follow or precede changes in technology cannot be answered conclusively.

For instance, did birth-control technology produce public attitude changes toward sex and reproduction or, conversely, did changes in the social context produce a change in attitudes that led to acceptance of and therefore encouragement for the development of new methods of birth control? Some observers have opted for the latter explanation. They see social security and the threat of overpopulation as undermining older arguments against limiting family size, an attitude that results in support for more reliable birth-control methods (Department of Health, Education, and Welfare [DHEW], 1978: 5). These observers assert that "innovations in biobehavioral technology represent responses to other, larger social changes in the patterns of social policy, individual behavior, and ethical belief" (DHEW, 1978: 1). There is little doubt that the effects of technology on society are substantial, but there is also much evidence that technology is strongly responsive to societal inputs.

Technology and American Culture

Many observers have noted that American culture is dominated by a technological orientation (Ellul, 1964; Calder, 1970). According to Sinsheimer (1978: 34), we are addicted to technology: "We rely evermore upon it and thus become its servant as well as its master." Boorstein (1978: 60) asserts that our technological orientation can be traced to the experimental spirit reflected in the United States Constitution. "American experimentalism — in its older form of American federalism and in its more modern generalized form of American technology," he argues, has become the "leitmotif of American civilization." Gaylin (1975) adds that the mass successes of science and technology have made it an indispensable part of our culture.

The profound influence of modern technology on American society has led some critics to contend that the technological society is bound to fail for a variety of reasons. Marcuse (1964) exclaims that technology is by necessity a system of social control. Every advance in technology represses individual freedoms and blinds people to their real interests. Galbraith (1967) expresses concern for the emergence of the "technostructure" — the technical elite required for complex technical decision making. Most critical is Ellul (1964), who envisions a technological trap leading to progressive dehumanization and warns against the domination of human values by technique.

On the other hand, John Fletcher (1974: 99) does not agree that a technological society leads to dehumanization. As people make culture and take the initiative in the culture-making process, "the roots of dehumanization lie deeper in us than feedback from technique or technology." Fletcher states that we must look at values, not technology, for the root of our dehumanization. Callahan (1973: 260) adds that these "preachers against technology" offer little more than "provocative bedtime reading" because they fail to account for the "psychological principle of reality — that contemporary man cannot and will not live without technology." Emphasis should be shifted toward development of an "ethic of technology" that, according to Callahan, starts with the "tangible, ineradicable fact of technology."

Ferkiss (1969) goes further, noting that the danger lies not in the dominance of technology over society but in the subordination of technology to the values of bygone eras. To him, it is crucial that the "new technological man" fully understand the environmental and social consequences of each innovation and take responsibility for them. To many theorists, technology, culture, and the environment are inseparable and society must channel and control technology but not condemn it. "Just as technological invention cannot remove the need for social invention," Spilhaus (1972) warns, "neither should our slowness in changing outmoded social practices, institutions, and traditions be allowed to slow technological realization of potential benefits to all." Calder (1970), for instance, proposes new forms of social control to direct the "staggering new powers" of technology toward perfection of the human condition.

Partially in response to the critics of technology, Weinberg (1972) introduced the concept of "technological fix" as a solution to the myriad social problems we face, including those created by technology. For instance, if we pollute the environment, we can develop new enzymes to break down the oil, neutralize the chemical wastes, and so on. Even though these measures do not solve the core problems, they might delay or obscure the consequences until a day when we are able to overcome them. In the meantime, these intermediate technological fixes might improve the world's condition without requiring major attitudinal or structural changes (Freeman, 1974: 50).

Although the concept of the technological fix has engendered discussion (Etzioni, 1973; Ellison, 1978), such transfusions not only fail to solve major problems but also might compound them for the future. By treating the symptoms, the core problems are left to fester and grow, often unnoticed, until it is too late. Sinsheimer (1978) notes that the application of one technological fix seems to lead to another, and another, and so forth. It appears that societies can no longer afford to depend solely on these expedient but short-term fixes that technology offers.

Although societal problems most likely will be approached through technological means, alterations in social structures, values, and perceptions of the problems are also necessary. More comprehensive and well-conceived strategies are needed for dealing with the complex problems that include social, moral, and political dimensions in addition to the technical.

As Kass (1971: 781) asserts, questions of the use of technology are always moral and political ones, not simply technical ones.

Technology and Politics

Politics is the primary means through which resources are authoritatively allocated to the various groups and individuals in society. Within the political arena, each interest attempts to resolve conflicts over the distribution of social goods in its own favor, thereby maximizing its relative social advantage. Much decision making in politics therefore revolves around the resolution of conflict. Technology is intricately related to politics, as it generates conflict by rewarding some interests and depriving others. Each technology brings with it forces that alter the existing competitive structure among these interests.

Technology inevitably is accompanied by costs and deprivations as well as benefits and new opportunities. Although the distribution of such costs and benefits varies from one innovation to the next, it is never socially neutral. Some groups are rewarded while others are penalized; certain interests gain a great deal while others record minimal or no gains. Often the costs are borne by groups that do not share in the benefits at all. Obviously, people who see a technological development in their interest will tend to support it; those who do not will oppose it or at least remain uncommitted. The wide diversity and large number of groups in the United States ensure that each technological development is a potential political issue. Contributing to this has been the trend in the United States over the last several decades toward broadened notions of participatory democracy, a trend that has encouraged many additional conflicting groups to enter the political arena to gain access to decisions and to press for their demands. In assessing any new technology, therefore, it is crucial to analyze the potential alterations in the distribution of resources in its application.

In addition to political conflict resulting from changes in the distribution of resources, technology also produces shifts between private and public interests and obliterates traditional distinctions between them. These alterations, in turn, have broad implications for the public-policy process as concern focuses on the expanded role of government in matters previously considered to be private (for example, procreation). Nelkin (1977: 412) sees democracy threatened by this tendency of a technological society to blur distinctions between private and public realms as well as by the utilization of sophisticated decision-making techniques that undermine democratic principles. Also of concern to Nelkin are the growing tendency to concentrate political power in those who control technical information and the danger of policy decisions becoming so technical that politicians defer to the technocrats. This interrelationship between technology and politics is critical in understanding why technologies are politically divisive.

Genes and Environment

A continuing controversy in social science, and one that has recently been fueled by the debate over sociobiology, relates to the degree to which human behavior is a result of genetic endowment. There is no attempt to discuss the intricacies of that argument here, but it is necessary to address the problem and demonstrate the need to include genetic components in our models. Obviously, how one views the need for and desirability of human genetic intervention is dependent to a large extent on one's conception of the contribution of the genetic component. The opposition engendered by even suggesting the application of biological models to social processes is a preface to the intense disagreement over implementation of genetic policies discussed in this book.

Competing Models: Genes Versus Environment

The debate over the extent to which humans are products of genetic and environmental variation is best pictured as a continuum with one extreme representing the environmental determinist position and the other the genetic determinist position:

Genetic Determinism	Interactive Model	Environmental Determinism

The pure environmental model is based on the assumption of a tabula rasa, or blank state, in which all human beings are deemed to possess exactly the same potential at birth. Differences exhibited among humans, therefore, are the result solely of variations in environmental conditions. At the opposite extreme is the theory of genetic predestination, which holds that all differences among humans are the result of variation in genetic endowment (Darlington, 1969). Under this model, few attributes can be altered substantially because they are predetermined by the genes. According to Dobzhansky (1973: 31), traditional caste systems are organized on the basis of this extreme model.

Although few scholars today totally subscribe to either of these pure deterministic models, there is a tendency to gravitate toward one or the other end of the continuum. In general, social scientists and humanists find the environmentalist assumptions more consonant with their perception of reality. White (1972), for instance, suggests that the assumption of individual uniqueness of the genetic model runs counter to the accepted paradigm of the social sciences—that individuals are malleable through cultural and political processes. Conversely, traditional biological premises suggest a convergence of biologists toward the opposite pole, though there are many notable exceptions (e.g., Dobzhansky) near the center. There appears to be a growing awareness in most disciplines of the necessity to use more complex interactive models,[2] where genetic and environmental factors interact to produce a phenotype, but there are pressures in each field to retain traditional paradigms.

The Interactive Model: Genes and Environment

Despite these constraints and the built-in resistance to an interactive model, such a model is most accurate and meaningful for describing the complexity of human existence. Dobzhansky (1973: 25) states that sociological and biological variables are almost always intertwined in humans and that diversity is a joint product of genetic and environmental differences. Even at the micro level

> an individual's physical and mental constitutions are emergent products, not a mere sum of independent effects of his genes. Genes interact with each other, as well as with the environment . . . gene B may enhance some desirable quality in combination with another gene A_1, but may have no effect or unfavorable effects with a gene A_2. . . . For this reason . . . it is not at all rare that talented parents produce some mediocre offspring, and vice versa. [Dobzhansky, 1973: 35]

Although the interactive model presumes that both genetic *and* environmental factors must be considered intricate and essential components of human existence, it does not suggest that they are equally important in each case, nor that variation can be parceled out to each.

White (1972) applies an interactive populational approach to the political system. According to White, neither nature nor nurture solely explains human behavior; therefore we need a more complex paradigm in which the complete genetic endowment interacts with environmental influences to produce a phenotype (see Figure 1.1). The result of this interaction is twofold (p. 1215). First, "individuals with similar genotypes will vary significantly in their phenotypes as a result of environmental differences." Second, and with more direct political implications, is "the alternative possibility that within similar environments individuals with varying genotypes will differ accordingly in observed behavior."

The concept of genetic diversity suggests, then, that individual capacities do vary and beyond a certain threshold are limited, no matter how favorable the environmental conditions. Although most people would ac-

FIGURE 1.1
An Interactive Paradigm

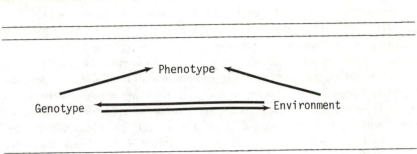

Source: White, 1972: 1215.

cept such a position as it relates, for instance, to artistic or musical abilities, environmentalists reject its applicability to most areas of human behavior. This concept often leads to cries of racism. White (1972: 1211), however, asserts that this represents an "unreasoning prejudgement" on the part of these critics and that they have, perhaps consciously, "compounded the problem by implying . . . that genetically-grounded approaches are necessarily racist." Populational thinking views discrimination applied wholesale to classes or races of people as without foundation. On the other hand, this fear of the environmentalists has been reinforced by the use (misuse) of genetic theories by some scientists (e.g., William Shockley) to demonstrate IQ differences by race.

Dobzhansky (1973: 44) contends that genetic diversity is a "treasure with which the evolutionary process has endowed the human species" and he sees no inherent conflict between genetic diversity and various social, economic, and political conceptions of human equality. Corning (1978: 25–26) points out that it is estimated that humans hold 95 percent of their genes in common and that 5 percent of each individual's genetic endowment is unique. As both are equally fundamental to the evolutionary process, it might be most natural to emphasize the 95 percent of the genes, held commonly, that define us as *Homo Sapiens*.[3]

White (1972: 1234) reiterates the political aspects of genetic diversity by stating that the "policy-maker—even more than the social scientist—must seek out rather than cover up individual differences." We must realize that each individual, despite his or her racial or social characteristics, is unique and must be treated so. As Ernst Mayr (1967: 833) points out, "Nothing is more undemocratic or more apt to destroy equal opportunity than forcing human beings with exceedingly different aptitudes and motivations through identical social institutions. There is only one way to cope with man's genetic diversity, and that is to diversify man's environment." It is clear that genetic diversity must be considered when public policies are created; it is also obvious that the cultural and social structures of American society make its inclusion a sensitive and difficult political problem.

Several problems with the shift from an environmentally oriented model to an interactive one, in addition to the political unfeasibility, are detailed by Marc Lappé (1976). Lappé asserts that there are serious cultural and social costs whenever genetic concepts are "assimilated into social structures" without a thorough questioning of their validity. He is mostly concerned with the treatment of intelligence, criminality, and disease as if they were primarily genetic attributes. For instance, he sees this narrow pattern of thinking as leading to a minimization of the environmental contribution to disease, which is substantial though often subtle, by focusing on the genetic components (p. 105). The emphasis on genetic models "also conflicts with norms that our society is deeply committed to," especially "our insistence on regarding the individual as the fundamental social unit" (p. 108). Despite his concern with the social costs of genetic models and his feeling that environmental factors should take precedence over genetic ones, Lappé agrees that "a balance needs to be struck between the monolithic acceptance of models of genetic determinism and those of social and environmental causation" (p. 108).

Our conception of the importance of genetic endowment to human existence in part determines how far we ought to intentionally alter our genetic composition and possibly modify human genes. Lappé and Roblin (1974: 20) go so far as to state that "genetic screening rests on the philosophic assumption that it is the genotype which has paramount importance in determining fitness." A pure genetic model must place top priority on genetic manipulation to improve our condition; conversely, a pure environmentalist would consider this of little or no importance and focus on manipulating the environment. A move toward an interactive model suggests that both genetic intervention and environmental adjustments are necessary in order to improve the human condition, and that neither approach should be used exclusively.

Assuming the acceptance of an interactive model, we should consider several questions concerning the use of human genetic technologies. First, should society attempt to reduce genetic diversity in humans? Mayr's assertion that diversification of the environment is the only way to deal fairly with genetic differences must be revised in light of the new technologies. No longer is the genetic element fixed: reproductive technologies, in combination with probable gene therapies in the future, provide the choice of modifying the genetic aspects and reducing such diversity. But is this the optimal or even a permissible option? If we intervene in the 5 percent of the genes that define human diversity, what impact will this have on the 95 percent that we share as members of a human species? According to Mayr, a gene is an exceedingly subtle and complex variable. The possibility exists, therefore, that manipulation of the genes might change evolutionary development in unanticipated and irreversible ways. A second question central to this study is the relationship between genetics and culture. According to Dobzhansky (1962), culture is built on a shifting genetic foundation. If we consciously alter the genetic base, value changes and disruptions are likely to follow, but in what direction? Because an interactive model presumes that both culture and genetic endowment define and affect humanhood, we must be aware of the implications of change in one aspect or the other.

It should be noted here that the discussion of human genetic intervention clearly illustrates the interdependence of genetic and environmental factors. Ironically, the concept of genetic intervention through medical techniques (screening, diagnosis), legal means (compulsory sterilization, marriage restrictions), or social methods (structural and value pressures for eugenic action) implies an environmental control over evolution or, in H. J. Muller's term, a need to "guide evolution." By altering the medical, legal, and social elements, heredity can be altered. To this extent the implication is that we will try to do through science what we have failed to do by attempts at social modifications alone. Dobzhansky (1973: 113) contends that humanity has gained the ability to adapt its environment to its genes as well as its genes to the environment. The availability of new genetic technologies leads us to ask whether we now desire to modify the genetic composition of society and its future extensions through a combination of environmental and genetic interventions.

Environment and Genetic Change

Although this book focuses on the social context of human genetic intervention as well as the impact of such developments on society, particularly the political aspects, it must be noted that at a more basic level, social and behavioral changes effect genetic change. That the genetic and environmental aspects of human life are inextricably related is illustrated by the increasing occurrence of the sickle-cell gene as slash-and-burn agricultural techniques have promoted the spread of the malaria-carrying anopheles mosquito.[4] The carrier state for the mutant form of hemoglobin S—i.e., the sickle-cell trait—protected children prior to the development of their mature immune response. As a result, more of those children with the sickle-cell trait survived malaria to promote the spread of the gene, which ultimately increased the frequency of sickle-cell disease. Despite reduction of malaria through technological advances, the gene that once had a protective purpose proliferates among populations that originally occupied parts of Africa and the Mediterranean region where this type of malaria was widespread.

The evolution of sickle-cell anemia is a clear example of the interrelationship between genetics and the environment. Two other examples of social changes resulting in genetic alterations are the increases in albinism among certain Indian tribes where albino men stayed at home with the women while other men hunted, and the increased frequency of certain traits in socially isolated groups (e.g., the Amish) where inbreeding is unavoidable. These cases also demonstrate that there is a considerable time difference between environmental and genetic changes, the latter being much more gradual. Indeed, one question of this study is whether we should utilize more direct genetic intervention techniques as soon as they become available, given the possibility of more serious long-term consequences resulting from the complex relationship between environment and genetics.

Recently, there has been much concern expressed about social-technological changes that might have a direct mutagenic effect. Research on mutation due to environmental contaminants, both chemical and from radiation, demonstrates substantial increases over natural mutation rates. Chromosomal abnormalities have been tied not only to high-dose external radiation from the atomic bombs but also to direct radiation from X rays. Although data on the mutagenic effects of chemicals are less conclusive, evidence is accumulating. According to Stine (1977: 369):

> On the basis of over 75 years of scientific investigation, it appears that an increase in the human mutation rate (by any means, radiation or chemical) would prove detrimental to humankind—both present and future generations. On the basis of such knowledge, the greatest caution must be exercised in avoiding human exposure to mutagens. Furthermore, the investigation of mechanisms, causal factors, and effects of mutations, in order that we avoid the suffering of inherited diseases, must be continued.

We live in a society dependent on chemicals; our environment abounds with over one-half million varieties of them (Williamson, 1969). Most prevalent are: over 3,000 approved chemical food additives, 900-plus agents registered for use as pesticides, and the wide variety of drugs used to enhance the growth of cattle and poultry. The use of these substances along with fertilizers and chemicals in most nonfood products to a large extent has allowed Western society to reach the high standard of living it enjoys. Any attempt to reduce dependence on these chemicals, therefore, is seen by some as a threat to this life-style. Similarly, our society has become increasingly drug oriented, with drugs produced for almost every conceivable purpose. The impact of prolonged use of various psychotropic drugs is not yet established, but it does not seem unreasonable to assume that infusion of chemicals into the human body could produce genetic changes. Neel and Bloom (1977: 102) reiterate the gravity and uncertainty of this situation: "The demonstration of even a small genetic effect of a drug in the first post-exposure generation implies a larger effect to be spread over subsequent generations; if we introduce mutagens into the environment, it is not so much ourselves as subsequent generations who pay the price."

There is as yet no definitive evidence of mutagenic damage produced by the use of chemicals and drugs, despite Cairns's (1978: 97) assertion that "nearly all known chemical carcinogens turn out to be mutagens." Also, certain chemicals, including LSD, cyclamates, and methyl mercury, have been linked with chromosomal damage in preliminary studies (Stine, 1977: 368). Although it is still uncertain to what extent congenital malformations (teratogenesis) are due to genetic damage, tissue injury in the developing embryo, a combination of factors, or environment interaction manifested only in genetically susceptible persons, evidence of the teratogenic effects of a variety of drugs is growing. Thalidomide is the most conclusive and obvious example, and other drugs, including the widely prescribed Valium, are suspected. Nonmedical drugs such as caffeine, alcohol, nicotine, and marijuana are also suspected, although evidence is limited.[5]

Finally, other social and behavioral changes that potentially alter the genetic composition of the population relate to altered reproductive patterns. These include changes in childbearing age, family size, and mate selection. Japan's legalization of abortion in 1947, for instance, is credited not only with a dramatic decrease in the birth rate but also with the 40 percent reduction of the incidence of Down's syndrome and with a decrease of 20 percent in deaths resulting from congenital malformation (Gottesman and Erlenmeyer-Kimling, 1971: S3). Some have suggested that any attempts at population control should include limits on parental age at time of childbirth in order to reduce the frequency of chromosomal abnormalities that are directly related to maternal age. Neel (1973: 366) asserts that 25 to 30 is the optimal age range for childbearing. This alteration of reproductive behavior, in addition to the examples noted above, demonstrates the profound interaction between the environment produced by a society and the genetic composition of its population or of future populations.

Explaining Behavior: The Genetic Component

Any attempt to explain human behavior will fail unless a wide variety of factors is incorporated in the model. The exclusion of any one of these results in distortions of the relative importance of any single factor if such a determination is possible or meaningful. The genetic aspect itself includes innate determinants that are species-wide: altruism, aggression, greed, and so on. It also encompasses genetic variation, which manifests itself in differences in inherited genetic potential and serves as the focus of this study. Similarly, the environment is a multifaceted concept that comprises cultural factors (prevailing values and beliefs) as well as contextual factors, including the social, political, economic, and educational frameworks. Furthermore, any explanation of behavior must comprise several factors that best represent the link between genetic and environmental determinants, including psychological and physiological dimensions. Behavior, then, results from a complex and little-understood synthesis of many aspects of human existence. Although this book focuses attention on the genetic component, through the technology that surrounds it, the complexity of human existence and the interactive nature of the various dimensions of reality must be kept foremost in mind.

Characteristics of Human Genetic Technology

The threat of new technology to traditional values and institutions is not a recent phenomenon. Today, technology is expanding into previously uncharted directions at an accelerated pace, making it more crucial to assess the social costs of each potential innovation. The diminishing lead time between initial technological innovation and widespread application and the potential irreversibility of such techniques demand that technology be controlled before the research is conducted (Kieffer, 1979: 418). Freeman (1974: 29) agrees that technologies must be assessed before "unwanted, unanticipated and damaging" consequences inflict "intolerable amounts" of harm to mankind. He is concerned that by the time their negative consequences are discovered, technologies are often "frozen" into technical and institutional patterns. In such cases, planned change to correct and control the adverse consequences is extremely costly and difficult. Although it is by no means clear that society is a captive of technology or that it lacks the capability to regulate technology, as Ellul and others contend, human genetic technology does pose crucial challenges that must be faced.

The Progression of Technology

Attempts to abstract reality into a series of distinct and identifiable elements are prone to oversimplification and, therefore, to distortion; despite the dangers, it is helpful at times to do just that. In order to place the topic of this book — human genetic technology — in perspective, it is useful to demonstrate how the emphasis on technology has progressed and how the focus of attention has changed. As the goal of technology has shifted from modifying our physical environment to improving physical and psychological health, and finally to altering our genetic composition, the issues and the stakes have become much greater.

Until recently, technological development has been concentrated on altering the environment for either political or economic motives. For instance, much of the effort of technology has been directed toward the production of new consumer goods to provide economic advantage. Similarly, much of the most sophisticated technological development is in the areas of defense and, more recently, space exploration, both of which are designed primarily to gain political advantage. During the last decade, some attention has shifted to technologies that overcome problems created by prior technologies, such as the reduction of air and water pollution or the manufacture of products less damaging to the environment. In general, however, society has embraced technology directed at altering, not necessarily improving, our environment.

Attempts to intervene in the physiological and psychological elements have surfaced as by-products of environmentally directed technology. The goal of creating physically healthy individuals through biomedical and agricultural technology is generally accepted, though the motivation is often economic. Better nutrition, protection from a wide range of diseases through immunization, and improved medical treatments have produced physiological changes with reasonable success. Less accepted has been the use of technology in the psychological dimension. Technology in pharmacology now offers an incredible variety of drugs to alter moods; for example, reduce depression, anxiety, and insomnia. Psychosurgery and electronic stimulation techniques have been introduced with mixed success and great controversy, to provide more long-term alterations in personality. Although some of these technologies have met with resistance, generally their development is accomplished without emotionally charged opposition. In the move from physical to psychological intervention, however, increased hostility is met in applying the technologies. Strongly held values regarding manipulation of the brain, plus concern over drug dependency and the question of social control, cause technology here to become more controversial. To some extent, current skepticism and hostility toward psychological intervention stems from the shift to techniques that are viewed as more intrusive.

Until the last decade, little emphasis was placed on technology designed to alter the genetic component in humans. Despite a long history of efforts to control heredity through social means, such as taboos on certain marriages, sterilization, or isolation from society of those deemed to have hereditary defects, a genotype was seen as a given. While genetic manipulation of livestock and plants, presumably with a solely economic purpose, thrived, human genetic technology was constrained. Not until the dramatic discovery of DNA and more recent knowledge about gene structure and action did direct human genetic intervention emerge as a potential technology for the reduction of genetic disease and the improvement of the human species.[6]

As a result of recent genetic research breakthroughs, we now find ourselves on the threshold of being able to alter factors that throughout time have been considered immutable and that, according to the values of many today, should not be altered. The object upon which these new technologies operate is not the environment but the human species itself (Kass, 1971). Society has committed itself to improving the human condition through alteration of a wide variety of environmental factors and to a lesser extent through modification of the physiological and psychological composition of its members. However, the same cultural heritage that envisions technology in most areas as progress still assumes the genetic base to be unalterable. It is not surprising then that technology that challenges this assumption and those who see its application as desirable are perceived as a threat by many individuals. It is in the application of technology modifying the genotypes of humans that traditional values and technological potential are most likely to clash, as it is those values that help define humanhood. In Häring's (1975: 4) words, now is the time to "face the question to what extent methods and attitudes suitable for shaping man's environment can be applied to the shaping of human society and the realm of human life and human relationships."

The Immediacy of the Problem

Due to the complexity of the questions raised by human genetic technology, the suggestion that we delay consideration of these matters until technology develops further is attractive. As the most controversial of these technologies (i.e., gene surgery, gene therapy, human cloning) are but theoretical possibilities, it does make sense to focus attention on more immediate forms of genetic intervention, as this book does. However, this does not mean that we can retain a naive, complacent attitude that reacts only to immediate and critical problems. According to Bender (1974: 74), "At best assertions of the right not to know might buy time, but the real costs of delay, individual and social, are incalculable. By putting off difficult decisions today, we may force far more drastic decisions in the future." The very nature of the intrusive and irreversible potential of most human intervention argues strongly for comprehensive examination of the real and potential issues now.

The urgency of the problems raised by genetic technology is noted by Callahan (1973: 255), who contends that the history of technology demonstrates that it cannot for long remain a matter of choice for individuals or societies. It is difficult to think of any older technology that has not become mandatory, either by law, custom, or social structure. Any new technology should be judged with the assumption that it will soon pass from being a voluntary matter to becoming a socially enforced requirement. Heim (1975: 264) adds that the need for reformulation of moral and legal positions on new developments before their widespread use is more crucial now than ever before, because "the changes are more fundamental in nature, are less likely to be reversible in the individual or in his descendents, and most importantly, are changes in human nature itself." Callahan (1973: 259), too, emphasizes the idea of the irreversibility of technology. We can never go back (e.g., deinvent the atomic bomb), so we find ourselves impelled to go forward and seek whatever technology promises to deliver.

According to some theorists, the most critical and immediate problems raised by genetic technology are ethical and political, not technical. For Toffler (1970: 436),

> technological questions can no longer be answered in technological terms alone. They are political questions. Indeed, they affect us more deeply than most of the superficial political issues that occupy us today. This is why we cannot continue to make technological decisions in the old way. We cannot permit them to be made haphazardly, independently of one another.

Unfortunately, those most able to formulate rules for acceptance or rejection of technology have not shown much interest in doing so. Social scientists have failed to delineate broad principles and politicians have consciously avoided such issues (Heim, 1975). Within this context of inaction by those outside of science, Toffler (1970: 205) suggests that it is "safe to say that, unless specific countermeasures are taken, if something can be done, someone, somewhere will do it." Conscious assessment and regulation of technology becomes imperative as technology itself advances at unprecedented speed. Sophisticated criteria are needed to avert avoidable disasters as well as to discover tomorrow's many opportunities. Nowhere is this more true than in the field of human genetics.

It has been estimated that knowledge in the field of genetics is expanding at a faster rate than in any other area of science. Each advance produces many new questions, most of which are highly volatile. Most of the new techniques are extremely controversial; terms such as eugenics, genetic screening, fetal research, and genetic engineering automatically trigger emotional responses from large proportions of social scientists and the public. Images of Nazi human experimentation are alluded to and terms such as racism and genocide are frequently mentioned. Others condemn these efforts as attempts to play God or point to the dangers of tampering with human nature. Despite these emotional attacks, it appears likely that advances in genetics will continue, probably at a faster rate than expected. Ludmerer (1972: 205), for instance, notes that American society offers only ambiguous and contradictory signs regarding the future of eugenic applications while "contemporary medical research is concentrating more and more earnestly on controlling hereditary conditions."

Although technologies are pursued largely as a means to social goals, they alter significantly the goals as well as the basic character of the individuals and communities that choose them. Tribe (1973: 621) contends that society's technological capabilities have "moved out of phase with our capacity to understand and direct their development" and to "integrate their evolution with our cultural and natural lives." Ellison (1978: 141) adds that cultural values "still lag behind the revolutionary changes in our social structure created by the new biological technologies," and Spilhaus (1972: 714) notes that technological developments have not been matched by social and cultural developments. Genetic research, whose purpose is to cure genetic disease, is likely to greatly influence our society. The uncertainty of its future use is what frightens many people. Tribe (1973) and Kindig and Sidel (1973) argue that the promised benefits of genetic research are too clear to warrant opposition solely on the ground of potential misuse. Tribe, however, does see genetic technology as a fundamental threat to the concept of a human being as a unique and intrinsically valuable entity, and he suggests caution on that basis. Unfortunately, he says (1973: 648), "we cannot avoid the necessity of making technological choices in the present" — our decisions concerning genetic research must be made before its impact on society can be analyzed.

The Expanding Scope of Genetic Intervention

The immediacy of concern in human genetic intervention arises partly from the newness of the technologies and their expanding scope. As recently as a decade ago, genetic intervention was primarily a negative process dependent on sterilization laws designed to end reproduction of individuals considered genetically or otherwise "unfit." Sterilization was supplemented by laws forbidding marriage of particular couples, supposedly on genetic grounds. Within a relative vacuum of knowledge concerning the transmission of genetic disease, these often ill-informed attempts to rid society of the defectives represented the entire arsenal of the early eugenic movement. Under such circumstances, the limited "technology" available offered a relatively straightforward dichotomy between acceptance or rejection of genetic intervention. The choice was simple: either for sterilization and restrictive marriage laws or against them.

The choices are no longer as simple or direct. The dramatic expansion of human genetic technology in the last two decades has greatly complicated the ethical choices in intervention. The presence of prenatal diagnostic techniques (such as amniocentesis and carrier and neonatal screening tests) has added an entirely new dimension to genetic intervention and has redefined the lines of disagreement. What once were exclusively eugenic motivations are now intertwined with therapeutic capabilities and means of providing couples with more complete genetic information about themselves and the risk of having affected children.

In addition, emphasis has moved from "negative" eugenics with its dependence on sterilization to "positive" eugenics.[7] This change has been brought about by the advancement in artificial insemination techniques, in vitro fertilization, and technology proceeding toward the possibility of embryo transplants. Intervention, under such conditions, produces an entirely new set of concerns not perceived several decades ago. Similarly, the potentiality of direct genetic engineering in humans through gene therapy and possibly gene surgery for certain monogenic or chromosomal disorders or for metabolic dysfunctions will shift emphasis toward treatment and even further away from the current focus on termination of affected fetuses. These developments necessitate a continuous reevaluation and more precise applications of our moral premises to each technology independently of our predispositions to support or reject all such technologies. Thus the dimensions of concern have expanded with the technology.

In a recent report (1978), the Department of Health, Education, and Welfare suggested that the widening scope of medicine has made it increasingly difficult to differentiate between medical services and other human or social services designed to improve the quality of life. As medicine has expanded progressively from pastoral, curative, and preventive orientations toward corrective and augmentative ones, health matters have come under increased public scrutiny and governmental intervention. These changes have produced many social and political problems, to some extent because our institutions respond very slowly to such changes. Under such dynamic conditions existing institutions and practices are liable to become obsolescent. "Some of the most urgent problems raised by innovations in 'biobehavioral technology' are, precisely, those concerned with monitoring the functioning of our institutions and administrative structures, so as to anticipate and guard against this kind of institutional obsolescence" (DHEW, 1978: 22).

The evaluation of various human intervention techniques demands a clearly defined distinction between individual health concerns and societal eugenic concerns. It is quite possible that one might be willing to accept a technique on individualistic grounds and reject the same technique if used as a conscious eugenic policy (a distinction that is examined in depth in Chapter 3). For instance, the use of in vitro fertilization in conjunction with sperm banks could be justified as a means of allowing couples, who are otherwise unable, to have children. Conversely, the same procedure, without the elements of individual choice and self-determination, could represent a conscious policy of social control. One must be certain, therefore, to distinguish between the desired goal of a particular application and the technology itself. The acceptance of any intervention technique depends heavily on the implementing policy. A policy that allows maximal individual choice rather than state coercion would be most acceptable from an individualist orientation. On the other hand, those who perceive human genetic intervention as solely eugenic in scope would argue that it must be compulsory in order to be successful eugenically.

Definitions of Human Life and Death

More than most other technologies, human genetic intervention challenges our conceptions of humanhood: it "will profoundly alter what it means to be a human being" (Tribe, 1973: 649). Gustafson (1973a: 46) suggests "that the question of what constitutes the normatively human is the most important issue that lurks in all the more specific and concrete problems we face . . . in the field of genetics." Increased capabilities to maintain life offered by recent biomedical innovations have been instrumental in modifying the concepts of human life and death among some lawmakers as well as the public. These changes have been accelerated by a series of well-publicized court cases, most notably that of Karen Quinlan (Kennedy, 1976), dealing with issues surrounding maintenance of life beyond limits previously thought impossible. The introduction of "living wills"[8] by California and other states and the attempts to redefine death by state legislatures have reinforced this interest.

Until recent decades, human life was equated with *biological* functioning. Traditional clinical and legal definitions of death were based on the loss of those biological functions. Although the loss of these functions (i.e., heartbeat, respiration, stereotypical reflexes, and such) is still indicative of death, the capability of technology to maintain them artificially implies that simple preservation of such biological functions by these means is not so obviously tantamount to human life. As a result, emphasis has transferred to the concepts of *intellectual* and *social* life as determinants of human existence. Social life is composed of one's behavior and interpersonal relationships, the products of a life-long process of socialization. According to Furlow (1974), social life is the most vulnerable and usually the first aspect of life to die, resulting in social isolation. Intellectual life is generally considered that part of a human being separating it from other species.[9] It includes consciousness and the rational interaction derived from the highest region of the brain. Even though biological life can and does exist with the aid of modern technology, Furlow contends that dehumanization follows social and intellectual death.

This shift in emphasis to the social and intellectual dimension of human existence is logical within the development of these technologies, but there is a danger that such a progression could result in the establishment of very narrow criteria of humanhood (Fletcher, 1979) and the exclusion of those who fail to pass the test. Euthanasia of the old, the retarded, and newborns who do not meet the criteria certainly is more readily acceptable under revised definitions of death. The apparent change in values toward these new conceptions of life and death also produces new categories of "life" that have broad implications for treatment of people at each level. For instance, Murphy, Chase, and Rodriguez (1978: 365) warn that we might easily be misled into believing that our own distaste for characteristics of certain genetic diseases must correspond to the views of the affected individual and that given the choice the person would rather not have been born. Although it is easy to exaggerate the ramifications of biomedical technologies on our conceptions of human life and the value we assign to it, at the least these technologies have produced confusion and challenged traditional values. They have come into direct conflict with emotionally charged and intense beliefs in the dignity and sanctity of life. Green (1973: 390) states that genetic technologies are "troubling possibilities" as they relate to the "very identity and dignity of man and his relationship to society and his government."

Selectivity of Genetic Disease: High-Risk Groups

In addition to the tendency of genetic issues to produce conflict among the most central values relating to human life vis-à-vis the state, the nature of genetic disease accentuates already sensitive divisions in society. Most genetic diseases occur at highly varied rates among different groups in the population. Certain racial or ethnic groups are highly susceptible to particular genetic diseases due to unique environmental factors and generations of inbreeding. Table 1.1 presents a listing of selected genetic diseases and the corresponding high-risk populations.

Although no race or ethnic group is without its share of genetic diseases and no single disease is found exclusively in a particular group, any attempts to intervene with respect to a specific disease entail concentration on a high-risk group. Obviously, this is bound to compound already sensitive relations among groups in this diverse society. This is most critical when intervention attempts are aimed at minority groups that are already

TABLE 1.1
High-Risk Populations for Selected Genetic Disease

Disease	High-Risk Population
Alpha thalassemia	Chinese
Cystic fibrosis	Caucasians
Diabetes mellitus	Jews, Polynesians
Galactosemia	Blacks
Glaucoma	Icelanders
Nieman-Pick	Jews
Neural tube defects (anencephaly, spina bifida, meningomyelocele)	Caucasians
Phenylketonuria (PKU)	Irish
Rheumatoid arthritis	American Indians
Sickle-cell anemia	Blacks, Mediterranean
Tay-Sachs	Ashkenazi Jews
Thalassemia major	Mediterranean (Greek, Italian, Armenian)

Source: Stine, 1977: 384-387; 402, 409-410.

the subject of discrimination. Unless great care is taken in clarifying the nature of genetic disease both to the target group and the population as a whole, stigmatization and bitter feelings will result. The early sickle-cell screening programs of the black population, for instance, were poorly planned and implemented and resulted in much unneeded anxiety (Cerami and Washington, 1974). The first reaction of many members of such groups is one of resentment and fear. Given the general population's ignorance of genetic disease and the sensitive nature of genetic intervention, it is not surprising that members of some groups view such attempts as a form of genocide. Although well-designed programs can reduce these social problems,[10] the selective distribution of genetic disease magnifies its potential impact on values and its susceptibility to political maneuvering.

Human Genetic Technology in Context

One premise of this study is that at all levels genetic technology must be examined within a broad multidimensional context. Genetic and environmental factors can be analyzed separately, but in reality they seldom operate independently. In order to understand the human condition, both sets of factors must be included in any model. At the same time, each technological innovation, genetic or otherwise, develops within a complex social and political context. The political implications of human genetic technology are examined in later chapters; the cultural, ethical, and social frameworks are summarized here.

Cultural Context

Earlier in this chapter it was stated that any technology is both influenced by and has influence on social values and institutions. At the base of these social structures is the foundation provided by the most central values that define a culture. It has already been demonstrated that American culture is predisposed toward progress through technological means. Capron (1975: 123) suggests that this value extends to medical technology through a deep commitment to the belief that medicine will progress and give us even greater powers over disease. A reinforcing value, according to Lappé (1972: 413), is a "deep-seated aversion to chance in the Western psyche." This desire for control is crucial to understanding attempts at genetic intervention. Presumably, equating the reduction of uncertainty with progress would facilitate acceptance of reproductive technologies. In a culture less disposed to progress and change, it undoubtedly would be more difficult to accept technology that challenged the status quo.

Another value central to perceptions of genetic intervention relates to society's conception of disease. Certainly our views toward genetic disease and those affected by it determine in large part our view toward genetic technology. Conversely, our beliefs about disease and those affected might be altered by changes in technology. Sorenson (1975: 220) contends that the success of medical advances is dependent on a prevailing value system in which disease is interpreted as a natural event and our active intervention to control disease is approved. American culture, however, fails to provide such unambiguous guidance. In spite of new knowledge disseminated through the media and a few successful educational efforts, the population as a whole is woefully ignorant of the workings of genetic disease. Ambivalent beliefs remain regarding the cause of genetic disease and existing values often result in guilt and shame for parents who bear genetically defective children. This ambivalence is compounded by the wide scope of genetic abnormalities, ranging from color blindness to Tay-Sachs disease, which precludes any simple classification. In addition, the fact that genetic anomalies often fail to exhibit consistent phenotypic manifestations normally associated with a "disease" reduces the ability to assign such a status to many genetic abnormalities (e.g., the XYY complement and Down's syndrome, discussed in Chapter 2). Similarly, the targets of genetic screening often are those individuals who carry a specific gene, but carrier status does not meet traditional definitions of disease and therefore cannot logically be treated as such. With so much ambiguity, it is not surprising that there is considerable controversy over the extent to which genetic intervention is or is not warranted.

The application of genetic technology also depends on values relating to human life and individual autonomy. Strong cultural constraints can be expected to exist on actions perceived as contradicting human life. This might vary substantially from one culture to the next. For instance, in the United States there is much debate over when fetal life begins, but there is virtual unanimity that persons once born have fundamental rights to continue to live, precluding certain forms of intervention that would lead to termination of those rights. It is not likely that the current value system would support the National Institute of Death (Lejeune, 1970: 125), which, among other things, would dispose of newborns not reaching minimal standards of normalcy. Although this might be acceptable in some cultures (see Neel, 1970), no U.S. policymaker would dare propose infanticide as a means of reducing the incidence of genetic disease. Even though it would be more effective and efficient than prenatal screening, infanticide is inimical to the basic value placed on life in our current cultural context.

Culture, then, reduces the number of options available and channels actions into acceptable forms. "The eventual role of applied human genetics," says Sorenson (1975: 20), "will reflect the complex intertwining of existing values and beliefs with increasing technological capacity." Just as applications of genetic technology reflect the values and perceived needs of society, so new technological capacities will influence culture.

Cultural Pluralism

Observers of American society, since Alexis de Tocqueville in the nineteenth century, have commented on the uniqueness and internal diversity of values among its citizens. This pattern of values has been viewed as a reflection of the historical development of the United States, especially the break from the feudal system and the continuous westward expansion. American values have been seen as products of, alternately, heavy dependence on the liberal tradition (with its emphasis on individual self-determination and freedom) and a fundamental consensus on the value of individual human life. Certainly the current political and social institutions reflect this unique American experience (Devine, 1972). Within this broad cultural context the belief has developed that each person's views should be heard and that all interests should be represented. The result has been a proliferation of competing interests on most issues of public concern. Social and political institutions have proved remarkably resilient and adaptable, given the diverse population and tradition of individualism; still, cultural pluralism has produced a large number of potential lines of stress in society.

The issues raised by human genetic technology, for example, threaten to produce levels of stress with which the system may not be able to cope, at least by traditional means. Kieffer (1979: 9) argues that the ethical premise that one position is as good as another is a principle with limited serviceability for biomedical issues: "There is a point at which ethical diversity and freedom ceases to be valuable. At least in matters dealing with the public good, it is rarely possible to honor all values simultaneously. Most of us do not find the societal good served by a do-your-own-thing tolerance." The issues surveyed here relate directly to the meaning of human life and force a distinction between the quality-of-life and sanctity-of-life perspectives that are at the core of our value system. These issues also center on conceptions of the role of society versus the individual and hence come into conflict with the liberal tradition and its emphasis on the individual. Although Kieffer (1979: 9) sees a need for a "new ethic" based on the proposition that the ethical dilemmas produced in the life sciences must be societal, not individual, this requires a major shift in values in a very short period of time. Even though values respond to technological innovations and alterations in society, value change is an incremental and gradual process. Values relating to one's conception of human nature are especially resistant to change. Although Callahan's (1973) perception of a current conflict between the individualistic and community-oriented cultural movements is no doubt accurate and is supported by certain patterns of change in public opinion, individualism permeates the core of American culture and has been firmly institutionalized for two centuries. This is unlikely to change without severe political and social disruptions.

Despite these problems, Callahan (1973: 262) argues that the present ethical individualism cannot be sustained in light of new technologies:

> It cannot handle those problems where people with diverse values must work together to deal with common problems, cannot create the necessary sense of trust which must undergird any community and cannot, in particular deal with those problems of technology where, because their implications and consequences are communal, the values by which they are judged and controlled must also be communal.

Agreeing with Kieffer, Callahan (1973: 268) proposes a social ethic or consensus but warns that the community cannot be given "moral preeminence" without the potential of persecution in the name of the common good. Tyranny of survival is just as dangerous as tyranny of individualism. The only "viable public morality" is one that sets limits on the government as well as on individuals. He sees an urgent need to recognize the valid claims of the community that, although necessarily repressive, also provide their own measure of satisfaction. The individual must always bargain with society. Instead of promoting a better bargain, however, technology is making it more difficult.

Ethical Perspectives

The interaction between culture and technology is manifested most clearly in the divergence of views concerning the application of human genetic technology. Kieffer (1979: 9) suggests that Western culture, with its emphasis on individual freedom of choice, has produced a great variety of ethical orientations. This moral pluralism, in combination with the rapid advances in genetic technology in the last several decades, has resulted in a proliferation of ethical perspectives on the moral implications of genetic intervention and a vast array of publications in the developing field of bioethics.

One reason for the very rapid growth of bioethics is that the ethical issues raised by genetic and biomedical technology strike directly at our conceptions of human existence. Genetic technology offers the possibility of deliberate modification, not of the environment, but of the human organism itself. Applications of this technology promise to reduce or eliminate genetic disease, relieve human suffering, and perhaps control the quality of human life in ways never before perceived. Even though there appears to be a consensus in our society to improve the quality of life through social and environmental means (Sonneborn, 1973: 5), there is no agreement as to whether this should be applied to genetic means as well. At the core of this diversity of ethical perspectives, then, is the question of the extent to which we ought to consciously and intentionally condition and modify the human genetic composition. Should we utilize available genetic technologies and continue to conduct research in human genetics? If so, what are the acceptable boundaries of human genetic intervention?

For purposes of simplification (and at the risk of doing a disservice to the complexity of these perspectives), the ethical orientations surrounding such questions are classified into one of three categories: (1) the pro-interventionists, (2) the anti-interventionists, and (3) those who are termed moderates for lack of a better descriptive term.[11]

Pro-interventionists. The most committed proponents of direct genetic intervention tend to be biologists and geneticists who focus their attentions on human species survival. Their concern is based on the assumption of a decreased natural selection rate resulting from advances in medical science over the past century that allow persons born with genetic defects to live and reproduce. Instead of the deleterious genes being "selected out," as under natural evolution conditions, they are passed on to future generations at an escalating rate. Furthermore, Cavalli-Sforza and Bodmer (1971: 785) note that through modern medicine, diseases are gradually being reduced to their most resilient core — those of genetic origin — thereby shifting emphasis to management and treatment of genetic diseases and extending this process of selection. The weakened natural selection process, combined with increased mutation rates that accompany population growth or result from environmental mutagens (such as radiation, chemicals, and drugs), leads to a threat to human survival as well as to a lower quality of life in the short run. Muller (1973), a Nobel laureate and long-time proponent of genetic intervention, states that

> the amelioration of our present biological burdens by modern medicine, sanitation, and all the other artificial aids to living is only temporary: since these devices save for reproduction many of the more defective individuals who would otherwise have died off. . . . they will continue to operate in this manner until, many generations later, the average individual, even with the best medical care is likely to meet genetic extinction as was the man of the stone age. Moreover, he will be as much dragged down by his natural disabilities as that man was. The only way to avoid this anticlimax would be for the people bearing heavier genetic loads to refrain from reproducing, even though medical and other aids had made them able to live and reproduce.

Thus, only by reversing this deterioration of the gene pool by genetic intervention can survival of the human species be assured. According to this view, humanitarianism means nothing if the species does not exist.

This assumption has led to a variety of suggestions for and support of human genetic intervention. Muller would depend heavily on semen banks to reverse deterioration, while another Nobel laureate, Joshua Lederberg (1966), perceives human cloning, among other means, as useful: "If a superior individual . . . is identified, why not copy it directly, rather than suffer all the risks of recombinational disruption, including those of sex? . . . Leave sexual reproduction for experimental purposes; when a suitable type is ascertained, take care to maintain it by clonal propagation." Linus Pauling (1968: 269), another Nobel winner, explains that carrier screening programs, combined with tattooing symbols for carrier status on the forehead, would reduce disease by eliminating procreation among those identified: "It is my opinion that legislation along this line, compulsory testing for defective genes before marriage, and some form of public or semipublic display of this possession, should be adopted." Dwight Ingle (1973) also suggests criteria for those who should and should not have children, based on the assumptions presented here, and proposes that public programs be established to facilitate this. He comes to this conclusion despite his statement (1970: 385) that "no one knows with certainty what is happening to the pool of genes that limit physique and intellect."

Other proponents of various types of genetic intervention include Crick and Watson, discoverers of DNA, the molecular basis of heredity. They have suggested that the legal status of newborns might need reevaluation. Tests could be given to each newborn infant regarding its genetic endowment; if it fails these tests, it forfeits the right to live. Watson (1973: 13) indicates that a three-day waiting period would be sufficient to allow all parents the choice that only few are currently given. This approach is more rational from a utilitarian or efficiency perspective than present procedures, as many defects cannot be identified until after birth, but there is little chance of the acceptance of this infanticide under present cultural constraints. It is this potential alteration in values that many opponents of intervention fear.

Among nonscientists, Joseph Fletcher, a theologian, is without doubt the most outspoken proponent of human genetic intervention of almost every type. He accepts the genetic-pool argument as a given (1974): "Each of us has a genetic 'load' of three to eight defects. This could double in two hundred years if we go on spreading genetic disorders through random sexual reproduction, multiplying the illnesses and costs that result from bad genes. This increase used to be offset by death and natural selection, but now the weak are preserved and protected." On the basis of this assumption and his concern for the reduction of human suffering, Fletcher (1966, 1974) sees the conflict reduced basically to sanctity of life versus quality of life, and he opts for the latter. His "situational ethics" places emphasis directly on the principle of proportionate good. He contends that one must attempt to compute the gains and losses that would follow from several possible courses of action (or nonaction) and then choose the one that offers the most good. The common welfare has to be safeguarded by compulsory control if necessary, according to Fletcher (1974: 180): "Ideally it is better to do the moral thing freely, but sometimes it is more compassionate to force it to be done than to sacrifice the well-being of the many to the egocentric 'rights' of the few."

Anti-interventionists. As a group, the anti-interventionists oppose, for a variety of reasons, all or most attempts at human genetic intervention, especially those of a coercive nature. The most adamant opponents are those who might be classified as holding a strict "right-to-life" orientation. Most Roman Catholic and fundamentalist religious philosophers are opposed to intervention, though not uniformly. Those who would intervene genetically are accused of attempting to "play God" (Goodfield, 1977; Howard and Rifkin, 1977) and are attacked as irreverent in their attempts to bypass natural human biology (Martin, 1978). Rice (1969) sees the entire complement of genetic and reproductive technology as a threat to the reverence for life. With few exceptions, those who reject abortion on moral grounds can be counted among the anti-interventionists.

A logical and consistent ethical orientation against human genetic intervention comes from Protestant theologian Paul Ramsey. Ramsey (1975: 238) contends that "procreation, parenthood, is certainly one of those 'courses of action' natural to man, which cannot without violation be disassembled and put together again." He vigorously defends the right of individuals to unique genotypes and sees germinal engineering as immoral: "The practice of medicine in the service of life is one thing; man's unlimited self-modification of the genetic conditions of life would be quite another matter" (1970: 95). Ramsey asserts that although the end results might be attractive, acquisition of the means necessary to reverse the growing genetic load is not morally permissible because it involves risks to life and health of individuals not yet born, through experimentation on fetuses (see Ramsey, 1975). Ramsey, then, provides a link between those opposed to genetic intervention on strictly right-to-life grounds and those opposed for broader social and moral reasons. C. S. Lewis (1965: 70–71) sees intervention as foreclosing options and weakening those who follow us: "If any one age really attains, by eugenics and scientific manipulation, the power to make descendents what it pleases, all men who live after it are patients of that power. They are weaker, not stronger."

Marc Lappé (1972: 421) is disturbed by the current advocacy of societal intervention in childbearing decisions, denial of medical care to the congenitally damaged, and sterilization of carriers. He contends that society has no right to intervene in childbearing decisions except in very rare exceptions. For Lappé (1979: 77), "even the most 'reasonable' breeding programs for the 'selection' of the brightest would necessarily involve the most repressive measures and an elitism . . . which runs completely counter to our political principles." He adamantly rejects the genetic load or genetic burden arguments of the pro-interventionists, contending that "imminent 'genetic deterioration' of the species is, for all intents and purposes, a red herring" (1972: 419). As evidence, he cites conclusions reached by an American Eugenics Society six-year report ending in 1970, which stated that "neither present scientific knowledge, current genetic trends, nor social value justify coercive measures as applied to human reproduction." Kass (1972: 18–19) points out that the world today suffers more from the morally and spiritually defective than the genetically defective and that efforts must first be made to reduce pollution and other problems of modern life. The case for society's concern for the genetic welfare of the population and its rights in imposing sanctions on the individual rests on a yet unproven "clear and present danger of genetic deterioration." According to Lappé (1972:

427), "The notion of a genetic 'burden' imposed on society by individuals carrying deleterious variant genes is a misleading concept: the 'burden' of deleterious genes is borne by families, not society." Society has an obligation to provide maternal and postnatal care, even at the cost of survival of the congenitally handicapped, and to provide optimal conditions for their development. To do otherwise would "jeopardize the moral tone of society itself." Lappé does not reject genetic intervention in all cases, as do the strict anti-interventionists, but he does oppose any application through which individual prerogatives are reduced and dismisses the basic arguments of the pro-interventionists.

Another concern of those opposed to more sophisticated forms of genetic intervention is that their widespread application would work to reduce human genetic variation. Murphy, Chase, and Rodriguez (1978) argue that constant environmental change implies that the "ideal genotype" is also changing. Despite the desirability that selection operate to some degree "lest the gene pool become so choked with defects that few individuals are healthy," reduction of genetic diversity could be disastrous:

> If there were no uncertainties about the future pattern of the environment, eugenic policy could be usefully directed to eliminating those currently detrimental genes for which there will be no further use. Actually, we eradicate any particular gene at our peril. By favoring those genotypes that would give the maximal possible chance of survival to the individual we might harm — perhaps even jeopardize — the chances for survival of the species. [P. 386]

Still another concern that has produced opposition to genetic technology is the fear that these techniques are readily adaptable as means through which the state can control social behavior. Although most attention until now has been directed toward technologies of more obvious behavior modification potential, such as drug therapy and psychosurgery (Scheflin and Upton, 1978; Schrag, 1978; Bach-y-Rita, 1974), the scope of this criticism is broadening to include genetic technologies. Given the sensitive nature of genetic intervention and its unforeseen and possibly irreversible consequences, it will continue to be open to these attacks. Although each of the techniques of human genetic intervention conceivably could be used to achieve either desirable or undesirable goals, some critics (e.g., Restak, 1975; Howard and Rifkin, 1977) focus on the least desirable of the alternatives and see these technologies as leading to governmental control over the procreation process and ultimately over decisions of who shall live based exclusively on genotype.

Moderates. Between the two divergent orientations discussed above fall many observers who accept or reject particular applications of human genetic technology on the basis of their specific social or moral implications. The moderate approach is represented in many recent works that examine the social impact of genetic technology (Etzioni, 1973; Reilly, 1977; Ellison, 1978). As it is also the orientation of this book and is reflected throughout, this approach is discussed only briefly here. In large part, moderates approve technologies directed at the amelioration of genetic disease and human suffering as long as they are conducted in a manner that protects the prerogatives and freedoms of individuals, and they reject technologies conducted for eugenic purposes. Moderates who do accept the assumption of gene-pool deterioration minimize its relative importance vis-à-vis more immediate social and medical concerns. For instance, Bentley Glass (1972) notes that "not many will deny the need for some measures to prevent the slow but inevitable deterioration of the human gene pool" (p. 329), but he goes on to argue that "man should pause on the threshold of these ominous powers over his own reproduction and evolution and take stock" (p. 335). Although he supports various genetic technologies in principle, Glass contends that a high priority must be placed on betterment of the environment.

Bernard Häring (1975: 188) also expresses caution regarding the use of genetic technologies and indicates that "man has a limited right of self-modification" and must "carry it out with wisdom and responsibility for future generations." Although Daniel Callahan (1973) defends the right of parents to bear defective children if they so desire even if the costs to society are high, he also feels that they should not be forced to bear them. Therefore, much additional genetic research is necessary in order to provide the most options to the parents. Again, the emphasis is shifted to the manner in which technology is applied and away from a wholesale acceptance or rejection of the technology per se.

Social Context

Any examination of the context of human genetic technology is incomplete unless it accounts for current social patterns and attitudes that constitute the immediate social environment. These attitudes reflect basic cultural and ethical dimensions and are also affected by current events and the pressures of everyday existence. At times the social context of a particular technology, therefore, will be inconsistent with underlying values of the society. Due to varying interests and concerns of the many groups within society, the social context often presents a conflicting and ambiguous framework within which a technology develops. For instance, Twiss (1974) finds evidence for support of at least five models of genetic responsibility in the United States.[12]

Despite the hesitation expressed concerning manipulation of human selfhood (Shinn, 1974: 113) and the substantial conflict of genetic intervention with basic values concerning individual rights and human life, Ludmerer (1972) notes that the public as well as decision makers historically have tended to embrace eugenic attempts, often without any scientific justification. Furthermore, Reilly (1977: 131) contends that the legal history suggests that strong support can be gathered for intervention programs that "contemplate major invasions of personal freedom," in spite of the strong presumption of individual rights in American culture. Apparently, a common perspective is to view eugenics as directed at those other than oneself and therefore to support it as not only acceptable but also necessary for the good of all concerned. In addition, there are many current social forces that appear to lead toward increased support for a variety of such technologies. These trends certainly are not unambiguous and continue to reflect the many divisions in society, but some appear to be quite strong. As the acceptance or rejection of human genetic technology ultimately depends upon public support, it is crucial to examine the social context for the 1980s.

Central to much genetic technology is the perception of the fetus either as a human being, a potential human being, or a subhuman organism. At the core of the debate over prenatal diagnosis, for instance, is acceptance or rejection of abortion of fetuses identified through amniocentesis as genetically defective. According to Kass (1976), any discussion of this technology unavoidably is "haunted by the ghost called the morality of abortion." Likewise, in vitro fertilization depends ultimately on acceptance of a higher risk of abortion and on the manipulation of human eggs and sperm. Although amniocentesis procedures and related techniques such as artificial insemination continue to be intensely rejected by some elements in society, the public opinion polls over the last decade have demonstrated dramatic shifts toward support of them by the public at large. These data are examined more extensively in Chapter 4, but it is important to note here the changing views toward abortion, as acceptance of abortion serves as an indicator of support for more specific applications.

The data in Table 1.2 indicate these attitude changes between 1966 and 1976 under several circumstances. In each case, the public has become consistently more supportive of abortion. In the case of a "child that may be born deformed," 54 percent supported abortion in 1966; in 1976 the corresponding figure was 82 percent with 2 percent uncertain. In 1974, 90 percent of the public agreed that abortion should be legal if the mother's health is threatened, and 52 percent favored abortion when the family is too poor.

This recent move toward more positive views concerning abortion has facilitated acceptance of prenatal diagnosis and provided a more favorable

TABLE 1.2
Attitudes Toward Abortion, 1966-1976

	Reason	Response	1966	1972	1973	1974	1975	1976
1.	Defect in	yes	54	74	83	83	80	82
	Baby	no	32	20	16	14	17	16
		DK	14	5	3	3	3	2
2.	Mother's Health	yes	77	83	91	90	88	89
	Threatened	no	16	13	8	8	9	9
		DK	7	5	2	2	3	2
3.	Family is	yes	18	45	52	52	51	51
	Poor	no	72	48	45	43	44	45
		DK	10	7	3	5	5	4
4.	Pregnancy	yes	-	74	81	83	80	80
	Result of Rape	no	-	20	16	13	16	16
		DK	-	6	4	4	4	4
5.	Mother Wants	yes	-	38	46	45	44	45
	No More Children	no	-	58	51	51	52	52
		DK	-	6	3	5	4	3

Sources: Gallup Opinion Index (1966, 1975, 1976);
         National Opinion Research Center (1972-1974).

climate for the use of a wide range of techniques. Harris (1975: 65) contends that the "rapidity with which moral views about abortion in general
have changed swept aside much of the resistance that might have been expected to develop against prenatal diagnosis and selective abortion." No
longer is the fetus seen as inviolable by a majority of citizens. Reinforcing
this change has been a growing awareness of quality of life as expressed in
"the right to be born healthy" attitude. In combination, these changes result
in the acceptance of abortion of those fetuses deemed not to have the potential for a "meaningful human existence." In part these opinion changes have
been brought about by technology through celebrated cases, such as Karen
Quinlan, that focus on the conflict between reverence-for-life and quality-
of-life perspectives. There is a growing attitude that life should be defined
in other than strict biological terms. Although these changes in attitude are
in themselves important, they must be seen within an even broader alteration in the social context of the late 1970s.

In addition to value changes relating to abortion and life-death matters
in general, other social forces appear to be creating a public mood that

might be more sympathetic toward genetic intervention attempts in the future. For example, since the late 1960s pressures for population control have mounted. Certainly, part of the concern for the quality of life has been the result of emphasis on the perceived need to limit the quantity. An increasing population is now viewed as an immediate threat by some proponents of population control (see Hardin, 1972), and although "zero population growth" has received diminished emphasis in recent years, the assumption that steps must be taken to keep the population within manageable bounds is widely held. Large families are no longer in vogue, and couples who fail to limit the number of children are coming under increased criticism. This may influence acceptance of genetic technology. As Twiss (1974: 235) asserts, "Many concerned parents are carefully planning for children; and because of perceived social expectation and pressure to produce a limited number of children, there is an increasing parental concern for the genetic health of each child."

Perhaps an extension of this concern for controlling the population growth is the concern over the increasing costs of supporting the elderly, the infirm, and the handicapped. Just when the government is finally moving to provide equal rights for these elements in society, there appears to be a growing feeling that society can no longer afford to carry these individuals along. Most of the decisions concerning screening programs at some point focus on the costs to society if those affected are not identified and eliminated. Questions are more frequently asked as to how long society can afford to pay $250,000 for lifetime support of a person with Down's syndrome, or to pay out billions each year to provide hemodialysis for the small segment of society with nonfunctioning kidneys. In other words, priorities in spending for various health programs are being questioned by the public as well as by the decision makers.

In the past, even in times of abundant resources, those affected by genetic disorders and other unfortunates have received minimal support. In times of scarce resources, it is likely that those at the bottom will be the targets of cost saving and increasingly will be seen as burdens to society. Greater pressures to reduce this burden would seem to be translated readily into support for programs aimed at eliminating or reducing the number of those affected. For instance, in his review of the recent restructuring of California's mental-health system from the state-hospital setting to an emphasis on community treatment, Cameron (1978) concludes that the most severely retarded are virtually left out as attention concentrates on voluntary patients. As the United States faces a probable drop in the standard of living over the next decades, and resources become even more scarce, it would not be surprising to see genetic intervention programs receive more emphasis and public support. Without doubt the growing "squeeze on money for research provides us with an opportunity to rethink and reorder priorities" (Kass 1971), but it seems unlikely that there will be a massive shift toward humanitarian concern for those affected most severely with genetic disease.

Related to the concern over costs of maintaining victims of genetic disorders and other infirmities is the growing resentment against people on welfare. As the size of the welfare population has grown and fostered succeeding generations of recipients, public opinion has been aroused. Taxpayers' revolts (e.g., California's Proposition 13) and other actions indicate a widespread wish to restrict the rights of those "feeding from the public trough." One perennial demand is that mothers on welfare be sterilized if they have more than a specified number of illegitimate children. This viewpoint reinforces the acceptance of reproductive intervention as a legitimate infringement of procreative rights based on some economic standard.

Another trend that Charles Frankel (1976: 24) sees as contributing toward a growing tolerance of eugenics is the decline of the family and of the marital idea. Kass (1971: 784) argues that the breakdown of the family threatens to destroy our sense of continuity with the past and the future, as it is the family through which we acquire links with the past as well as a sense of commitment to the future. He sees this trend as one that depersonalizes society. Parenthood means less than in past generations and results in ready acceptance of abortion of unwanted children. In part because of concerns for population and the cost of raising children, but also due to changing conceptions of the family, parents are opting to have fewer or no children. The technology of the pill and other birth-control methods has made this goal of limited families feasible. Perhaps nothing manifests this interplay between technology and values more clearly than the dramatic increase in vasectomies to men with one or two children. In addition, the acceptance of new life styles has provided alternatives to the traditional family, and the high divorce and remarriage rates complicate the notion of family. In any case, changing values regarding the centrality of the family to human existence have helped create an atmosphere (or are another manifestation of it at least) in which traditional parent-child relationships are more easily defined from an individualistic perspective.

Frankel (1976) also sees the growing cynicism regarding the possibility of social improvement through institutional means as adding to this movement. Despite the great social programs to fight poverty, improve housing, and remove urban problems, the ills of society are perceived by most as getting worse instead of better. According to Frankel (1976: 24) this leads to a political climate in which "on the right, people can look with sympathy on eugenics, envisaging the program's being tried on others, not on themselves. And on the left, biomedicine speaks to the hope, ever rising from the ashes, that the human race can still be made over by proper planning."

Finally, Twiss (1974: 245) contends that "an almost euphoric ethos in our culture and society regarding the control and elimination of genetic diseases" has been produced by rapid advances in genetic technology. It has created an atmosphere of expectation that control of these diseases is now possible or imminent and has infused our social consciousness with the conception of responsibility toward future generations. Although he does not see such a shift as necessarily desirable, he suggests that "changes in cultural and societal attitudes and practices may be leading to a virtual demand for programs in applied human genetics."

Complementing this attitudinal change in the population as a whole is the heightened awareness among particular ethnic groups that they are at high risk for certain genetic diseases, that genetic screening is available to identify carrier status, and that such screening is desirable. Screening programs for Tay-Sachs disease among eastern European Jews and more recent efforts by blacks to establish sickle-cell screening programs at the community level are examples of this new awareness. According to Twiss (1974: 245), "Insofar as certain of these high-risk populations have some degree of community identity and organization, they are likely to develop a distinctive sense of genetic responsibility and to support genetic screening programs relevant to their respective medical problems." Such a pattern would be expected to increase in intensity and scope as community education and counseling programs expand and as genetic screening and therapy technologies advance.

These contextual factors as a whole appear to provide a favorable social framework for the development of eugenic programs, but their presence does not ensure implementation. Countering these trends are basic cultural values relating to the dignity of the person and to self-determination. The liberal value system in the past has worked to protect the fundamental rights of all people, regardless of their condition. It is this value system that is being challenged by situational changes, including advances in genetic technology. Despite the social trends outlined above and the wide discrepancies that exist in distribution of goods and services, the value system does reflect a concern for the human as something special. The extent to which these current social patterns accelerate the "erosion of the idea of man as something splendid or divine" (Kass, 1971), and replace it with the view that man is not unique and therefore can be manipulated genetically, will depend in large part on how the issues are presented to the public and how public decision makers perceive them.

Political Context

Although the political context is less obvious than the social or ethical, ultimately all technological decisions are made within a political-economic context. Furthermore, the disputes that necessarily result when technological innovation challenges established social values and structures are resolved through legal and political institutions. More than any other technology, genetics produces highly sensitive political questions because it deals with the bases of human behavior and existence: "It is not surprising that genetics has been so involved in twentieth century American politics, for its intellectual context bears directly upon political matters in a way unlike that of any other science" (Ludmerer, 1972: 203). As noted earlier, the nature-nurture debate is most likely based on oversimplified assumptions; still, it has had substantial political impact.

Although genetic technology itself is highly political and therefore takes place within a dynamic political context, several current political trends imply that the relationship will become more critical in the future. One major trend in the 1970s was the growing public role in biomedical research. Hanft (1977: 19) sees this emergence into the public debate as a result of a combination of inflation, multiplying health-care costs, and the general freedom-of-information climate. This trend also indicates that as the costs of genetic research and application increase, public debate over priorities will expand. As a large proportion of the funding comes from public monies, decision makers must scrutinize particular expenditures more closely, producing an even greater dependence on the public sector. Moves toward nationalized health insurance will accelerate the role of government in this direction. Genetic research is presently subject to budgetary constraints and will face even stiffer competition for health dollars in the coming years.

Another political trend that defines the context for genetic technology is increasing activist orientation. The U.S. political system, with its numerous check points and relative ease of access, provides organized groups a reasonable opportunity to block or at least delay implementation of technology. Due to this, as well as to a propensity of Americans to organize, many groups have been established for that purpose. The most visible of these groups continue to focus on nuclear power or environmental issues, but recent public confrontations over recombinant DNA research and prenatal diagnosis suggest that more action will be forthcoming as the issues become more salient.

Supplementing this trend toward activist intervention is the emerging interest of the mass media in publicizing many of the genetic issues. In vitro fertilization, human cloning, and DNA research have all made the headlines in recent years and are viewed as highly newsworthy items. Although this coverage often has been oversimplified and the real issues have been obscured, prolonged visibility through the media promises to maximize public awareness and concern over these issues. Coupled with the ability of the activist groups to gain access to the media, the interest of the press will assure a continued public scrutiny of genetic technology.

Human genetic technology raises crucial questions relating to (1) the proper goals of society, (2) the proper means of achieving such goals, and (3) the proper role of the government in implementing genetic intervention programs. Does a democratic society have the duty to reduce the occurrence of genetic disease and, if so, to what degree can it preclude certain individual freedoms in order to achieve this goal? Certainly any decision in such matters requires caution, as the criteria of genetic good set up by persons or societies will always be culturally conditioned. Shinn (1974: 115) warns that particular "societies or powerful cliques within them claim for their particular prejudices the status of norms for all human life for all time." Increasingly, the decisions we make today will foreclose the options of those who follow, thereby preserving our prejudices.

Technology has always produced conflict as it clashed with traditional social values and established institutions, but genetic technology is unique as it acts directly on us instead of on our environment. The potential impact on the human condition and possibly on human nature itself is enough to demand serious attention. The questions raised by biomedical technology are new because the manipulation of humans leads to questions "vastly more fundamental than previous ones" and because incorrect decisions could seriously degrade the quality of life (Heim, 1975: 263). This, along with the uncertainty of long-range consequences and the potential irreversibility of certain genetic techniques, reinforces the need to carefully evaluate each technology within a democratic framework before its widespread application.

At the same time, we must be aware that all technology, including genetic, is highly responsive to societal inputs and that development and application are channeled by cultural, social, and political factors. As the technologies advance, we can expect the tensions among the varied elements in our pluralistic society to be accentuated and questions regarding equity and efficiency of genetic intervention programs to emerge as critical policy issues. "Biomedical technologies . . . are producing or are likely to produce some of the most profound effects on social mores and behavior of the future. It is likely that public policy issues will soon arise from this area in great numbers, and . . . will be profoundly interwoven with religious, social, economic, cultural and ideological factors" (V. T. Coates, 1972: 26). Whether we like it or not, the government, through its various institutions, increasingly may be called upon to make controversial — and political — decisions on these issues.

2
Applications of Human
Genetic Technology

The technologies reviewed in this chapter are collectively referred to here as human genetic technologies.[1] The author is aware of the distinction between technologies of an obvious genetic nature, such as genetic screening and gene therapy, and those classified primarily as reproductive technologies, such as in vitro fertilization and artificial insemination. When examining human genetic intervention, however, this distinction is of questionable value, as the potential use of reproductive techniques for genetic purposes is substantial. Amniocentesis, used in conjunction with carrier screening and genetic counseling, remains the single most important technique for genetic intervention. In vitro fertilization, artificial insemination, and sterilization are among a varety of techniques that, although not inherently genetically oriented, are included in this discussion because they might serve as means by which human genetic intervention is achieved. The use of these primarily reproductive techniques for genetic purposes depends on the motivation behind their application: In vitro fertilization, for example, might be viewed as a means by which a couple's desire to have children is fulfilled when not otherwise possible, but the same procedure could serve eugenic ends just as sterilization has in past decades.

This chapter reviews the state of current applications in human genetic intervention and also directs some attention to reproductive techniques with potential genetic applications. Collectively, these present and future technologies offer a powerful array of mechanisms for genetic intervention. When coupled with more distant, directly genetic possibilities such as gene therapy and surgery and human cloning, the full impact of these technologies on societal structures and values can be fully appreciated. By focusing on current genetic applications, suggesting future applications of various reproductive technologies, and noting the impact of possible developments (now at the theoretical stage), this chapter attempts to provide a well-balanced and realistic assessment of the status of human genetic intervention techniques. Discussion of technologies of less immediate con-

FIGURE 2.1
Life Stages: Levels of Potential Genetic Intervention

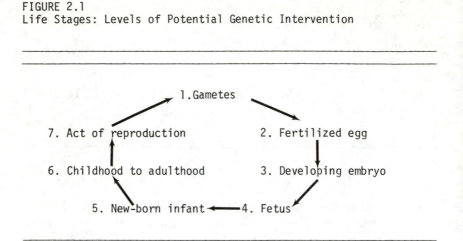

cern for human genetic applications, such as recombinant DNA research, is minimized here.[2]

There are at least seven levels of possible genetic intervention. Figure 2.1 shows these stages as separate elements in a continuous life process. This emphasizes the difficulty in drawing clear lines of distinction and demonstrates that stage one is always a continuation of stage seven in the preceding generation. In other words, the reproductive level, rather than some final stage, is a prelude to a renewal of the process. Clearly, intervention at each level has direct implications for all succeeding points in the circle. Intervention in the reproductive process, presumably for genetic reasons, has long been traditional in most cultures. Restrictions on consanguineous marriages as well as compulsory sterilization of large categories of people have been justified, in many cases wrongly, on genetic grounds. Additionally, genetic intervention from childhood to adulthood is available on a limited scope through attempts to treat and keep alive those born with certain genetic problems. Treatments such as surgery for cleft palate and administration of insulin for diabetes allow most of these individuals a near-normal existence.

Similar efforts to treat and keep alive newborn infants have extended intervention to that level. Screening of newborns for phenylketonuria (PKU) and other metabolic disorders and the implementation of dietary treatment are widespread and largely successful. On the other hand, genetic intervention at the newborn stage can also result in the elimination of those with gross genetic defects. Although presently infanticide is not accepted in principle by Western cultures, in practice treatment is frequently withheld from infants with severe neural tube defects or other abnormalities. As a matter of public policy, Britain denies treatment to neural tube infants classified as "severe." Still, there is much debate in the medical profession over the proper course of action in such cases.

Intervention at stages one through four represents the major thrust of current efforts in genetic research, but projected technologies appear to be directed toward the earliest life stages. Presently, fetal intervention is primarily based on prenatal diagnosis through amniocentesis and ultrasound followed by termination of fetuses identified as genetically defective. Although few therapeutic options are now available at the early life stages, future work in gene therapy might substantially increase such possibilities. This study, being primarily concerned with the impact of current genetic technologies, will focus on interventions at the fetal stage and later. However, it must be reiterated that intervention at the reproductive stage has direct repercussions on the early stages of the next generation and thus on all generations that follow.

The Nature and Scope of Genetic Disease

Each year in the United States alone, between 100,000 and 200,000 infants are born with congenital malformations, single-gene hereditary disorders, or chromosomal anomalies. This represents approximately 3 to 5 percent of the three million annual live births. These disorders collectively are responsible for over 20 percent of all infant deaths, second only to prematurity and birth injuries. Furthermore, this proportion is expected to continue to increase as improvements in obstetrical care, improved nutrition, and other therapies reduce the relative contribution of other disorders to infant mortality.[3] In addition, genetic disorders are the second leading cause of death in the one-to-four age group and the third leading cause in the 15-to-19 age group (National Center for Health Statistics, 1978) and contribute to a substantial proportion of miscarriages (Crandall and Brazier, 1978).

Congenital defects and hereditary diseases are important causes of mental retardation and physical disability as well. It is estimated that at least 40 percent of all individuals with an IQ of less than 50 in the United States have either a chromosome disorder, a single-gene disease, or a severe developmental disorder (Stein and Susser, 1978). In addition, many chronic disabling conditions such as cystic fibrosis, Duchenne muscular dystrophy, and sickle-cell anemia are genetic diseases with substantial morbidity (National Institutes of Health [NIH], 1979: 29).

In view of these figures, it is no surprise that 25 to 30 percent of admissions to acute-care hospitals for those under age 18 are for conditions of genetic origin or for disorders strongly influenced by genetic factors (Childs, Miller, and Bearn, 1972). Also, many individuals with genetic-related diseases who survive infancy must be institutionalized for all or part of their lives. NIH (1979: 30) estimates that "of the 210,000 individuals with mental retardation institutionalized in U.S. facilities in 1970, the etiology for their retardation could be ascribed to genetic or genetically in-fluenced conditions in 20 to 25 percent of the cases. This generates an an-nual institutional cost of $315,000,000 for such individuals (1970 dollars)." Lifetime institutional cost for an individual with Down's syndrome who survives the first five years of life approximated $300,000 in 1970 (Swan-son, 1970) and is increasing. The net future commitment of society to the maintenance and care of those affected with chromosomal abnormalities alone is over $3 billion per year (Milunsky, 1973).

   In addition to the role genetic-related factors play in fetal and infant mor-tality, mental retardation, and chronic disability, and the considerable medical care and institutional costs frequently required in the care and management of affected individuals, is the psychological impact on parents, families, and communities. "The guilt, anxiety, despair, and unrealized hopes and ambitions of some individuals in families associated with hereditary disease and congenital defects can lead to family disruption, life-long stigmatization, and altered life styles and avocation" (NIH, 1979: 30–31). Limited evidence suggests that the psychological impact on the family may be profound (Drotar et al., 1975).

Categories of Genetic Disease

   Although it is reasonable to treat all types of genetic-related problems as one category of disease when discussing their joint health impact, it is crucial to distinguish them when focusing on genetic concerns. Any at-tempts to intervene prenatally must be directed toward specific types of disease. Actually, the term "genetic disease" can refer to a broad range of incredibly diverse disorders, anomalies, and conditions. Unless these distinctions are clarified, any examination of human genetic technology will be confusing and possibly misleading. Categories of genetic disease are themselves simplifications of a complex set of phenomena, but they do il-lustrate the scope of the topic at hand and demonstrate problems inherent in the identification and treatment of these conditions. The three most com-monly discussed types of genetic disease are: chromosomal abnormalities, single-gene disorders, and multifactorial (or polygenic) disorders. Brief descriptions of each type of disorder and examples of each are presented here. More technical and complete coverage of these categories is available in several excellent genetics textbooks including Levitan (1977), Stine

(1977), Lerner and Libby (1968), and Cavalli-Sforza and Bodmer (1971).

Chromosomal Abnormalities

It has been estimated that each adult human has approximately 10^{14} cells, all derived through the process of cell division (mitosis) from a single cell. In a normal adult each of the cells has 46 chromosomes, 23 contributed by the father's gamete (sperm) and 23 from the mother's gamete (egg). Before the gametes can unite, however, the total complement of each must be reduced from 46 to 23 in order to result in a cell with a normal complement of 46. This process is called meiosis and is responsible for the incredible number of possible combinations of chromosomes of any two gametes and thus for variations among humans and all other biparental organisms. Meiosis also assures the formation of individual gametes that contain one member from each pair of chromosomes. It is crucial that one chromosome from each pair be included in each gamete because each pair has a specific set of functions based on its unique DNA sequence (Cavalli-Sforza and Bodmer, 1971: 14). If the process is successful, the fertilized egg (zygote) will contain 46 chromosomes (22 pairs of autosomes and 2 sex chromosomes, XY for males and XX for females).

Chromosome abnormalities occur when something goes wrong at some stage in meiosis. This might result in either changes in the amount of chromosomal material (usually a change in number) or changes in the arrangement of the chromosomal material (Levitan, 1977: 66). The most common forms of chromosomal abnormalities are those involving either a loss or an excess of chromosomes. A *trisomy* is the condition caused by an excess chromosome, and *monosomy* refers to cases in which one chromosome from any pair is missing. In general trisomics and monosomics result from the failure of a pair of chromosomes to separate during meiosis (Stine, 1977: 131). This failure, *meiotic nondisjunction,* causes the vast majority of chromosomal disorders. Nondisjunction occurs in females at a much higher frequency than males and increases with the age of the mother. Figure 2.2 illustrates a normal and abnormal meiosis of chromosome 21.

In addition to the abnormal inclusion or exclusion of entire chromosomes, there are four types of chromosomal aberrations involving the loss, addition, or displacement of a major portion of a chromosome. *Translocations* and *inversions* alter the arrangement of genes in the chromosomes but do not necessarily affect their quantity and quality (Stine, 1977: 132). Translocation occurs when a segment of one chromosome is transferred to another, usually reciprocally, and inversion is the 180-degree rotation of a section of a chromosome. In contrast to these rearrangements, *deletions* and *duplications* alter the normal quantity and

FIGURE 2.2
Nondisjunction and Normal Meiosis

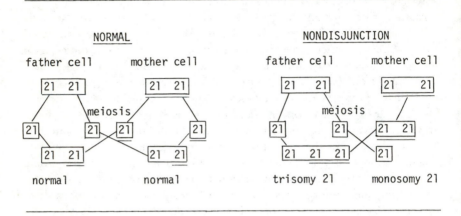

quality of genetic material, extending anywhere from one gene to an entire chromosome. Although there have been over 300 different forms of chromosomal abnormalities detected, and the possible number of mutations is unlimited, the discussion here will focus on a few of the more common anomalies.

The most frequent and well-known chromosomal abnormality is Down's syndrome. Over 15,000 infants are born each year in the United States with a debilitating chromosomal disorder; 3,000 of them are afflicted with Down's syndrome. Moreover, it is estimated that spontaneous abortion occurs in two-thirds of all fetuses with this syndrome (Creasy and Crolla, 1974). Although Down's syndrome can be transmitted through translocation,[4] the most common form is trisomy 21 (an extra chromosome in the 21st pair). Trisomy 13 and trisomy 18 (an extra chromosome in the 13th and 18th pairs, respectively) are rarer and more likely to be fatal early in life. Most chromosomal syndromes are associated with mental retardation, from mild to severe, with important exceptions such as XXX, XO, and XYY, where phenotype symptoms might be slight or nonexistent. Table 2.1 presents the incidences of the most common abnormalities as reported by Stine (1977: 150). In addition, at least 175,000 spontaneous abortions of such fetuses occur each year in the United States (NIH, 1979: 48).

With the exception of Turner's syndrome (XO), all of the disorders listed in Table 2.1 increase dramatically in frequency with maternal age (see Table 2.2). One theory suggests that this is caused by the increased chance

TABLE 2.1
Frequencies for Selected Chromosomal Abnormalities in
Live Births

Karyotype	Clinical Condition	Incidence at Birth
Trisomy 21	Down's syndrome	1 in 600-700
Trisomy 18	Edward's syndrome	1 in 4000
Trisomy 13	Patau's syndrome	1 in 6000-7000
XO	Turner's syndrome	1 in 2500 females
XXX	Triple X	1 in 1000 females
XXY	Klinefelter's syndrome	1 in 400 males
XYY	YY syndrome	1 in 250 males

Source: Stine, 1977: 150

that chromosomes will attach to each other as the ova progress in age (Stine, 1977: 75). Carr (1970) offers a basis for another hypothesis. He asserts that if the sperm does not penetrate the egg within 24 hours after ovulation, there is evidence that an aged egg will give rise to various malformations including dispermy (two sperms enter one egg resulting in a triploid condition in which the zygote has three sets of chromosomes). According to Carr, women tend to have sex less often as they age, so the time between ovulation and fertilization is bound to be on the average longer, therefore increasing the possibility of chromosomal abnormalities. Regardless of explanatory theories, evidence tying maternal age to cytogenic disorders is overwhelming.[5] Table 2.2 presents recent data for Down's syndrome.

Single-Gene Disorders

The largest number of inherited disorders is the result of single-gene defects, often related to a specific enzyme or protein production. Over 2,500 such conditions have already been catalogued (McKusick, 1978), and an average of 100 are added to the list each year (Stine, 1977: 253). Although the incidence of most single-gene disorders is rare, collectively it is estimated that 1 to 2 percent of all live-born infants will manifest such a condition at some point in their lives (NIH, 1979: 51). Although these disorders have in common the malfunctioning of a single gene, three distinct patterns of inheritance are discernible: dominant, autosomal recessive, and X-linked recessive.

Dominant. Over 1,000 genetic disorders inherited in a dominant fashion

TABLE 2.2
Risk of Giving Birth to a Down's Syndrome Infant
by Maternal Age

Maternal Age	Frequency of Down's Syndrome Infants Among Births
30	1/885
31	1/826
32	1/725
33	1/592
34	1/465
35	1/365
36	1/287
37	1/225
38	1/176
39	1/139
40	1/109
41	1/85
42	1/67
43	1/53
44	1/41
45	1/32
46	1/25
47	1/20
48	1/16
49	1/12

Source: Hook, E.B., and Lindsjö, A. (1978: 19).

are passed from parent to child directly. Each child born to a parent with a dominant disorder has a 50 percent risk or receiving that single-gene aberration from the affected parent and thereby expressing the trait. Dominant diseases do not skip generations and generally strike men and women equally. They often are manifested by abnormalities in physical structure such as the presence of an extra finger or achondroplastic dwarfism, but also might involve a change in structural protein.

One of the most publicized dominant disorders is Huntington's disease, a progressive degeneration of the nervous system causing a slow, painful, and dehumanizing deterioration of the patient.[6] The estimates of those affected in the United States range from 20,000 to 100,000 (DHEW, 1977: 3; and Stine, 1977: 270). The symptoms of Huntington's disease generally are not manifested until after the reproductive years. From the onset of symptoms, the patient steadily deteriorates for 10 to 15 years at great expense,

TABLE 2.3
Three Patterns of Inherited Single-Gene Disorders

Dominant	Autosomal Recessive	X-Linked Recessive

	a	A			a	b			X	Y
a	aa	aA		a	aa	ab		X	XX	XY
a	aa	aA		b	ab	bb		X_a	XX_a	X_aY

aa: normal 50%	aa: normal 25%	XX: normal female
aA: affected 50%	ab: carrier 50%	XXa: carrier female
	bb: affected 25%	XY: normal male
		X_aY: affected male

both financially and emotionally, to the family. The disease is expressed in loss of memory, choreic-like movement, loss of physical mobility, and a decrease in mental activity.

Autosomal Recessive. Recessive diseases exhibit a Mendelian pattern of inheritance and can occur only when two carriers of a particular gene reproduce. In each case, the child of such a union has a 25 percent chance of being affected and a 50 percent chance of being a carrier (see Table 2.3). When the affected gene is a part of a chromosome other than X or Y, it is termed autosomal recessive. Among the 1,000 or so single-gene disorders of this pattern, there are more than 100 inborn errors of metabolism. Approximately 75 of these 100 can be identified prenatally through biochemical tests. These diseases serve the basis for most of the neonatal and carrier screening programs as well as prenatal diagnosis. They include: phenylketonuria, galactosemia, sickle-cell anemia, Tay-Sachs disease, and cystic fibrosis.

X-Linked Recessive. When the recessive genes are found on the X chromosome, only males would be expected to manifest the abnormality in question. Most X-linked recessive disorders are rare; hemophilia (1/10,000) and Duchenne muscular dystrophy (1/5,200) are the more common chronic diseases caused by gene aberrations on the X chromosome. Each male will have a 50 percent chance of being affected. Female offspring will not be affected, as they will also have a normal X chromosome, but 50 percent of them will be heterozygous for the trait (i.e., carriers).

TABLE 2.4
Frequency of Multifactorial Genetic Disorders at Birth

Disorder	Whites	Blacks
Anencephaly	1/700	1/2450
Spina bifida	1/1800	1/1900
Cleft lip and palate	1/750	1/2450
Congenital heart defects	1/500	1/550
Club foot	1/230	1/355

Source: Chung and Myrianthopoulus (1968).

According to Milunsky (1977: 174), there are a few "sex-limited" diseases, such as uncontinentia pigmenti, that are confined to females.

Multifactorial Diseases

This category includes disorders involving multiple gene aberrations (polygenic) and conditions caused by an interaction between genetic and environmental causes. Most of the major birth defects and malformation syndromes are included in this category. Most common are cleft lip and palate, neural tube defects, congenital heart defects, and club foot deformity (see Table 2.4). It is estimated that 1 to 2 percent of the newborn population in the United States is affected with such a disorder (NIH, 1979: 53). Severity of these conditions varies substantially and surgical techniques are available to treat all but the most severe neural tube defects.

Genetic Screening

The most advanced state of genetic technology application is in the area of genetic screening and prenatal diagnosis. Although all genetic screening applications are similar in their objective to reduce genetic disease, the vast array of genetic disorders requires many different approaches and techniques. Some screening efforts are aimed at the general population; others are targeted at selective high-risk populations. Screening can also be conducted at various life stages: prenatal diagnosis is central to screening for Down's syndrome and other chromosomal abnormalities, PKU screening is conducted in newborns, other metabolic disorders are most effectively screened in adolescence, and detection of carriers of recessive genes is best accomplished in screening young adults. The techniques and procedures used to accomplish each of the three major types of screening (prenatal, carrier, neonatal) are summarized here and the status of current applications for each is reviewed.

Prenatal Diagnosis Techniques

Amniocentesis. The most controversial form of screening entails the prenatal detection of genetic disorders through the use of amniocentesis followed by abortion of the defective fetuses. Amniocentesis is an outpatient procedure in which approximately 20 cc of amniotic fluid is withdrawn from the amniotic sac. Although this procedure has been conducted as early as 14 weeks, Golbus et al. (1979) and others have concluded that 16 to 18 weeks from the beginning of the last menstrual period offers the maximum number of viable cells as well as optimal safety. Currently, the amniotic fluid or cultured cells, or both, can be used to detect virtually all chromosomal abnormalities in the fetus, approximately 75 serious inborn metabolic disorders, and approximately 90 percent of fetal neural tube defects (those associated with increased alpha fetoprotein in the amniotic fluid) (NIH, 1979: 4). Peter (1975: 202) suggests that eventually screening for all metabolic and chromosomal disorders might be conducted from amniotic fluid cells through routine monitoring of pregnancies.

Initial concern over potential medical risks of amniocentesis has largely dissipated. A major control study conducted by the National Institute of Child Health and Human Development (NICHD Amniocentesis Registry, 1976) concludes that "midtrimester amniocentesis is a highly accurate and safe procedure that does not significantly increase the risk of fetal loss or injury." Golbus et al. (1979: 157), in an analysis of over 3,000 consecutive amniocenteses, agree that prenatal diagnosis is "safe, highly reliable, and extremely accurate." The overall accuracy of amniocentesis in the assessment of chromosomal constitution and establishing the presence or absence of a detectable inborn error of metabolism exceeds 99.4 percent (NIH, 1979: 61).

Not surprisingly, the use of amniocentesis has increased dramatically since 1968. Of the estimated 40,000 procedures performed from 1968 to 1978, approximately 15,000 were performed in 1978. Despite the rising cost of amniocentesis (now $250–$700), especially the cell culturing process, which takes from two to three weeks, it is expected that the pattern of increased use will continue. The procedure is now regarded in most areas as accepted medical practice (Culliton, 1975), and several recent lawsuits against physicians who failed to advise this procedure will likely accelerate its use.

Ultrasound. The very recent developments in ultrasound techniques (pulse-echo sonography) have provided a supplementary method for prenatal diagnosis as well as for fetal monitoring (NIH, 1979 supplement). High-frequency sound waves are directed into the abdomen of the pregnant woman to gain an "echo-visual" representation of the fetus, placenta, uterus, and such. Ultrasound has broad medical applications but is used in prenatal diagnosis primarily to locate the placenta and head of the fetus prior to amniocentesis, especially where multiple births are suspected. In many medical centers, amniocentesis is conducted under ultrasound so that the needle can be safely guided into the amniotic sac. The widespread use of ultrasound in this way will reduce even more the risks associated with prenatal diagnosis. Evidence concerning the safety of ultrasound is less solid than for amniocentesis, although most studies have found no harmful long- or short-term hazards to the patient or the fetus (Frankel, 1973: 9; and NIH, 1979: 7).

Fetoscopy/Placental Aspiration. A wide variety of hereditary disorders (including hemophilia, sickle-cell anemia, and possibly Duchenne muscular dystrophy) not detectable via amniotic samples might be found through fetoscopy.[7] This procedure offers direct visualization of the fetus and access to fetal blood samples. It also has a therapeutic use in intrauterine transfusion of fetuses with hemolytic disease. Despite its potential, fetoscopy, especially in conjunction with aspiration, remains only an applied research technique, due to several hazards, including a miscarriage rate of 3–10 percent and an increased rate of prematurity (NIH, 1979: 9).

Other Related Technologies. The measurement of alpha fetoprotein in the amniotic fluid to identify approximately 90 percent of neural tube defects is now routinely performed at many prenatal diagnostic centers and will most likely increase as the technique becomes more precise. Fluorescent staining promises to increase the accuracy and reduce the time for karyotyping (studying chromosomes) and has the potential to identify certain chromosomal translocations undetectable through traditional karyotype analysis (Frankel, 1973: 9). In addition to the use of fluorescent screening, computer karyotyping promises more efficient diagnosis of chromosomal disorders.

Applications of Prenatal Diagnosis

Currently, approximately 85 percent of amniocenteses are conducted for chromosomal evaluation, and about three-fourths of those are for women over 35 years of age (NIH, 1979: 68). Previous birth of a child with Down's syndrome or other chromosomal abnormality, parental chromosome abnormality, and severe parental anxiety are other reasons for chromosomal evaluation. In 1978 in the United States about 7 percent of pregnant women 35 or over had an amniocentesis (though the rate in some medically sophisticated urban centers is much higher[8]), up from 3.6 percent in

1975-1976 (NIH, 1979: 151). The reason for the concentration on women over thirty-five is obvious, given the data in Table 2.2 demonstrating the relationship between Down's syndrome and maternal age.

The remaining 15 percent of prenatal diagnoses are usually indicated by previous offspring or close relatives with neural tube defects, the possibility of a sex-linked disorder, or carrier status of both parents for an inborn metabolic disorder. The screening for neural tube defects through amniocentesis is bound to expand with more widespread use of maternal-serum alpha-fetoprotein screening (NIH, 1979: 69). Except for Lesch-Nyhan disease,[9] recessive X-linked diseases cannot be diagnosed prenatally. At present sex determination is made for fetuses at high risk. If the fetus is a male, it has a 50 percent chance of having the disorder, and abortion is an option. If the fetus is identified as female, there is virtually no chance that she will have the disease but a 50 percent chance that she will be a carrier.

To date, most amniocenteses conducted to detect recessive diseases, especially inborn metabolic disorders, have been applied in families with previously affected offspring. This pattern is shifting, however, due to the increased availability and use of carrier screening programs (discussed below). For example, Tay-Sachs screening directed at high-risk Ashkenazi Jews, in combination with prenatal diagnosis of all offspring of carrier couples, provides a means of eliminating this dreaded disease. Recent prenatal diagnostic techniques can identify up to 65 percent of fetuses with the sickle-cell trait as well. Close to 80 biochemical disorders can be diagnosed prenatally today, only ten years since the first (Tay-Sachs) was possible.

Finally, amniocentesis can be used to detect Rh incompatibility between the fetus and the mother. This condition occurs when the fetus inherits the gene for Rh + blood from the father while the mother is Rh – . If some Rh + red blood cells cross the placenta into the Rh – blood of the mother, antibodies formed in the mother against the Rh + antigen can lead to severe anemia, brain damage, and possible death of the fetus (2,600 per year in the past). The development of Rh immunoglobulin, however, makes it possible to prevent this process from occurring. Early diagnosis of Rh incompatibility coupled with treatment has successfully reduced the frequency of Rh hemolytic diseases caused by incompatible Rh-factor pregnancies (Stine, 1977: 461). This represents one of the few current examples of amniocentesis used in conjunction with treatment of the disorder.

The Process of Prenatal Diagnosis

Due to the increasing use of amniocentesis and the attention it evokes from critics of genetic intervention, there is a tendency by some to equate prenatal diagnosis with the amniocentesis/abortion sequence. Although amniocentesis is the central technique through which diagnosis is accomplished, it is only one element in the entire process. Also, abortion may be the outcome in the case of a positive test, but the argument that amniocentesis leads to abortion is misleading. First, only 3 to 5 percent of all amniocenteses result in abnormal findings; in over 95 percent of the cases, the fetus is found to be normal and the pregnancy is continued. Second, there is evidence that, had prenatal diagnosis not been available, many at-risk parents automatically would have had an abortion or would have refrained from having children at all (NIH, 1979: 130; Carter et al., 1971).[10] According to Kaback, Becker, and Ruth (1974: 146), amniocentesis "dramatically alters the mechanism by which genetic disease is prevented. In the past genetic disease prevention was achieved through limitation of further reproduction in these families. Now at-risk couples can reproduce and, at the same time, selectively prevent further cases of the disorder in question, if the new alternative is acceptable to them."

Prenatal diagnosis is an integrated process extending over a period of four to six weeks or more. The complete prenatal diagnostic process presented in Figure 2.3 demonstrates its complexity and the roles of the many experts involved. Some of the techniques, especially in cell culturing, enzyme assaying, and karyotyping, require sophisticated technical skills. Although amniocentesis itself is a straightforward and relatively simple medical procedure, the support activities are extensive. For example, radiologists are needed to operate the ultrasound equipment while the physician conducts the amniocentesis. Genetic counselors provide initial explanation of the procedures and describe the options available during the process.[11] The need for continued counseling in the case of positive results is indicated by reports of depression by up to 92 percent of women who underwent abortion for medical reasons after prenatal diagnosis (Blumberg, Golbus, and Hanson, 1975).

Much investment in skills, knowledge, and equipment is required to provide a successful prenatal diagnostic program. Although the amniocentesis procedure can be done in any obstetrician's office, the laboratory facilities for cytogenic and biochemical analyses are usually located in major medical centers. The use of more sophisticated electronic monitoring equipment in larger centers suggests that a shift toward such facilities in the future is warranted (Powledge and Fletcher, 1979: 170). At present, no single laboratory has the expertise needed to perform the variety of enzyme assays now possible. Obviously, it would not be efficient to develop such skills at each location. The resulting concentration of prenatal programs in major research institutions, however, has contributed to the maldistribution of genetic services in the United States and denied ready access to large por-

FIGURE 2.3
Prenatal Diagnosis Procedures

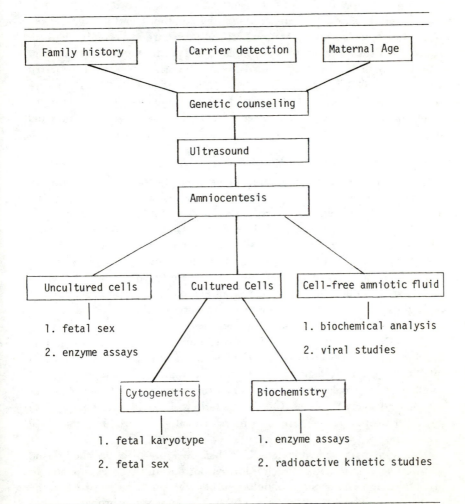

tions of the nonurban populations. One of the problems for the implementation of prenatal diagnosis programs in the future, then, is to provide a realistic service delivery system, given the technical incentives to centralize. Currently, most of the amniocenteses in the United States are conducted in university hospitals, ranging in capacity from 1,000 to 1,200 tests per year (NIH, 1979: 153). Those looking into possible certification of facilities have recommended a minimal cutoff capacity of 500 tests per year, which would further reduce access to prenatal diagnosis. Another trend in high-density urban areas, where transportation costs and time are not prohibitive, is illustrated by the megalab concept, which would permit high-volume testing. The first such facility is scheduled for New York City with a projected capacity of 4,000 prenatal tests per year (NIH, 1979: 153). Clearly, a central concern of policymakers must be to balance the technical pressures for centralization and the human needs for wide dissemination of prenatal diagnosis services.

Special Problems of Prenatal Diagnosis

One form of chromosomal abnormality that has become the center of screening controversy is the presence of an XYY complement. Early statistical data (Jacobs et al., 1965) demonstrated a high incidence of this complement among prisoners. When it was found that XYY "supermales" were overrepresented in prisons and that some tended to express antisocial behavior, in addition to being tall and having below-average IQs, efforts were made to establish a test program to identify young boys with this genotype. Although there is much disagreement over what XYY means, and no causal link has been demonstrated between this genotype and aggressive behavior, controversy has raged since the first XYY was identified in 1961 (Dershowitz, 1976: 63–71). For instance, Witkin et al. (1976: 554) conclude that the elevated crime rate of XYY males might be related to low intelligence but not to aggression. They argue that attempts to identify and single out XYY males would serve no useful purpose, as intelligence is not determined solely by genes. Others, including Beckwith and King (1974) and Pyeritz et al. (1977), are even more critical of research into the XYY syndrome.

Although mass screening for XYY has never been established,[12] the question of what to do with such information, once it becomes available in prenatal diagnosis, persists. Should parents with an XYY son be told the truth under these circumstances? There is at least some probability that their knowledge of this might be self-fulfilling: they might be looking for the predicted behavior, with the resulting stigmatization imposed on a healthy normal boy. Powledge and Fletcher (1979: 171) argue that such information should not be withheld despite its disputed importance. They suggest full discussion of such possibilities during counseling prior to amniocentesis with the option of disclosure stated on the consent form. The parents' request for disclosure or nondisclosure should be honored in all cases. Another question is whether or not an XYY complement should be grounds for dismissal of criminal proceedings. In other words, if XYY is really linked to antisocial behavior, can society treat that person as a criminal? Should criminals with abnormal chromosome complements be sent to prison at all if they are genetically predestined to behave in a particular manner?[13] Prior to 1961 this was of no concern. Again, increased knowledge presents us with new dilemmas.

An additional dilemma arising out of prenatal chromosomal technologies concerns its use for sex predetermination. As the sex of a fetus is easily identified through amniocentesis, it is obvious that persons desiring a child of a particular sex could use prenatal diagnostic techniques for that purpose. Prenatal diagnosis for sex determination is controversial for two reasons: first, there are ethical objections to the use of abortion for such a reason; second, there is a question as to whether a scarce medical resource such as amniocentesis ought to be used for that purpose (John Fletcher, 1978). Despite these considerations, abortion for sex choice is legal under *Roe* v. *Wade*: The state has no interest in refusing an adult woman the right of self-determination in reproduction through the second trimester of pregnancy. Some doctors may object to performing amniocentesis solely to identify fetal sex (except in cases of X-linked diseases such as hemophilia), but such information must be made available to parents who desire it under the prevailing law.

John Fletcher (1979: 553), although concluding that "it is not ethically required that physicians withhold amniocentesis from fully informed parents who may use the results in deciding to abort for sex choice," offers three counterarguments. First, when there is a genuine scarcity of amniocentesis in any center, its use for sex choice should be given lowest priority and the parents should bear all expenses. Second, because of even minimal risks to the mother and fetus, the procedure should be performed only with adequate counseling and high-quality laboratory work. Finally, concern should be directed to the long-range consequences of sex preselection on the family and society. Coombs's (1977) findings that women are much more likely to prefer sons than daughters suggests possible social implications should the process become widespread. Etzioni (1968) and Westoff and Rindfuss (1974) contend that if sex predetermination were widely available it would lead to an additional 7 percent surplus in males, resulting in social changes. Emphasis will most probably shift away from this method of predetermining sex in the near future as progress apparently is being made on several other fronts including special types of diaphragms and pills and a sperm treatment in which the X and Y fractions are separated and the selected element is inseminated artificially (Largey, 1972: 379–382)

At the center of such prenatal diagnosis is the role of the state. Milunsky (1976: 58) argues that although a voluntary program of amniocentesis followed by voluntary abortion of genetically defective fetuses is equitable, evidence implies that such an approach is not effective. A mandatory program of amniocentesis (most probably based on maternal age and other risk factors) followed by voluntary abortion would increase the effectiveness of the preventive program, but serious ethical and legal questions make this approach difficult to accept.[14] Questions of invasion of privacy and religious freedom arise, and at least one observer (Friedman, 1974: 92) contends that mandatory amniocentesis for any reason would be challenged on grounds of violating the Fourth Amendment proscription of "unreasonable search and seizure." Any efforts at mandating prenatal diagnosis are likely to fail because, at present, there is no evidence that the state has any compelling interest to warrant intrusion into the procreation process on genetic grounds. Prenatal diagnosis should be available to those who desire it; any effort to mandate such procedures, however, has little support.

The very presence of the ability to diagnose genetic diseases prenatally results in an ethical dilemma centering on the attitudes of society toward those who bear children with conditions that could have been diagnosed if the parents had desired. Callahan (1973: 248ff) sees a potential danger to the right of self-determination, for instance, if such screening becomes routine and therapeutic abortions automatic. Even if the decision of the parents is voluntary, this precedent would establish a "causal logic" in bearing a defective child. By giving the parents "freedom of choice" through advances in screening, we are also making them responsible for the choices they make. Callahan (1973) argues convincingly that it is only a short step to distinguishing between responsible and irresponsible choices under such conditions. The social pressure on parents to make the "responsible" choice might be powerful. Although they would, in principle, retain the right to carry a diagnosed defective fetus to term, it is not difficult to imagine the inherent pressures on them to abort for the "good of society" and the potential child. By providing full, informed freedom of choice, then, advances in prenatal diagnosis techniques might result in the abrogation of such freedom.

The ultimate medical goal of prenatal diagnosis is to identify and treat the fetus while in the womb. Abortion of the fetus is the only means available at present to prevent the majority of genetic diseases, and it certainly is not an ideal approach or even an acceptable one for some observers. John Fletcher (1974: 96), for instance, contends it is wrong to designate abortion of an affected fetus "therapy," as that term implies the curing of a disease rather than the elimination of the diseased person. In addition to treatment available in cases of Rh incompatibility, galactosemia and a few other disorders [15] can now be diagnosed prenatally and treated successfully, thus averting mental retardation and in some cases early death. Milunsky (1977: 177) states that progress in prenatal treatment for genetic disorders will be forthcoming "provided that fetal research is not even further interdicted by state legislation." With continued support for medical research in this area, opportunities for early treatment or prevention will increase, thus reducing the need for the major option today, abortion.

Carrier Screening

Prenatal diagnosis for most recessive diseases can be effectively conducted only after the birth of one affected child, but developments in the identification of carriers (heterozygotes) among those of reproductive age offers a means of directing attention to high-risk couples before they have children. The prospective parents can then be given the option of prenatal diagnosis to determine the status of their offspring, only 25 percent of whom will be affected. Carrier screening is most practical when the disorder occurs predominantly in a well-defined population *and* when a simple, accurate, and inexpensive method to identify heterozygotes is available (NIH, 1979: 43).

The primary objective of these programs is to diagnose the carrier status of individuals for specific genetic traits and educate them as to their chances of having affected offspring, with the hope thereby of reducing the number of children born with that disorder. This objective might be accomplished by discouraging them to reproduce or by providing prenatal diagnosis, if available for that particular disease. Obviously, this type of screening intrudes into the procreation process and provides an excellent example of the potential conflict among parental rights, societal needs, and the rights of the potentially affected individual (discussed in Chapter 3). Also, as the carriers do not have the disease, the screening process is indirect and not beneficial to the health of those screened but rather to potential persons who have a one-in-four chance of having the disease if they are conceived and born.

Tay-Sachs Disease. The most extensive and successful heterozygote screening attempts in the United States are for Tay-Sachs disease. Tay-Sachs is a fatal neurodegenerative disease that is 100 times more common in Jews of eastern European background than in any other population.[16] An unfortunate aspect of Tay-Sachs is that an affected baby appears normal and healthy for the first six to eight months of life. Gradually, however, the nervous system degenerates and death results by age four or five after a long and painful confinement. Paralysis, blindness, and severe mental retardation are common, and the care approaches $40,000 per year (Powledge, 1974). In addition, the emotional toll of watching one's apparently normal baby deteriorate is heavy.

Since 1969, more than 200,000 childbearing-age individuals in North America have voluntarily submitted to the Tay-Sachs screening test. Furthermore, "it is estimated that as many as 600 pregnancies at risk for Tay-Sachs disease have been monitored through amniocentesis. . . . The births of approximately 150 infants afflicted . . . have been prevented" (NIH, 1979: 43–44). Screening for Tay-Sachs is unusual because both carrier detection and prenatal diagnostic tests through amniocentesis are available at this time. As a result, prospective prevention of the disease is feasible, as (1) it occurs primarily in a specific population where selective screening can be effective; (2) there is a simple, accurate, and inexpensive carrier detection test; and (3) the condition can be detected early in pregnancy, enabling selective abortion if the parents desire. Despite its adaptability to mass screening because of these factors, Tay-Sachs also reflects the problems posed by carrier screening. Unless the program is conducted with care and utmost concern for human values, it, too, can be counterproductive. Still, the success of Tay-Sachs screening in several communities, such as Washington, D.C., offers hope for similar screening of other diseases (Kaback and O'Brien, 1973).

Sickle-Cell Anemia. Sickle-cell anemia is an autosomal recessive disease found primarily in American blacks, of whom approximately 10 percent are carriers of the trait. Approximately 50,000 persons suffer from the disease, which can lead to early and painful death but also might allow for a relatively normal life span. The cost of care for sickle-cell anemia is high, and no treatment is available. As there is no comprehensive prenatal diagnostic test available at present, selective abortion is not always an alternative. Often the only option is to identify carriers and counsel them on the risks of having an affected child if both parents are heterozygotes. Current technical advances in prenatal detection through amniocentesis, coupled with restrictive enzyme-recombinant DNA techniques with uncultured amniotic fluid cells (Kan and Dozy, 1978), promise to lead to expanded carrier screening and monitoring; at present, though, screening for sickle-cell anemia leaves carriers with fewer choices than Tay-Sachs carriers.

The early 1970s saw a great amount of interest in sickle-cell legislation. At both the national and state levels politicians embraced the concept of attacking this long-neglected disease and, in some cases, rushed into passing screening programs that were haphazard and poorly planned (National Academy of Sciences, 1975: 117). In many statutes, little distinction was made between the carrier status and the disease, and much unnecessary anxiety and confusion resulted. Education of the public in some cases came after rather than prior to screening and was generally insufficient. Despite the fact that the first laws were often written and sponsored by black legislators, the negative repercussions in the black community were not anticipated. Opposition to mandatory screening was strong, and voluntary programs also came under attack, primarily because of the stigmatization attached to being a carrier of this highly selective disease. Fear of discrimination by insurance companies and employers accentuated this opposition.[17]

Table 2.5 illustrates that about one-third of the states offer screening for sickle-cell anemia. Legislation in a handful of these states makes screening mandatory. The National Sickle Cell Anemia Control Act passed in May 1972 allocated $85 million over a three-year period to be used for screening and counseling. One requirement of the act is that the states administer screening programs on a voluntary basis in order to qualify for federal funds, and pressure is on the states to comply. This, combined with opposition from internal sources, resulted in Massachusetts' decision in 1974 to amend its earlier compulsory legislation to provide sickle-cell testing on a voluntary basis. The present state of knowledge about the disease and the sensitive nature of the issue certainly favor voluntary screening based on adequately funded education programs. Obviously, these programs also require full support of the target population if they are to succeed.

Carrier Screening Problems. The process of carrier identification produces a major dilemma. It is clear that for many recessive diseases such as Tay-Sachs, sickle-cell anemia, and thalassemia, the incidence among members of particular ethnic groups is significantly higher than the population as a whole. Economically and logistically, screening such high-risk groups is practical, but screening the entire population would be a waste of money because of the low overall incidence of carriers. When certain groups already are the target of social discrimination, however, identifying them as carriers of a genetic disease can be further stigmatizing. This is especially true in screening for the sickle-cell trait, as there is little medical value in detecting carrier status unless it is used to influence the reproductive decision of two carriers contemplating having a child.

Another problem is that in screening for carriers, one is not dealing with a treatable disease. Usually there is no disease, only the existence of heterozygous carriers of the particular genes. The stigmatization attached to carriers causes much misplaced apprehension and bitterness, even under the best of circumstances. Therefore, screening of this type presents an even greater dilemma than mass PKU testing programs. Any state considering carrier detection programs must be certain to have the support of

TABLE 2.5
Sickle-Cell Anemia Screening Laws, 1977

State	Voluntary	Preschool Testing	Premarital Testing	Confidential Results	Counseling Program	Public Education
Arizona	yes	yes	yes	no	no	no
California	no	yes	yes	no	no	no
Georgia	yes	no	yes	no	yes	no
Illinois	no	yes	no	no	no	no
Indiana	no	yes	yes	no	yes	no
Iowa	yes	yes	yes	yes	yes	yes
Kansas	yes	no	no	yes	yes	no
Kentucky	no	no	yes	no	yes	no
Louisiana	yes	yes	no	no	no	no
Massachusetts	yes	yes	no	yes	yes	yes
Mississippi	no	yes	no	no	no	yes
New Mexico	no	yes	no	no	no	yes
New York	no	yes	no	no	no	no
North Carolina	yes	no	no	yes	yes	yes
Ohio	yes	no	no	no	yes	yes
South Carolina	yes	no	no	no	yes	yes
Virginia	yes	no	no	yes	yes	yes

Source: Data from Philip Reilly, Genetics, Law and Social Policy (Cambridge: Harvard University Press, 1977), p. 85.

the affected population and must be willing to expend significant resources on education and publicity before the actual screening begins. Even then, screening will be controversial because it restricts certain individual prerogatives, either implicitly or explicitly.

Neonatal Screening: Phenylketonuria (PKU)

According to Hansen, Shahidi, and Stein (1978: 246), screening for PKU is "one of the largest and most successful of recent preventive public health programs." Since 1962, an estimated 20 million infants have been screened for this autosomal recessive disease caused by inactivity of the enzyme phenylalanine. This metabolic defect results in severe mental retardation if it is not identified soon after birth and treated. With early detection and administration of a diet low in phenylalanine content (see Reyzer [1978] for a description of the diet), mental retardation can be averted. PKU cases previously accounted for about 1 percent of residents in mental institutions; since systematic screening was introduced, there has not been one admission of a child with mental retardation caused by PKU (Mac-Cready, 1974).

In the early 1960s Robert Guthrie developed a bacterial inhibition assay test that could be automated to provide for mass screening of PKU. Since that time, the test has been improved and multiple tests for other metabolic disorders have been used in combination with the Guthrie test (Guthrie, 1973: 229–230). Although PKU screening has enjoyed widespread public support and is viewed by most observers to be a valuable screening effort for a treatable metabolic disorder, early PKU testing met with criticisms of its inaccuracy, especially relating to false positives. For example:

> The tests are not accurate: they miss a number of cases of PKU and yield false positive reactions in an even greater number. Given a positive test, the physician will very probably put the child on a low phenylalanine diet. . . . But a child who does not have PKU is actively endangered by the diet and can suffer physical deterioration at the least; a number of children have died from being treated for PKU, and it is likely that they did not have the disease. [Bessman and Swazey, 1971: 51]

Stine (1977: 507) also criticizes the fact that such tests were made compulsory before sufficient knowledge was available to make an informed decision. Nitowsky (1973) asserts that the state-mandated laboratory tests do not detect PKU but instead indicate high blood phenylalanine levels, which can have causes other than PKU. Although it is now generally agreed that quality-control improvements and new procedures have minimized though not eliminated this possibility (Hansen, Shahidi, and

Stein, 1978), PKU screening continues to elicit criticism.

Despite a virtual consensus that the diet therapy can be discontinued at about age six or seven without adverse effects (Holtzman, Welcher, and Mellitis, 1975), recent evidence suggests that it might be better if the patient remains on the diet until the teen years. Also, there is increasing concern for mothers who had been treated for PKU as children. Data suggest that a previously treated mother who is not on the diet during preganancy will poison the fetus and up to 70 percent of fetuses will die even if they themselves are free of PKU. Murray (1979) contends that the mother should be placed on a low phenylalanine diet extremely early in pregnancy, preferably before she becomes pregnant and throughout the pregnancy. This problem suggests the need for continual follow-up and educational programs for those with PKU and demonstrates the complexity of genetic disease.

The history of PKU screening legislation has been a short but active one. Within two years after passage of the first mandatory testing program in 1962, 31 states followed suit. By 1970, 42 states plus the District of Columbia had passed PKU legislation.[18] About half the states now provide multiphasic testing for other less common metabolic errors.[19] Although the specifics of PKU screening legislation vary, most states mandate the testing of newborns. Most of these states, however, provide for exemption on religious grounds.

Reilly (1977) is critical on several grounds of the legislation written by many states. First, most of the states do not provide guarantees of genetic counseling to parents of affected children or provide counseling of the affected person at appropriate ages. Second, only a handful of the states fund public education programs or provide follow-up testing. Also, few state laws consider the confidentiality of test results or specify the manner in which such data should be stored, if at all. Reilly (1975: 334) concludes that "the passage of shoddily written genetic disease screening laws" suggests the need for model legislation drafted by a committee of concerned individuals. This would help ensure "comprehensive and reflective treatment of medicoethical issues by a panel of experts that no single group of state lawmakers could amass" (Reilly, 1975: 336). The passage of comprehensive federal legislation to combat genetic disease appears to be increasingly likely.

Despite technical testing problems and the difficulties of applying many state laws, PKU screening of newborns is the most widespread form of genetic screening.[20] As such, it serves as a model for screening programs for other metabolic disorders such as galactosemia. It is unlikely, however, that the haste in passing PKU screening legislation will be duplicated for other diseases (Lappé and Roblin, 1974). One reason for this is that legislators are less likely than a decade ago to commit funds to untested health-related programs. Another reason is that among all the screening procedures, PKU is probably the least controversial because it results in the treatment of the disease. Most importantly, the stigmatization and sensitivity of PKU screening are more limited than for programs in which the target population is both well defined and already the subject of discrimination.

Implications of Genetic Screening and Prenatal Diagnosis

Mass genetic screening, whether through amniocentesis, carrier testing, or neonatal tests, remains controversial. Even among scientists there is a "typical lack of professional agreement on proper procedures" (Powledge, 1974: 32). Although Pole (1971) sees mass screening as cost effective in saving physician's time, Black and Riley (1973) urge that low priority be given to patient monitoring and population screening because it is too costly and not very useful.

Out of this controversy has come a series of studies proposing guidelines or standards for genetic screening. The National Academy of Sciences (1975) recommends that genetic screening is an appropriate form of medical care only when the following conditions are met:

1. There is evidence of substantial public benefit and acceptance.
2. The benefits outweigh the costs.
3. Appropriate public education can be carried out.
4. Informed consent is feasible.
5. The means are available to evaluate the effectiveness and success of each step in the process.

Obviously, each of these conditions is open to a broad range of interpretations, although together they serve as a useful initial set of guidelines. Nitowsky (1973) offers further technical criteria regarding sensitivity of the tests, treatment of false positives, and prompt study of suspected positives to distinguish among variants. The most comprehensive guidelines for genetic screening are contained in a report of a research group from the Institute of Society, Ethics and the Life Sciences (Lappé et al., 1972). They concentrate on the ethical and social issues emphasizing community participation, equal access, voluntary compliance, informed consent, provision of counseling, and protection of the right to privacy. More recently the institute promulgated similar guidelines for prenatal diagnosis, placing even greater emphasis on privacy, confidentiality, and access (Powledge and Fletcher, 1979).

In spite of the mixed success in PKU screening, Lappé and Roblin

(1974: 10–12) suggest caution in establishing new screening programs. They recommend creation of pilot research screening programs to assess variability of the disease and efficacy of proposed treatments before mass screening. These and other concerns will be discussed in detail in later chapters when the role of the government in genetic intervention is explicated. Before consideration of the political and social issues surrounding genetic technology, it is necessary to review the current status of a variety of available reproductive technologies that might serve as powerful forms of genetic intervention.

Artificial Insemination and Sperm Banking

The most widespread form of reproductive technology today is artificial insemination. Annas (1979: 14) estimates that approximately 250,000 children have been born through artificial insemination (AI) and that a "home insemination kit" might not be far off. Estimates of annual AIs in the United States range from 10,000 (Annas, 1979) to 20,000 (Finegold, 1976: 121). The first recorded use of AI in humans was conducted by John Hunter in the eighteenth century (McLaren, 1973: 3), but the technique has enjoyed wide application only since the late 1940s. Recent innovations in sperm banking, combined with an increasing scarcity of adoptable children in the United States, promises to expand the use of artificial insemination for personal and potentially eugenic purposes.

Artificial insemination is a relatively simple medical procedure, although its success depends on a number of technical factors including the quality of the semen specimen and the timing of insemination (McLaren, 1973). After the semen is obtained by masturbation, it is deposited by means of a syringe in or near the cervix of the woman's uterus. Due to uncertainty as to exact timing of ovulation, insemination is usually conducted on several consecutive days to increase the chance of pregnancy. A success rate of 70 to 75 percent pregnancy within three to four months of the start of treatment has been achieved (McLaren, 1973: 3). Although few systematic, long-term studies have been conducted, there is no evidence of increased mortality or abnormality rates in babies born via AI. Iizuka et al. (1968) have concluded that physical and mental development of the AI children was in no way inferior to those in a control group and that in IQ they significantly exceeded the control group.[21]

Although the procedures are identical, there are two basic types of AI, depending on whether the sperm used is the husband's (AIH) or a donor's (AID). Although biologically it is irrelevant whether the semen is provided by a husband or a donor, the ethical, psychological, and social problems surrounding AID are more severe. Also, indications for the use of each technique differ. In the past AIH was limited to the infrequent situation in which physical or psychological difficulties precluded fertilization through sexual intercourse. Recently, with the capability to freeze and store sperm, it has become possible to pool several ejaculations from a male with a low sperm count (oligospermia) and concentrate them by separating the spermatozoa from the semen.

Artificial insemination with a donor is medically indicated when the husband is wholly infertile, there is severe Rh incompatibility, or the husband is known to suffer from a serious hereditary disorder such as Huntington's disease. In addition to its strict medical uses, AID encompasses a range of possible eugenic applications. By selecting donors according to some predetermined genetic characteristics, AID could be used to extend propagation of males with such qualities. This positive eugenics approach, according to Muller (1961), would benefit human evolution, but there appears to be little support for this use of AID (Medawar, 1969). On the other hand, it could be argued that those with certain genetic diseases should refrain from propagating (Purdy, 1978). Under these conditions, AID could be used as an alternative means of "having children."

The potential application of artificial insemination for eugenic purposes has been extended by the introduction of technologies designed to freeze and preserve sperm at low temperatures (see Mark Frankel, 1973a). The most accepted technique of "cryopreservation" is the immersion of sperm in liquid nitrogen at $-196.5°C$ (Mark Frankel, 1978: 1446). Sperm banks are now available in many U.S. cities to store the frozen semen. Such facilities have raised the specter of parents going to the bank and selecting sperm of donors with superior genotypes with the hope of propagating little Einsteins or Van Cliburns, or even Shockleys.[22] At present, however, the majority of clients are men who contemplate undergoing vasectomy but who wish to maintain a "fertility insurance" against unforeseen circumstances such as the death of a child, new marriage, or change of mind (Reilly, 1977: 203). Sperm banking also facilitates administrative convenience and allows for expanded use of donors,[23] as well as providing a mechanism through which characteristic selection of one's progeny is simplified.

It is estimated that about 1,000 infants have been born after fertilization with sperm stored at low temperatures. The procedure is still considered experimental, as its genetic and biological consequences are unknown. So far few pregnancies have resulted from sperm frozen for more than six months (Mark Frankel, 1978: 1446). It is known that the fertilizing capacity of human sperm frozen for several months drops to about two-thirds of that of fresh semen (McLaren, 1973: 5), but less is known about the prolonged effects of freezing. The possibility of irreversible genetic damage of the sperm during the freezing still exists, despite early successes. This uncertainty is enough for Kass (1971) to consider experimentation with human sperm and zygote banking as immoral and to argue that it should not be conducted.

Zygote (fertilized egg) banking is not yet available for humans, but in vitro fertilization, initiated in 1978, suggests that it is only a matter of time. Although it would be similar in principle to semen banking, zygote banking would entail more complicated medical procedures. Eggs would first be removed from the female ovary by a minor surgical operation called laparoscopy. Then, the egg would be fertilized in the laboratory by the sperm of either the husband or a donor. Finally, the fertilized egg would be implanted in the uterus of the natural mother or a surrogate mother for normal gestation and birth. Obviously, zygote banking could extend the possibilities for manipulating the reproductive process, and the ramifications could be dramatic.

Major ethical questions raised by artificial insemination center on its impact on the meaning of marriage and parenthood. According to Dunstan (1973: 51), no major Christian church has explicitly favored the practice of AID, and the Roman Catholic and Jewish orthodox teachings have condemned it as adulterous. Ramsey (1970) opposes AID because it dehumanizes parenthood and relegates procreation to the laboratory. Similarly, Piatelli-Palmarini (1973: 24) is hesitant to accept such techniques because of the potential loss of identity of the individual produced. In addition to the possible effects on the "stepfather" and donor, "we must consider whether the very person thus created is also merely a means for gratifying a frustrated maternity." Dunstan (1973) criticizes the deception and concealment that frequently accompanies AID and asserts that the act of compassion to a would-be mother might result in injustice to the child. On the other hand, Joseph Fletcher (1954: 100 ff.) argues that the need to love and care for a child is central to marriage. AID, then, can be a truly human act of love on the part of both parents, not a contemptuous act. Sherman (1973) suggests that the benefits of sperm banking and AID outweigh the risks. Finegold (1976: 121–125) offers examples of the joy expressed by couples who had children through AID and concludes that the "gratification exhibited by the 'parents' of the AI child" probably encourages sterologists to continue the practice in spite of the legal pitfalls and religious-ethical objections.

Despite the widespread use of AID during the last three decades, legal questions abound. As the children resulting from AID are not the biological offspring of the parents, their legitimacy has been frequently questioned, especially in estate or divorce proceedings. After a series of court cases in which the AID child was declared illegitimate,[24] a California appellate court in 1968 held that the term "father" could not be restricted to its biological sense.[25] The court ruled that "the determinative factor is whether the legal relationship of the father and child exists" and that consent of the father prior to AID was both legally binding and irreversible. Since that decision, at least 15 states have enacted laws to regulate artificial insemination, although none has yet written a comprehensive statute (Reilly, 1977: 200). Although there is some variation by state, in general they agree that AID children are legitimate if the husband consented prior to the procedure.

With the debate over legitimacy of AID children apparently resolved in the few states that have faced the question, concern now has shifted toward criteria for donor selection. Curie-Cohen, Luttrell, and Shapiro (1979), in a survey of 379 practitioners of AID, found a general lack of standards in donor selection, inadequate genetic screening of prospective donors, and a failure to keep adequate permanent records on donors.[26] They also suggest that the process often places the interests of the physician and donor above that of the child. Although Reilly (1977: 202) agrees that donor selection requires more consideration and that properly drafted legislation would clarify the situation, he suggests caution in legislating elevated standards of care. He asks why the AID process should be scrutinized more carefully than natural insemination, as Curie-Cohen and associates imply in their appeal for extensive genetic screening of donors.

Many other legal questions remain unanswered. The legal status of the donor, for example, is questioned in many states (except California, where the statute excludes the donor from being designated the natural father). Also, the standardization of records for personal or genetic purposes is bound to become a legal issue in the future as some of the children born through AID attempt to "find their roots." Finally, there is the question of the liability of sperm banks. For instance, what if they mislabel a deposit, resulting in the birth of a mulatto to two black parents (Reilly, 1977: 204)? What if the semen is accidentally destroyed by power failure or such?[27] What happens if a depositor fails to pay the annual storage fee? As it appears that a greater proportion of semen banking in the future will take place in commercial enterprises, what guarantees does a depositor have of continued service? These and many other legal questions will certainly occur in the near future, as no state as yet has any laws covering sperm banks.

As in the case of screening programs, public policy lags far behind the technological advances in artificial insemination. The legal system has offered conflicting decisions, and most state legislatures and Congress have ignored the problems raised by sperm banks, AID, and possible zygote banks. The eugenic potential of these technologies is substantial and will emerge as an issue of importance as the various genetic and reproductive technologies are used at accelerating rates. As Reilly (1977: 206) concludes,

"It is clear that AID is a firmly established clinical procedure whose use will increase as screening for genetic disease becomes more sophisticated."

In Vitro Fertilization and Embryo Transfer

In vitro fertilization is the procedure through which eggs are removed from the ovaries via laparoscopy and are fertilized outside the body, generally, though not always, with the sperm of the husband. Embryo transfer is the procedure through which the fertilized egg, cultured to the 16- to 32-cell stage, is implanted in the uterus of the woman. For clarification purposes, both procedures together are labeled IVF. The most common medical indication for IVF is tubal occlusion (blocked oviducts), which does not allow the egg to pass through the fallopian tubes to be fertilized. It is estimated by the National Research Council (1975: 20) that between 0.5 and 1 percent of all American women who are otherwise unable might be able to bear children through IVF. A recent estimate by the Ethics Advisory Board (1979) sets this figure at 280,000 women.

Until 1978, discussion of IVF was directed at potential applications and limited to a handful of ethicists and scientists. However, the birth of the world's first confirmed "test-tube" baby on July 25, 1978, in England immediately expanded awareness of the issues. Although Louise Brown represents the first successful attempt to bring an ovum fertilized outside the body to a full-term pregnancy, this single event was not the dramatic breakthrough heralded by the mass media and was not unexpected in the scientific community. Earlier (1973), Steptoe and Edwards had been successful with in vitro fertilization and implantation in the womb for short periods of time.

Due to the public and media attention caused by this development, as well as the significance of the event, the Secretary of the Department of Health, Education, and Welfare (DHEW) directed the Ethics Advisory Board to study the "profound scientific, ethical, legal, and social aspects" of IVF (for previous action, see Reilly, 1977: 209–211). The findings were to help DHEW make decisions on the funding and conduct of such experiments. Although the board concluded that a prohibition of such research is "neither justified nor wise" and could find no ethical objections to the funding of IVF research with federal monies, it expressed grave concern for the ethical complexity raised by this technological application. The board also recommended a fourteen-day limit on the length of time embryos should be sustained in vitro, strict research guidelines, and the development of a "model law to clarify the legal status of children born as a result of *in vitro* fertilization."

Despite the acceptance of IVF research by the Ethics Advisory Board, the ethical, legal, and social issues raised by IVF promise much future debate in the political arena. The ethical issues center on the disposition of the embryos as well as the intervention in procreation. (The complexity of these ethical dimensions is reviewed thoroughly in an excellent article by Walters [1979]). In general, though, the three ethical perspectives (pro, con, and moderate) toward human genetic intervention reviewed in Chapter 1 apply here as well. Against the use of IVF are Kass, Ramsey, and Lappé, among others. Their opposition varies in substance and intensity, but Kass (1972: 49) summarizes it well: "My point is simply this: there are more and less human ways of bringing a child into the world. I am arguing that the laboratory production of human beings is no longer *human* procreation, that making babies in laboratories—even 'perfect' babies—means a degradation of parenthood." Both Ramsey (1972) and Kass (1972) favor additional research on oviduct reconstruction as an alternative to IVF and argue that clinical research on IVF should not be continued.

Taking more moderate yet cautious positions are Curran (1973) and Hellegers and McCormick (1978). Although they have no inherent moral objections to IVF in cases where conception is not otherwise possible, they are concerned about the risks to potential offspring as well as the desirability of proceeding with the research at this time. Kieffer (1979: 205) cautions that "there is at present no way of finding out whether or not the experimental procedures of *in vitro* fertilization . . . or any other exotic reproductive technique will result in congenital anomalies, sterility, or mental or physical retardation in any of the progeny." Hellegers and McCormick (1978: 77) also question whether it is justifiable to expend limited resources on life-creating technologies in view of more immediate health and nutrition problems.

Joseph Fletcher again is the most vocal ethical proponent of reproductive intervention. By focusing on the end result of a healthy child, he concludes (1971: 776) that the human need to bear children justifies the choice to use IVF. Despite his personal hesitancy, Rosenfeld (1978) contends that clinical use of IVF can easily be justified on ethical grounds. Most of the other supporters of IVF are clinicians and researchers such as Shettles and Edwards who argue that the procedure has been well tested in animals, has proved safe, and is justified for clinical application in humans (Walters, 1979: 26).

In addition to the continuous ethical debate, IVF raises legal questions. It shares all of the legal problems of AID, as many of its procedures and results are similar, and presents several new ones. One major question is the legal status of the preimplanted embryo: Is it a person, the property of the couple, or what? The recent award of $50,000 in damages to a woman whose preimplanted embryo was destroyed at a New York hospital suggests that although the embryo is not a legal person (under *Roe* v. *Wade*), the special interests of the donors in the embryo give it great value. Reilly (1977: 214) contends that the legal status of the embryo must be defined so that laboratory technicians and clinicians will be aware of their responsibilities. Reilly (1977: 213) concludes that the rights of reproductive autonomy guaranteed by the Supreme Court extend to the use of IVF and that the legal right of the woman to seek treatment for infertility outweighs any state interest to protect her health or the health of the embryo.

The ethical and legal problems become even more complex when logical extensions of IVF are considered. In addition to the clinical use of IVF to overcome the problem of blocked fallopian tubes are its applications in combination with donated ova and surrogate mothers. There is no known biological reason why the egg ultimately implanted in the woman must be her own. In certain cases an "adopted embryo" might be produced from fertilization of a donor egg with the husband's sperm. This represents the female counterpart to AID. Medical indications for this procedure include cases of maternally carried dominant genetic disorders, women whose eggs do not accept fertilization, and infertility due to ovarian failures of undetermined causes. Edwards and Steptoe (1973) explain that relatively few women would need a donor embryo to alleviate infertility.

The most controversial use of IVF occurs when a couple undergoes in vitro fertilization and has the embryo implanted in another woman's uterus to carry to term. Usually this would entail the hiring of a surrogate mother to, in effect, rent her womb for nine months. The legal and ethical implications of this application are staggering. For instance, what if the surrogate mother decides to keep the baby, or the natural parents attempt to prohibit the surrogate from smoking or drinking during pregnancy to protect "their" baby? Many of these questions might be worked out before the procedure begins, but the emotional and psychological problems may persist.

Although there are limited medical indications for IVF in a surrogate, such as cases in which a woman has a diseased or absent uterus but functional ovaries, it would more likely be used to avoid pregnancy for reasons of career, convenience, fear, or vanity. Some argue that this rationale could lead to disruption of the traditional family and produce classes of surrogates who carried babies as a profession. Reilly (1977: 218) suggests that the state might wish to permit surrogate motherhood to women incapable of childbirth but forbid it to women who choose to avoid gestation for other reasons, but he rejects state interference with the right of individuals to contract for surrogate-motherhood services: "Women should also have the legal right to carry any embryo to term for any reason they wish."

A final set of concerns over IVF relates to the laboratory uses to which this procedure might be put. Some of those who support in vitro fertilization to help infertile couples oppose what they view as close to experimentation with human subjects. These nonclinical uses include the production of embryos through in vitro fertilization to develop and test contraceptives, investigate abnormal cell growth, determine certain causes of cancer, and study the development of chromosomal abnormalities (Edwards and Steptoe, 1973: 14). Other potential genetic uses include attempts at altering gene structures, preimplantation repair of genetic defects (Walters, 1979: 38), and preimplantation screening for chromosomal abnormalities and genetic defects. Some of these areas of research promise many future benefits, but they do so through experimentation with embryos and are therefore highly controversial.

Cloning of Humans

Cloning is a process through which the original nucleus of an egg with its genetic code is removed and replaced with a nucleus from a body (somatic) cell. In the case of humans this would require the acquisition of an egg from the woman via laparoscopy, the chemical or laser destruction of the nucleus, and the "fertilization" with the nucleus of the somatic cell. This "fertilized" egg would then be implanted in a womb and brought to term. The result of cloning, if successful, is an exact genetic duplicate of the organism from which the somatic cell was taken. This process is based on the premise that the entire genetic code of any organism is present in each somatic cell and that when inserted properly in the egg it will produce a duplicate of the entire organism. Obviously, this is a much more difficult and drastic intervention process than any of the current reproductive technologies because the product is not a unique genotype.

Although human clones have long been a central aspect of science fiction and futuristic works, including Huxley's *Brave New World* (1932), only recently have the possible consequences of cloning been publicly debated. In large part this controversy was generated by David Rorvik's claim of the first human cloning in his book *In His Image* (1978). Although few scientists took his claim seriously, due to current technical obstacles, it led to wide and sensational coverage by the mass media and therefore a greater awareness by the public. It also resulted in a suit to gain access to federal grants involving cloning being filed in federal court by a group of scientists (Kieffer, 1979: 206) and in the first congressional hearing devoted to human cloning, conducted by the House Subcommittee on Health and Environment in May 1978. Although the hearings were inconclusive and resulted in no legislation, and the public furor and press coverage has been inactivated, cloning has quickly become a recognized though misunderstood term in the United States.

Despite the attention, human cloning at this stage is theoretical. The process has been successful in frogs, but as yet no mammal has been cloned. Also, no organism, including frogs, has been cloned from adult somatic cells; only embryonic cells have been used. Although James Watson (1971: 74), codiscoverer of DNA, projects that a human being will be produced by means of clonal reproduction in 20 to 50 years, there is still disagreement among scientists as to whether it will ever be even technically feasible. With the stakes in animal cloning, especially of livestock, so high, however, research in that area is expected to continue. If it is successful, most informed researchers predict that the time lapse before humans can be cloned will be short.

Why clone humans? What are the advantages? Some of the more serious reasons that have been offered are:

1. Replication of adults proved to be healthy (bypassing the risk of disease inherent in the chance mechanism of sexual recombination);
2. Replication of individuals of great genius or beauty to improve the species;
3. Provision of children to infertile couples;
4. Control of the sex of future children (always the same as the donor nucleus);
5. Acquisition of children with genotypes of the parents' own choosing;
6. Production of embryonic replicas of each person to be frozen until needed as a source of organ transplants (with no rejection problem);
7. Dispensable beings for use in war or other dangerous activities; and
8. Acquisition of large numbers of genetically identical humans for scientific studies (e.g., on nature versus nurture).

Other reproductive technologies, discussed earlier, that would achieve objectives 3 and 4 are available or imminent. The other objectives, except perhaps the 6th, would most effectively be achieved through cloning—if they can be considered in any way desirable.

Although not as immediate a concern as the other technologies discussed here, there is much debate over whether research dealing with human cloning ought to proceed. Perhaps the most consistent proponents of human cloning are Joseph Fletcher (1974) and Nobel laureate Joshua Lederberg (1966). The latter asserts, "If a superior individual . . . is identified, why not copy it directly, rather than suffer all the risks of recombinational disruption, including those of sex? Leave sexual reproduction for experimental purposes; when a suitable type is ascertained, take care to maintain it by clonal propagation." Lederberg has been attacked by ethicists as well as by other geneticists who are either more cautious toward or totally opposed to further research in cloning. It has been cancer research, however, that has afforded the breakthroughs in cell-fusion techniques that might lead ultimately to cloning of humans, and few are willing to halt basic fusion research. According to James Watson (1971: 53), "Any attempts now to stop such work using the argument that cloning represents a greater threat than a disease like cancer is likely to be considered irresponsible by virtually anyone able to understand the matter." Watson contends that this matter is "far too important to be left solely in the hands of the scientific" community. He warns that any efforts to stop such research must be international in scope, as many countries will soon have the potential to pursue it even if the current British effort is stifled.

Reaction against the prospect of human cloning has come from a variety of directions. Kass (1972a: 44) states that "among sensible men, the ability to clone a man would not be a sufficient reason for doing so. Indeed, among sensible men there would be no human cloning." Cloning, as an extension of in vitro fertilization, depersonalizes the process of human procreation by placing it in the laboratory and thereby represents "voluntary dehumanization." Both Kass (1972a) and Ramsey (1970) argue that such research is immoral because it violates the rights of the unborn. The production and disposal of defectives and the destruction of unused embryos are common to such research and necessarily preclude any attempts at human cloning. Ramsey (1972: 14–17) expresses hope that the first experiments in cloning will produce monsters, that they will receive widespread publicity, and that public pressure will lead to abandonment of the endeavor. Otherwise, he says, we will continue to be led down the "primrose path" by the marvels of science.

In addition to ethical concerns relating to the actual research, there are vital questions concerning the results of cloning. What impact would cloning have on self-identity and self-determination? Would a clone be given all political and civil rights? Although a clone lacks a mother or father in a biological sense, it is assumed that it will be normal in every other respect. Unlike humans as they are presently defined, however, clones are not the result of some chance union of sperm and egg and thus are not unique individuals. Rather, the resulting organism is a biological extension of a donor, an exact copy of an existing genotype.[28] Does a person have the right to be genetically unique or at least not to be deliberately denied a unique genotype? Is not individual dignity and self-identification and actualization denied by a lack of genetic distinctiveness (Kass: 1972)? Certainly current values concerning human dignity, self-actualization, and equality would be directly challenged by the production of the first human clone.

Sinsheimer (1973: 344) suggests that these profound questions must be asked before we advocate "this seemingly attractive short cut to human genetic improvement." He questions how the clones would fit into society and what psychological pressures would be placed on a child that had been cloned for some special characteristics. Performance comparisons with the donor would, in all likelihood, occur and the child might be forced into a mold he or she might neither fit nor want. Kieffer (1979: 207) notes: "To aspire to genius is laudable, to be the child of a genius can be dreadfully difficult, but to be expected to be a genius because you are a genetic twin to one is or could be crushing." Certainly, the life of a clone would be quite different from that of the normally produced peers. The right to select one's own destiny would probably be denied, and other freedoms would be in doubt. Carroll (1974: 303) sees partial genetic manipulation as leading to two types of humans: well-bred "retort men" with inevitable special status, and average nonselected "commonplace men" who originate in the old-fashioned random manner.

Dukeminier (1970: 847) sees an immediate legal issue when cloning of humans becomes possible: the status of the clones. For example, what rights would they have if they were utilized for transplantation of organs to the original donor? "The issue would inevitably arise whether clones are people and thus entitled to the respect due to a human being and to equal protection of the law." Also, as they are technically the result of only one parent (the donor), what are their legal claims to inheritance? Are they legitimate human beings or a subhuman category? Surely, if they are designed to imitate the "best" of society, they will expect full rights — but will they get them? Many of these legal questions have been raised with AID but would be complicated even further with cloning.

Other Intervention Techniques

In addition to the "new" genetic and reproductive technologies emphasized here is a set of other techniques or behavioral patterns that might represent attempts at human genetic intervention. These include laws designed to restrict marriage, involuntary or voluntary sterilization, and neonatal euthanasia. Also noted here are several legal trends that might increase the use of human genetic technologies.

Marriage Restrictions

A common form of genetic intervention in a variety of cultures, practiced by law or custom, is the prohibition of consanguineous marriages. Although the laws prohibiting such marriages in the United States are primarily the product of religious and social motivation, they do have genetic support. Children whose parents are biologically related bear a higher risk of genetic disease as both parents receive their genetic complement from a limited gene pool. Biologically close parents have an increased chance of sharing genes, including those that are deleterious.[29]

Legal prohibitions on marriage vary substantially from one state to the next. All states except Georgia and Rhode Island[30] preempt marriages between parent-child, grandparent-grandchild, aunt-nephew, uncle-niece, and brother-sister couples. Thirty states prohibit marriages between first cousins, and 12 proscribe marriages of more distant biological relatives. Finally, to demonstrate the social and moral dimensions of these restrictions, 21 states prohibit marriages of affinal relatives (those established by marriage). The most common of these laws prohibits marriage to the spouse of a parent (stepmother or stepfather) and to the offspring of a spouse (stepson or stepdaughter). (The absence of a genetic rationale in these latter restrictions suggests that the primary incentive for such laws, generally written in the late nineteenth century, was social and religious, not eugenic.[31])

Sterilization

No other means of human genetic intervention has engendered more intense debate or produced more governmental activity during this century than sterilization. Similarly, none of the more recent technologies better illustrates the ambiguous relationship between the individualistic and eugenic applications of reproductive intervention (Gray, 1976). Although the most common references to sterilization distinguish between voluntary and compulsory or involuntary sterilization, the techniques are identical, only the motivation and means of ensuring compliance vary. The substantial technological change sterilization is undergoing as it becomes a reversible process promises to complicate the debate and modify the structures through which it is implemented.

Voluntary sterilization, conducted with free and informed consent, is the most effective method of ensuring freedom of choice in having children. For this reason, surgical sterilization is the most common form of fertility control in the United States, surpassing even oral contraceptives. It is estimated that about 10 million Americans have been sterilized in the United States (Gonzales, 1976), with an additional million or so added each year. Of these, 6 to 10 percent are federally funded, a fact that has led to much criticism from opponents of sterilization and those who feel that it is used in a coercive manner for persons on welfare. Prior to 1973, about 75 percent of sterilizations in the United States were performed on males through vasectomies (Largey, 1979: 136). Since that time, due to the development of safer and easier female sterilization techniques, an increasing proportion have been performed on females. Now over half of sterilizations are done on females.

Despite the fact that voluntary sterilization is legal in all 50 states and that over 80 percent of the public approves its use for birth control, Kieffer (1979: 105ff) explains that there are many barriers to effective implementation. Waiting periods of up to 30 days, written consent of spouse, confusion over insurance coverage, and the right of private hospitals and physicians to refuse to allow or perform sterilizations combine to make sterilization difficult in many places. Kieffer (1979: 198) suggests that special interest groups are responsible for blocking provisions designed to benefit the majority. Despite opposition from groups opposed to reproductive intervention, Westoff (1976) foresees a definite trend toward an increased use of sterilization for that purpose.

Compulsory sterilization until recently was at the core of eugenics. For its opponents, eugenics is still equated with the technique of sterilization conducted on those considered unfit, whether for genetic or other reasons. Voluntary sterilization might have a eugenic purpose (e.g., when a person with Huntington's disease is voluntarily sterilized) or a eugenic result (e.g., when the number of pregnancies to older women is reduced, thus reducing the prevalence of chromosomal abnormalities), but compulsory sterilization is a conscious effort to reduce the propagation of those considered unfit to have children. As a result of quasi-eugenic concern based on little, if any, scientific evidence, about half of the states have enacted compulsory sterilization laws since 1907 (see Reilly, 1977: 122–132).

Although some of these statutes are still in effect, a series of court rulings along with a shift in public attitudes have resulted in lack of enforcement.[32] For example, in *Wyatt* v. *Aderholt* (1976) the court ruled that all sterilizations for those under 21 are prohibited and no sterilizations for those over 21 are permitted without voluntary and informed consent. Significantly, the decision also stipulated that consent of parent or guardian was not an acceptable substitute (Soskin, 1977: 43). Subsequently, a court of appeals in San Francisco declared that courts cannot order the involuntary sterilization of a mentally incompetent person because it is an "extreme remedy which irreversibly denies a human being the fundamental right to bear and beget children." These decisions lead to a "catch-22" phenomenon in which those declared incompetent are left with no choice: neither they nor their guardians can decide in favor of sterilization and therefore they must bear the risk of having children. This is the reverse of past policy in which they had no choice but to be sterilized.

According to Largey (1979), it appears likely that sterilizations will soon be reversible and that public policy will have to be reformulated to account for this technological alteration. As noted in the court decisions above, the irreversibility of sterilization has been a major concern of those opposed to sterilization of the mentally retarded. Researchers have developed a variety of reversibility techniques, however, and report success in restoring fertility to patients, both male and female, who had been sterilized for as long as 10 years (Silber, 1977; Gomel, 1977; Diamond, 1977). In addition, reversible nonsurgical techniques are currently being tested and could replace the "older" methods of sterilization in the near future (Van, 1979). One method is to inject catalyzed silicone into the fallopian tubes, where it turns to a rubber-like plug. The silicone is inserted with the hysteroscope, which utilizes fiber optics to visually locate the ends of the tubes. To facilitate later withdrawal and subsequent restoration of fertility, each plug has a ringed tip to be used by the physician with a special instrument to remove it. Although they are still at the testing stage, such techniques hold the promise of easy, safe, and effective reversible sterilizations.

The opponents of compulsory sterilization have emphasized the irreversible nature of sterilization. Will the new reversible techniques stop the trend toward more stringent regulations on its use? Certainly it would be easier to justify a reversible procedure, though this raises questions of who can decide when to "pull the plug." Is there much likelihood that the technically "reversible" sterilization will ever actually be reversed, or is the knowledge of that possibility enough? Should the government pay the costs of reversing sterilization if it paid for or ordered the original procedure? (This is especially important in cases where informed consent was not clearly obtained for the sterilization.) The 1970s demonstrated an increased acceptance of sterilization of welfare recipients among many legislators. Although no such legislation was passed, at least several states considered laws that would offer incentives to welfare recipients to be sterilized. There also were many reports of sterilization of substantial numbers of the poor without full voluntary and informed consent (Spriggs, 1974; Rothman 1977). Will the introduction of reversible techniques accentuate such procedures and weaken regulations designed to reduce them?

Proponents of sterilization often are parents of deinstitutionalized retarded who want their children to be free of the risk of pregnancy. They argue that their children are not competent to bear and raise children of their own. Does society have the right to require that the retarded (or prisoners) undergo sterilization in order to be deinstitutionalized? Do children have the right to be born to sane and able parents, as Ingle (1973) argues? Retarded persons constitute only 2 percent of the population, but they produce 17 percent of retarded children (Reilly, 1977: 131). According to Reed and Anderson (1973: 118), the risks of retardation are "much higher among the offspring of retarded persons than among normals." Additionally, many people feel that educable retarded persons can lead relatively independent lives if they are not burdened with the care of children (Reilly, 1977: 131).

Reversible sterilization, then, will not solve the problems surrounding compulsory sterilization. Instead, it will probably lead to a reemergence of controversy, as it relieves sterilization of the irreversibility connotation on which its opponents have built their case. Given current negative attitudes of the public toward those on welfare, the increased emphasis on the population problem, the scarcity of public funds for welfare programs, and the emerging focus on the competency of parents, it would not be surprising if the availability of reversible sterilization gave impetus to pressures for widespread use of incentives (or coercion) to encourage (or force) sterilization of the poor, the retarded, and those otherwise deemed unfit.

Neonatal Euthanasia

New surgical innovations and procedures have allowed many newborns with congenital defects to survive. They also have produced serious ethical questions. Newborn intensive-care units are used to "save" premature infants weighing as little as 500 grams (17.5 oz.), despite the ignorance of a long-term prognosis. Similarly, congenital heart defects, spine defects, respiratory problems, and other congenital and genetic disorders can be treated and death averted. With these new capabilities, however, come hard questions as to whether we should use these technologies in every case. Are there situations in which life-support measures are inappropriate? As McCormick (1974: 174) states: "Granted that we can easily save the life, what kind of life are we saving?" Ought we to use available techniques to prolong the life of severely brain-damaged or grossly deformed infants, only to shunt them away from society as wards of the state?

Although there is agreement that cases exist in which it is wrong to initiate or continue life-support procedures on certain infants (Lorber, 1974; Shaw, 1973; Duff and Campbell, 1973), there is disagreement concerning the nature of those cases, the procedures for dealing with them, and the decision-making criteria (Robertson, 1975; Engelhardt, 1975; Tooley, 1972; John Fletcher, 1975). In addition to gene-pool and quality-of-life arguments, there are the considerations of the economic and emotional pressures on the family, as well as the cost to society of maintaining a growing number of grossly defective children. The decision to allow the infant to die — "neonatal euthanasia" — could be passive (withholding treatment) or active (giving a drug to induce death). In all cases, it is involuntary in that no consent of the infant is possible (Shaw, 1973).

The debate over neonatal euthanasia includes many of the same participants in the more general debate over the use of biomedical technologies. Here the proponents of neonatal euthanasia argue that we should not use available technology to save the infant and the opponents contend that we should. This is often the reverse of their orientations toward the use of genetic technologies in general.

Ramsey (1970) contends that the newborn possesses humanhood and we have a responsibility to maintain life despite the social costs. Human life is human life whatever its form. Diamond (1977) agrees that even the deformed child has the right to live and that the parents and physicians cannot decide to terminate that right, which takes precedence over all others. Conversely, Joseph Fletcher (1971 and 1973) views active neonatal euthanasia as "mercy killing." This is justifiable as such creatures are devoid of the characteristics that constitute personhood (Fletcher, 1972). Williams (1958) adds that it is cruel to maintain even a human life in agony. As Lejeune (1970: 122) notes, however, there is a distinction between euthanasia for terminal adult patients and euthanasia for newborns: "The purpose of euthanasia is to spare seemingly unnecessary suffering to *the patient,* while the goal of the suppression of a disabled child is to prevent suffering to *his family and to society.*" Again, the divergent assumptions concerning the definition of human life as well as the different conceptions of the responsibility of society to maintain or terminate a specific life result in an ethical standoff.

Despite the ethical objections of Ramsey and others (see Gustafson, 1973b), the rapid advances in the ability to maintain indefinitely even the most grossly retarded and deformed have given momentum to proponents of neonatal euthanasia, at least in its passive form. Milunsky (1977: 291) argues that parents and doctors ought to be able to determine whether to maintain life on a case-by-case method, without continued threat of prosecution. "Unfortunately, in the eyes of many people there are simply no grounds for withholding treatment; but these are probably mostly individuals who have never had to face personally these soul-destroying decisions." Kieffer (1979: 187) states that if it is affirmed that we have a duty to keep these persons alive, "then our social institutions must be restructured to accommodate them. Simply putting the deformed out of sight in custodial care institutions does not speak very highly of a society which freely subscribes to and encourages the principles of love, justice, and

humanity." This implies that any decision to maintain the life of these individuals also requires a commitment by those who carry it out to the continued support at optimal levels of the product of their success. If the
parents and doctors fail to assume this responsibility it falls on society. At
present it appears that society is largely unwilling to make sacrifices for
these unfortunates. Therefore, it is incumbent on opponents of neonatal
euthanasia to suggest how the fate of the deformed and retarded can be improved substantially.

3
Democratic Concepts and
Human Genetic Intervention

The political implications of the human genetic technologies presented in Chapter 2 can be examined at two basic levels. At the more practical level, concern focuses on the actual policymaking process in the United States through which decisions are made. The theoretical level places attention on how political concepts both affect and are affected by applications of genetic technology. What are the fundamental characteristics of a democracy and how might these be altered if human genetic intervention becomes widespread? Among the variety of democratic theories most crucial to the discussion of genetic issues are theories based upon utilitarian, liberal, or deontological assumptions. As much of the debate in politics revolves around the concept of "rights," attention will be directed to it. What rights are fundamental in a democracy, and under what situations can the rights of individuals be constrained? How ought conflicts among the rights of individuals be solved and what legitimate role can the government take in furthering the common or societal good? These and related questions concerning responsibilities, needs, and duties must be discussed before examining the actual policymaking process or suggesting how it might be modified to better resolve the questions raised by human genetic technology. This chapter, therefore, examines questions pertaining to how decisions ought to be made within a democratic context and notes how the new technologies are affecting this political dimension.

Through this discussion, more specific questions raised by genetic technology are faced. Does a child have the right to be born healthy? If so, what does this right entail? Should public health or eugenic considerations override human rights of privacy and self-determination? What particular restraints do various methods of human genetic intervention place on individual freedoms? Although none of these questions can be satisfactorily answered, it is critical to raise them within the context of democratic theory.

Alternative Frameworks for Democratic Choice

As the primary objective of this chapter is to explicate the policy implications and context of human genetic technology and not to explore ethical controversies surrounding their use, discussion of the philosophical groundings of political choice is limited to a brief review of selected approaches.[1] The emphasis is on the recurring conflict in democratic theories between those that assign preeminent value to the autonomy and self-determination of the individual and those that view societal or collective good as the predominant value to be attained. Most of the theories examined here attempt to provide for both but differ significantly as to where they place the greatest weight. Despite their varied assumptions and implications, theories classified as liberal place emphasis on individual rights and owe at least some of their substance to the natural–rights tradition. Similarly, several deontological ethical frameworks, including Judeo-Christian ethics and the sanctity-of-life approach, are critical to the views of many persons concerning decisions on genetic issues and reiterate the perception of the individual as the highest value.

Contrary to theories stressing individual rights is a strong philosophical tradition that assigns the greatest weight to the common or societal good. The utilitarian base of these theories shifts the emphasis from rights to the impact of particular decisions on society as a whole. Utilitarianism as reflected in the emphasis on pragmatism, the public interest, and situational ethics is "consequential" in that a moral or "right" decision is always contingent on the situation. Despite their differing conceptions of what the social good entails and their disagreement as to how it could be measured, these theories agree in their concern for the implications of each decision on some broader social interest. Individual self-determination is not negated but becomes of secondary importance.

Theories of Individual Rights

One danger of the utilitarian approach is that the interests of individuals and groups might be sacrificed for the sake of a social good they do not share. Although contemporary utilitarians such as Harsanyi (1975) express concern for individual rights, they assume that such rights are maximized through utilitarian calculations. In case of conflict between individual rights and utility, utility would seem to have a large advantage, and particular interests normally could be subjugated to produce the greatest overall good. Although early natural-rights theories are generally dismissed by contemporary political philosophers, alternative theories that place emphasis on individual rights and autonomy have gained wide support. Several of these theories are examined in detail here and will serve as potential theoretical options when discussing the political context of genetic technologies in the remaining chapters.

Natural Rights. The natural-rights approach is characterized by the presumption that there is a set of rights so basic to human existence that they are independent of existing legal principles of any society. Natural-rights theories evolved prior to the nineteenth century as a defense of human liberty and autonomy against the oppressive powers of the state. Every human is obliged to respect these natural rights of others — rights that are morally fundamental and inalienable. According to John Locke, the primary job of the state is to secure these rights for its citizens. Intuitively, natural-rights theories are attractive even though in practice they fail to provide much guidance in decision making, especially in the area of biomedical policy.

There are two basic problems in applying natural rights to questions raised by genetic technology. The first represents an inherent problem in the natural-rights approach: delineating specifically what "fundamental human rights" entail. There is some general agreement on this, but the inclusion of or emphasis on specific rights is subjective and varies from one theorist to the next. Most commonly these rights are stated only in general terms such as Locke's "life, liberty, and property," and the priorities of rights are often confused or unstated.

One basic distinction between rights as applied in natural-rights theories is that between negative and positive rights. Negative rights are those that impose obligations on others to refrain from interfering with the rights bearer. Locke, for instance, places almost exclusive reliance on the obligation to refrain from interfering with one's life, liberty, or property. Each person under such conditions has a sphere of autonomy that others cannot violate, but no one is further obliged to take positive action to provide that person with property, liberty, or life. In other words, one is entitled to protection of certain rights but has no claims on others.

Conversely, positive rights impose obligation on others (society?) to provide those goods and services necessary for each individual to have at least a minimally decent level of human existence. Feinberg (1973: 59) makes the distinction as follows: "A *positive* right is a right to other persons' positive actions; a negative right is a right to other persons' omissions or forebearances. For every positive right I have, someone else has a duty to *do* something; for every negative right I have, someone else has a duty to *refrain* from doing something." Although the level of positive rights necessary is not clearly defined, this additional dimension requires the presence of institutions that guarantee a certain level of material well-being, through the redistribution of goods and services if needed. Beauchamp and Childress (1979: 51) suggest that "much confusion in moral discourse about public policies governing biomedicine" can be traced to the failure to distinguish positive rights from negative rights. The negative-rights approach envisions the state as a referee among competing interests so that the natural rights of all are protected, while the inclusion of positive rights implies positive action by the state to provide for the welfare of its citizens. Those who focus exclusively on negative rights obviously would attack implementation of positive rights as an unjustified restriction on the liberty of those asked to take positive action to protect the rights of others. However it is approached, the natural-rights perspective fails to provide an objective set of rights. There are some general rights most might agree with, but distinctions are never sharp and clear. The question always remains: What are fundamental human rights?

A second problem that arises mostly in biomedical issues relates to who qualifies as a human; i.e., what characteristics are necessary for human existence? Obviously, this question is central to any definition of rights and obligations. If, as Bowie and Simon (1977) contend, rights give us basic human dignity and allow us to respect persons as ends in themselves, then the definition of "person" is crucial. It is easy to say that all humans have natural—i.e., "human"—rights, but in practice it has never been that straightforward. Society has always set arbitrary boundaries, whether by age or socioeconomic status, on rights considered basic. For instance, voting is considered a fundamental liberty and a protection of one's interests, yet there is no universal acceptance of the criteria for exercising this "fundamental" right.

Although there always have been problems in defining those who qualify to hold particular rights, within the context of biomedical technology it is becoming more and more difficult to define human life. For example, the irreversibly comatose patient is biologically alive and thereby retains certain natural rights, but it has been questioned whether such an existence is a fully human experience and whether a person in such a condition should continue to be afforded full rights (Hardin, 1974). A case more to the point for genetic technology is the controversy over abortion, which also is centered on the definition of "human" being. As much current genetic intervention revolves around the potential use of abortion, it becomes crucial to ask when and if the fetus has rights independent of the mother. In other words, at what point does the fetus receive protection afforded by natural rights: at conception, at viability, at birth, after one year of life if and only if it can pass required genetic tests? One problem with defining "human" at present is that biomedical technology has so drastically altered the conditions of life that our traditional definitions become meaningless or at least ambiguous. For instance, the introduction of the concept of brain death has produced great confusion in the political institutions designed to protect rights.[2]

Due to the problems of defining the boundaries of natural rights and defining "human" existence, natural-rights theories fail to offer much guidance in decisions involving human genetic intervention. It is too easy to define the problem away under such conditions. The lack of clear priorities of rights also results in failure of the natural-rights approach to be of much help when rights of one person conflict with the rights of another. For instance, assuming parents have the right to reproduce, is such a "fundamental" right unlimited? Given the possibility of overpopulation or of the birth of a defective child identified through amniocentesis, does the right to procreation take precedence? Or do the potential children and future generations have rights that at times counteract the rights of the parents? If natural rights are so fundamental and applicable to all humans, then why impose artificial time constraints?

With the inclusion of positive as well as negative rights, natural-rights theory is useful in helping delineate rights and obligations and in promoting human dignity, autonomy, and self-respect. Rigidity and the virtual exclusion of positive rights limit the ability of much of the natural-rights tradition to handle the complex moral issues raised by genetic technology and lead to its failure to provide adequate guidance for resolving conflicts among rights. Nonetheless, natural rights have contributed much through their emphasis on the state as existing primarily to protect the rights of citizens. Many of the concepts introduced through these theories are central aspects of more recent liberal theories.

Respect for Persons. Another philosophical orientation centering on the individual is that of respect for persons. Decisions here are made on the basis of reverence for human life. This approach would preclude certain areas of research on moral grounds. Ramsey (1975), for instance, declares live fetus research out of bounds on this basis. Many of those who would prohibit certain types of genetic research use respect for life as a moral rationale for their decision. As human life is precious, it is argued, the individual must be protected from any means that destroy his or her autonomy or dignity. The proponents of this basically deontological position usually delineate an inviolable concept and devise priorities on the basis of it. For instance, they often establish features defining human life that are regarded as unalterable and then attempt to achieve a binding moral consensus around them.

In discussing respect for persons, a basic question is: What is a person?[3] Although common sense dictates certain characteristics, the answer is far from clear. As certain genetic and medical techniques are improved, this question will become even more difficult to answer. Kant's definition of a person as a rational being able to choose freely among alternatives is quite narrow and would seem to eliminate many people in institutions, in states of unconsciousness, and so forth. It also becomes difficult to determine whether anyone would meet his criteria of reasoning from particular situations to general rules and then applying these rules consistently to oneself and others.

Another definition of humanhood is more inclusive than the rationalist one. Biological existence as a criterion of personhood is usually found in certain reverence-for-life or right-to-life theories. As medical science has advanced, however, these definitions have been challenged, as noted in Chapter 1. The Karen Quinlan case is one example of the problem of defining persons by biological existence alone. Biological life under this defini- tion could exist without many other qualities of humanness. The case of an anencephalic fetus illustrates this problem: A human-like form devoid of brain has little in common with most accepted definitions of humans, though it meets the strict biological criteria. Still another definition that is gaining acceptance is a capacity to communicate and be communicated with. Unlike the rational approach, communication here is broadly defined with both rational and emotional levels. Therefore, a mentally defective individual might be seen to communicate in terms very different from those envisioned in a Kantian manner.

Despite their distinctive definitions of person, a common feature of respect-for-person theories is their emphasis on free choice. A person is held responsible for his or her actions except for compulsion (either internal or external) or unavoidable ignorance (e.g., young children, senile aged, or mentally ill). Whether freedom of choice is an illusion as argued by Spinoza, based upon the motive of self-interest as described by Hobbes, or limited by one's concept of humanity and the association of feelings with others as outlined by Hume, in each of these approaches the individual is paramount. The values of the individual are placed above the value or benefit to society, thereby negating utilitarian criteria for just action. According to theories that emphasize respect for persons, each person is assumed to be equal and no amount of social benefit justifies the depersonalization of individuals. The right-to-life frameworks, currently being heard in debates over genetic intervention, reflect clearly these assumptions without concern for the changing circumstances brought about by biomedical technology. In their emphasis for life at all costs, they fail to account for the consequences of carrying out their principles in each case.

Liberalism. According to Nagel (1975), liberalism is the conjunction of two ideals: (1) individual liberty and (2) a democratic society controlled by its citizens and serving their needs and in which inequalities are not excessive. As we have seen, it is difficult enough to approach the concept of individual liberty alone. To pursue notions of equality in addition to liberty produces difficult dilemmas to which there is no solution. In such cases Nagel (1975: 136) notes that "liberalism tends to give priority to the respect for certain personal rights, even at substantial cost in the realization of other goods such as efficiency, equality, and social stability." Due to this tendency, liberalism has been attacked in recent decades from both the right and the left. Conservatives have argued that liberal democratic institutions result in too much freedom for the individual and lead to a social atmosphere lacking adequate restraints on behavior. Conversely, the left has attacked liberal society as racist, sexist, and inherently elitist.

In response to these criticisms, three contemporary political philosophers have published controversial defenses of liberalism. Although each of the theories of Rawls (1971), Nozick (1974), and Dworkin (1977) has distinctive assumptions and implications, together they illuminate the debate over the place of individual liberty in a liberal society. For instance, Dworkin (1979: 48) explains that all three approaches accept the "liberal attitude which insists that government must not force a conception of the good life upon its citizens, or justify political decisions by preferring one vision of human excellence to another." Due to their importance to the contemporary political-philosophical debate and their relevance to the discussion of rights, their major provisions are briefly reviewed here.

Nozick (1974) elevates liberty at the expense of all other values by arguing that individuals have certain rights that cannot be abridged by the state for any reason. So long as one does not violate the rights of others, one's rights to person and property are absolute. Nozick contends that all states systematically violate the rights of citizens and he concludes that the only morally permissible state is one limited to protecting individuals' person and property and punishing those who transgress the liberty of others. By focusing exclusively on negative rights associated with person and property, Nozick rejects any efforts by a state to redistribute wealth or provide minimal standards of living. Liberty may not be overridden even to do things for the broader common good. Furthermore, a person is entitled to any goods he can get either through working or by transfer from others, including inheritance, without state interference. Nozick rejects any theory that imposes on any distribution a fixed goal, whether utilitarian or egalitarian, and condemns any such attempt as an invasion of personal liberty.

The state, then, has no autonomous power as a separate entity with moral rights greater than those of any single individual. According to Nagel (1975: 141), individual rights and duties are the basis of what governments may do in Nozick's scheme. By assuming that the right to liberty is virtually absolute, this "libertarian" theory obscures the complexity of rights and responsibilities, ignores positive rights and corresponding obligations, and fails to account for the conflict in basic individual rights present in most decisions of human genetic intervention.

Nozick would deny the concept of equality due to its perceived incongruity with liberty. Dworkin (1979), however, asserts that individual rights and the notion of equality are in fact mutually supportive. Dworkin's objective is to defend liberalism from the charge by the left that it protects the individual at the expense of the welfare of those at the bottom. He argues that rights and the general welfare (or general good) are both "rooted" in the more fundamental idea of equality as independence. For Dworkin (1979: 48), the apparent opposition between rights and the general good is only on the surface. He suggests a combination of the two ideas: "allowing the general welfare to be a good justification of political decisions in the normal case but providing individual rights as trumps over that justification in exceptional cases." In other words, it is just as arbitrary to suggest that the general welfare is fundamental in importance as it is to argue that individual liberty is always predominant.

There is this mutual dependence of rights, equality, and the common good; when, if ever, is government intervention in individual rights justified? Nozick would answer never, and Dworkin (1977: 202) concludes that the government can restrict a right, but only with presentation of a compelling reason "that is consistent with the suppositions on which the original right must be based." A government "takes rights seriously" when it acknowledges that citizens have a right to break laws that contradict that right and gives priority to fundamental rights of citizens even when they conflict with the general welfare. Despite giving priority to rights, Dworkin does acknowledge that the common good might at times require violation of those rights. Dworkin's liberalism is more complex than Nozick's and requires equality as a foundation for individual rights as well as the general welfare.

No recent liberal philosophical work has generated as much critical reaction or been interpreted in as many ways as Rawls's *A Theory of Justice* (1971), in which he presents the conception of justice and outlines principles imbedded in a just society. Rawls is concerned primarily with the "way in which the major social institutions distribute fundamental rights and duties and determine the division of advantages from social cooperation." Rawls is most critical of utilitarian society, which, he contends, is intolerable for those at the bottom. Reliance on the greatest good for the greatest number undermines self-respect and results in enormous sacrifices from those already least well off. In its place Rawls proposes a contractual society that maximizes individual liberty and tolerates inequalities only if they work to the advantage of the least–well-off members. Individual liberty here is a much broader concept than that of Nozick and includes a heavy emphasis on positive rights and corresponding obligations to those with the fewest resources. Rawls sets out to provide procedures for resolving conflicts among competing interests and rights that inevitably arise and assumes that all self-interested persons would select his principles of justice under the conditions he establishes.

To an extent, Rawls's conception of the just society reflects traditional notions of the common good in which the well-being of society depends on the well-being of all the members. For Rawls all human assets are collective social goods: The distribution of goods and services is a cooperative effort, and an innate sense of respect for fellow human beings[4] compels each person to pay attention to those whose needs are the greatest. Under such conditions, political institutions exist to preserve and enhance both individual liberty and general well-being. Through concern for individual standards of living, attention is placed on equality of opportunity. Unlike Nozick, Rawls asserts that state intervention is justified to protect individual freedom and to minimize inequalities in wealth and other resources. Liberty, therefore, is not absolute as restrictions are necessary in order to strengthen the total system of liberty. Despite this, "Rawls' theory creates a very strong presumption against interference with fundamental freedoms" (Amdur, 1977: 446). Infringement of freedom is just only if it serves to protect those very liberties. Only when liberty has been fully protected are economic considerations warranted.[5]

Theories of Societal Good

According to the traditional notion of the "common good" as envisioned by such philosophers as Aquinas and Suarez, the sole purpose of the state is to provide for the common good of its members. This end is broadly defined as anything that promotes the general well-being of the society at large. Benefits are common in that they pertain to all members of society. They are good in that they represent genuine contributions to the well-being of the people, not simply what the people want. They are objectively beneficial and good in the moral sense. In this way the common good contributes not only to the material well-being of the members but also to the development and perfection of unique human qualities.

According to Douglas (1976), the common good in the traditional sense is more than just an aggregation of individual goals. Instead, the benefits are shared goods, not reducible to terms of private advantage. Their very existence depends on their being reciprocal; each person is critically dependent on his fellow citizens. In turn, the common good is treated as higher than that of the individual. Although the two normally coincide, there are situations in which conflict might occur. Under such circumstances, the common good takes precedence, although there are usually limits to the individual sacrifices necessary to achieve the common good. For common-good theories, the judgment of the government is accepted because it represents the genuine greater good of the community. The government alone has responsibility for protecting the good of its citizens. In addition, traditional theories of common good assume that rulers are duty-bound to intervene actively in societal decision to ensure furtherance of the common good when private initiatives fail.

Utilitarianism. The term "common good" has continued to be widely alluded to in contemporary political theories that emphasize societal interests, but its meaning has changed significantly. Although utilitarianism is not fully representative of collective-oriented democratic theories, it certainly has been the predominant system of theory during much of modern moral philosophy (Rawls, 1971: vii). Utilitarianism holds that social decision making is largely a matter of mathematical calculation in which the option producing the greatest overall benefit or utility is selected.

Even though the roots of utilitarian thought predate Jeremy Bentham, he has come to be identified as the theorist who first espoused the notion of societal good as a function of utility. Bentham's formula of "maximum happiness for the greatest number" provided a direct alternative to the predominant natural-rights theory of the early nineteenth century by dismissing concern for individuals and respect for human life and subsuming them under the concept of social utility. For Bentham, each person counts as one and no one counts as more than one. The right decision in each case will be the one that maximizes the overall balance of benefit over harm for society — the total *quantity* of happiness.

John Stuart Mill (1863) made this theory more palpable by adding the dimension of *quality*. According to Mill, one must take into account the kind as well as the amount of happiness resulting from alternative courses of action. In order to distinguish between lower- and higher-level pleasures, Mill depends upon the "competent judge." Mill admits, unlike Bentham, that although in theory the greatest-happiness principle is the only ultimate test of rightness, in practice it is difficult to use in solving dilemmas. Many problems of social morality require a complex balancing of one set of advantages against another. Despite this limitation, the "greatest happiness" remains the best test of rightness. For Mill, happiness becomes a more complex concept than for his predecessors. It includes various components, each desirable in its own right and not merely in the aggregate. According to Mill, happiness refers to all things that are of ultimate value in human life. He rejects the imposition of conformity for the sake of social benefit and emphasizes the quality of each individual life. The common good then becomes submerged under Mill's attempt to justify the greatest-happiness concept. The utilitarian framework presented by Mill and others shifts emphasis to more exclusive interests and provides a basis for much of the liberal public-interest assumptions of today.

It would be misleading to suggest that either utilitarian thought is a unified philosophy or it has not progressed beyond the "greatest good for the greatest number." In reality it is a loose label for a wide range of theories. One common philosophical distinction is made between *rule* utilitarians who justify action by appeal to rules, which in turn appeal to the principle of utility, and *act* utilitarians who appeal directly to the principle of utility in determining action in each specific case. Contemporary utilitarians have progressed far beyond the more narrowly hedonistic utilitarians (McDonald, 1978). Flathman's works on the public interest (1966) and on political obligation (1972) and Harsanyi's (1975) statistically sophisticated "expected-utility maximization" are two divergent paths contemporary utilitarian theorists have offered.

Utilitarian Influence on U.S. Politics. Out of the traditions of common good and utilitarianism has come a strong emphasis on the concept of the "public interest" in political decision making in the United States. Often the public interest is used to refer simultaneously to the common good and to some balance or weighted average of the various private interests in society. (The extent to which public interest has become the basis for decision making in the United States will be examined later in this chapter and the problems this creates will be examined more fully in Chapter 4.) Act utilitarianism especially appears to be at the base of American pragmatism in which political benefits and risks are weighed not on the basis of some absolute principles but rather on an estimation of the possible consequences. Decisions are judged right or wrong primarily to the extent that they maximize overall good—either to the individuals making the decision or to society, depending on one's perspective.[6] Politics, as currently practiced in the United States, then, has a clear utilitarian foundation.

Fundamental Rights in a Democracy

Central to the theoretical debate as to what constitutes a just decision in a democracy and what criteria are most crucial in such decisions is concern for the proper weight given to individual rights. Although few theorists have mentioned human genetic policies per se, the principles they set forth and assumptions they make have substantial relevance to genetic questions. Utilitarians who believe that moral action is defined by that which does the greatest good for the greatest number, or some similar formula, might be expected to favor any genetic intervention that would maximize overall genetic good. The violation of individual liberties in the achievement of this goal might be of secondary concern, but it would not in itself lead to rejection. Conversely, theorists who emphasize individual liberty and self-determination would tend to reject what they perceive as a violation of human rights. There might be rare circumstances in which certain rights might be precluded, but "societal good" would seldom in itself be justification to deny basic rights. All of these theories espouse the concept of rights but fail to provide specific guidance as to what are fundamental rights. Even the natural-rights approach, which is intuitively attractive regarding rights of individuals, fails to offer an inclusive set of such rights or provide any meaningful hierarchical ordering of them.

Despite the absence of agreement as to what the priorities of rights ought to be or even which rights ought to be included as fundamental to human existence, rights continue to be critical in examining an individual's relationships with others in a society. They serve to sharpen one's perception of society because they define not only the essence of citizenship but also, in a broader sense, the boundaries of human existence. "Rights define a man or woman as a human being and they spell out the individual's obligations as a member of society. The rest of society perceives each individual as a functional or superfluous man or woman largely on the basis of whether he or she has the option to exercise these rights" (Wald, 1975: 4).

The theories discussed here offer several perspectives, each distinct in the extent to which it emphasizes particular rights over others and the role of society in defining, protecting, or abrogating specific rights. Although there tends to be some unanimity among democratic theories in defining civil rights, treatment of personal rights is less consistent and generally ambiguous. The focus here is on personal rights that relate most directly to human genetic intervention, including privacy, procreation, and self-determination. Several basic documents are examined to ascertain how such rights are defined by societies.

U.S. Constitution

The Constitution and its amendments, although addressing themselves most expressly toward civil rights such as voting, provide a broad framework for defining personal rights as well. As usual in the case of general political documents, the Constitution introduces a series of consciously vague constructs, leaving them open to broad interpretation. The general-welfare clause of the preamble, the due-process clause of the Fifth Amendment, the due-process and equal-protection clauses of the Fourteenth Amendment, and protection from government encroachment afforded by the Ninth Amendment all have been interpreted at one time or another as defining the scope of personal rights. Not surprisingly, a large number of the most critical Supreme Court decisions have encompassed questions concerning these rights. Often the focus of inquiry has been the extent to which society, as defined by particular interests in the population, can proscribe or limit the rights of some on the basis of a broader social interest. As in other discussions involving rights, the decisions rendered have been far from consistent and reflect the uncertainty as to where one person's rights end and another's begin.

U.N. Declaration of Human Rights

The more modern (1948) Universal Declaration of Human Rights of the United Nations explicitly specifies a wide range of individual rights to serve as a "common standard of achievement for all peoples and all nations." Based on the presumption that "all human beings are born free and equal in dignity and rights" and "endowed with reason and conscience," it goes on to expand the notion of fundamental rights to include among other things: (1) the right to equal pay for equal work, (2) the right to a standard of living adequate for the health and well-being of individuals and their families, and (3) the right to rest and leisure including "periodic holidays with pay." In the area of personal rights, this document, whatever its practical worth, emphasizes the right to marry and "found a family" free from constraints. Men and women of "full age" are entitled to equal rights, and motherhood and childhood are to be afforded special care and assistance. According to Article 16, "The family is the natural and fundamental group unit of society and is entitled to protection by society and the State." Children are entitled to the same social protection whether they are born in or out of wedlock.

Despite its detailed enumeration of human rights, this document fails to provide much guidance for the kinds of questions raised by human genetic intervention or intervention in reproduction on grounds of population control. In fact, it presents the right to "found a family," presumably by having children, as an absolute to be protected by society. It says nothing about rights associated with those yet unborn, nor does it imply concern for future generations. Does a person have the unlimited right to procreate without any responsibility to others in society? This document does not explicitly state such a right, but its absolutist terminology and the absence of corollary limits suggest a failure to offer much assistance in questions relating to human genetic intervention.

Fundamental Rights in the United States

The President's Committee on Mental Retardation (Wald, 1975) detailed fundamental personal rights that are often taken for granted in the United States:

    1. the right to marry

2. the right to sexual freedom outside marriage
3. the right to bear children
4. the right to raise children
5. the right to family life
6. the right to be left alone
7. the right to be allowed to succeed or fail
8. the right to ignore gratuitous advice

To this list of fundamental human rights have been added the right to a unique genotype (Ramsey, 1970), the right not to know (Bender, 1974), the right to be born healthy (Murphy, Chase, and Rodriguez, 1978: 363), and others. In general, these specific rights appear to constitute multidimensional rights to privacy, procreation, and self-determination.

Wald (1975: 4) argues that rights as important to human existence as these should be denied to no one except under extraordinary circumstances. She asserts that "every human being should be presumed to have these rights unless someone can show an almost certain probability of disastrous consequences" if they are exercised. According to the Supreme Court, such basic relationships can be interfered with only if there is "compelling state interest." The key here is determining what "compelling state interest" entails, assuming that the rights are indeed that fundamental. We again are left lacking a clear and unambiguous definition of the boundaries of these basic human rights and are given little guidance as to what action is warranted when these fundamental rights conflict.

Rights and Responsibilities

The concept of "rights" is complex and heavily bound by cultural norms and beliefs. It is virtually meaningless to compare lists of rights proposed in various government documents without examining what they actually mean and how they are applied. Rights are defined not only by the perspective of the observer but also by the particular situation, natural-rights theories to the contrary. Rights are by nature ambiguous and open to interpretation and qualification.

Consider, for example, the "right to life," which has been a central concept of American culture and is also the basic human right as defined by the United Nations. Its meaning can vary substantially depending on one's conception of the point at which "life" begins and ends and of the minimal qualities that define a meaningful human life.

Even if we could ever agree on the definition of human life, which appears unlikely, the question still remains as to what should be done when the rights to life of two individuals conflict head on, as, for instance, when scarce medical resources preclude the life of one or the other. Does the life of a mother or of her unborn fetus take precedence? The law agrees that the mother's life does; this reflects the values of our society. What if the mother had only several weeks to live and the child if born would have a full and productive life? This is the kind of decision to which a rights approach often has little practical relevance. Another unanswered question relates to conflicts between rights themselves. Is a person justified in committing suicide based on a right of self-determination? Defining that person's behavior as irrational, and therefore not a reflection of self-will, seems to clarify nothing.

In addition to the problems inherent in attempts to define fundamental rights and establish their boundaries in a democratic society are questions that arise when the exercise of the rights of one set of individuals conflicts with similar rights of others. Neither the natural-rights, the utilitarian, nor the contract theories discussed above offer an adequate solution in cases of conflict among the rights of various interests in society. Each theory provides guidelines (from absolute to highly relativistic) for priorities among rights; none, however, provides a reasonable framework for the discussion of complex questions raised by human genetic intervention. Most of these theories appear to be best suited for describing abstract rights devoid of the dynamic interaction among various participants.

It is necessary, therefore, to introduce the dimension of "responsibility" when discussing genetic intervention, in order to provide a means of gauging the impact of each technology on the various participants and demonstrate how the rights of each are affected. Hellberg (1974: 38) contends that it is impossible to make progress in resolving biomedical issues until we combine rights with duties and responsibilities: "The legitimate rights of the individual can only really come alive if we put them in the context of a wider understanding of man and the interaction of rights with responsibilities." Responsibility, then, places rights in a relative social context and allows an observer to set priorities of rights according to the extent to which each interest is affected. In order to distinguish appropriate rights, each application must be analyzed carefully within this more complex and dynamic context. Responsibility of society toward these individuals or groups must be gauged and their freedom of expression and choice must be balanced against some broader responsibility for society.

In order to examine rights and responsibilities as applied to human genetic intervention in a meaningful manner, at least four categories of individuals must be discussed: (1) the affected or potentially affected person, (2) the parents and family, (3) society, and (4) future generations.[7] Society is defined here as individuals in the community other than the family or the affected individuals. Future generations refer to individuals beyond our great-grandchildren, thereby limiting it to our more remote descendants.

Most attention in the academic literature has focused on the rights of parents, specifically their prerogatives in reproduction, and in the potential conflict raised by genetic technology between their rights and some societal good. Comparatively little attention has been directed toward the rights of the affected persons, although they generally are noted in passing. Those who emphasize the deterioration of the gene pool concentrate on responsibility toward remote future generations and limit discussions of the rights of theoretically potential individuals. After reviewing this more complete framework, it will be clear that the major problems raised by genetic technology relate directly to the conflicts between these rights.

Affected Persons or Fetuses

It seems reasonable that in making genetic decisions the first responsibility ought to go to the person directly affected or potentially affected. This appears to be an obvious assumption, but there is a tendency among most observers to focus instead on the procreative rights of parents or on the needs of society (Freund, 1977; Murphy, Chase, and Rodriguez, 1978). This pattern is reinforced due to the fact that in many cases the affected "person" is a fetus being diagnosed through amniocentesis or the hypothetical product of a high-risk couple.

The responsibility to affected persons can relate either to those presently living with a genetic disorder or to potential persons who would be affected if they are born. It seems that the responsibility toward those already living is to protect their well-being and to provide all possible means of minimizing their problems. As has often been noted, however, the mentally retarded rarely are given rights commensurate with those commonly associated with full humanhood (Wald, 1975). Does one have the "right to be unhealthy" even at a high cost to others in society? Hardin (1974) questions how much society must invest to maintain individuals with hemophilia, for instance. The very presence of such questions implies that concern for those affected by genetic disease is far from unanimous. From other data on attitudes toward those with genetic disease (Sorenson, 1975) and spending patterns on the mentally retarded (Cameron, 1978), it is clear that the rights of those affected and living are not defined on the same basis as those who are "normal."

Fetal Rights. Discussion of rights and responsibilities for those affected by genetic disease becomes even more ambivalent when attention shifts to a fetus identified as having a particular disorder. In fact no single ethical issue is more sensitive and complicated than rights of fetuses. Although numerous works have been written on the subject, few provide a neutral framework for specifying whether there is such a thing as a "right of a fetus" that corresponds to freedom of choice in life-and-death situations. Much of the debate has centered on the "prolife" versus the "proabortion" dichotomy. Neither of these positions recognizes or allows for the right of choice for the unborn; both impose a decision on the fetus, a decision that reflects not the choice of the fetus but of the mother or society. In one case the fetus is forced to live, in the other it has no choice but to die.

Most observers place emphasis on the rights of parties other than the fetus and also fail to distinguish between healthy fetuses and those prenatally diagnosed with varying degrees of disorders and deformities. Consequently, the conditions of life imposed upon or denied a fetus are seldom distinguishable. Harris (1975: 70) notes this in stating, "When it comes to weighing what have been called the 'rights of the fetus' the matter is obviously much more obscure. But if the concept means anything in practical terms, its evaluation presumably turns on an assessment of the quality of the life the fetus may eventually come to have." Instead, most right-to-life arguments now center on whether or not a fetus is a person and reject the notion of a choice based on the expected quality of life. Those who contend that any abortion is acceptable if desired by the mother also fail to account for the possibility of fetal rights to choice in life and death, usually by rejecting the fetus as a person and dismissing or minimizing the concept of the fetus as a potential person.

One approach to the debate over rights of the fetus or embryo is to present the acquisition of rights as a progressive process. This precedent is not new and is commonly applied to citizens in all societies, with full rights granted only after reaching a particular age. When applied to the fetus, this model suggests an incremental cumulative application of rights. Full rights as a human would be accorded only after birth or perhaps even later if acceptable to society. An obvious question is: what constitutes basic rights at each stage of development? Specifically, when, if ever, does a fetus or its representative acquire the right to make a life-death decision independent of the mother and society? The concept of progressive rights fails to determine at what point particular rights are to be afforded the fetus. The lines between levels of rights remain arbitrary.

One position is to suggest that fetuses up to the point of viability have a right at least not to be terminated for experimental purposes. Kass (1976: 314) uses this argument to reject certain reproductive technologies and asserts that at the least a fetus is a living thing with some moral claim on us not to do violence to it. Such a logic implies that after viability the fetus has expanded rights, though it fails to define such rights relative to those of other members of society. Attention turns to the courts to resolve this question. In *Roe* v. *Wade* (1973) the Supreme Court determined that abortion at early stages of fetal development did not deprive the fetus of whatever "life"

TABLE 3.1
Typology of Fetus Rights

	No Fetus Rights	Fetus Has Rights
Keep Alive	I. Rigid Right-to-life Position -no choice for fetus or any person -life all-important -death is always worst possible alternative	II. Probability of Meaningful Human Existence -happiness to individual outweighs pain -any life better than none at all -rational person under like circumstances would be expected to choose to live

Let Die	III. Other-oriented Decision
	
	-what is best for society, mother, family?
	-cost/benefit
	-mother's choice
	  -moral decision
	  -convenience
	-costs to family
	-rights of next child in the queue
	-fetus is non-human organism/ dispose of when defective
		IV. Low or No Probability of Meaningful Human Existence
		
		-suffering outweighs happiness
		-lacks basic criteria for human life
		-rational person under like circumstances would choose to die

it had without due process, in part because the term "person" as used in the Constitution "does not include the unborn." Although the Court made a distinction between "viable" and "nonviable" fetuses, thus recognizing a concept of progressive rights, it has yet to define the rights of a viable fetus except to preclude abortions in the third trimester in all but extraordinary circumstances. Within the present legal framework, as distinguished from the range of ethical frameworks, fetuses do not have claim to "fundamental personal rights."

   A Typology of Fetal Rights. In order to clarify the full range of possible situations regarding fetal rights, a typology of fetal rights is presented in Table 3.1. Of the four possible positions only two are generally presented in the debate over abortion. Although there are problems with attempts to simplify such a complex area of conflict and place all approaches into distinct categories, typologies of this sort can be useful in delineating the boundaries of discussion. The focus here is on the theoretical rights of a fetus to choose whether to live or die, not whether life or death is justified under any particular situation.[8]

Interestingly, the two most common approaches to abortion fall under column 1: no fetal rights. Although distinctions are made as to the situation under which termination of a fetus is justified, proponents of abortion generally base their argument solely on the rights of the mother to abort a fetus. Less commonly, but especially in the cases of a defective fetus, the decision to allow fetus death is justified on societal grounds. It is argued that society cannot afford the costs or that the fetus can never be a productive member of society. These positions emphasize the interests of the mother and the family who must bear the direct material and emotional costs or the taxpayers who would also bear costs (though of a much smaller magnitude). They might also include concern for other societal members who might have better care by doctors and health institutions if they did not have to compete with the severely abnormal.[9] Those taking a proabortion stance, including those focusing on the abnormal fetus, tend to direct attention to the interests of the mother, the family, or society.

In the right-to-life position, which purports to base its concern on the right of the fetus to live, the fetus has no choice. Kass (1976: 314), for instance, argues that the "fetus has a right to continued life," but he makes no suggestion that it has a similar right not to live. In theory at least, it must live no matter what conditions are imposed upon it. Although many proponents of the right-to-life stance would make exception for abortion of the severely abnormal, their opposition to amniocentesis and other prenatal diagnostic techniques implies a rejection of distinction by condition of the fetus. Some (see Lebacqz, 1973) indeed see selective abortion as a greater moral threat than abortion for other reasons because it results in unequal treatment, thus violating the "fundamental moral and legal equality of all human beings." Lebacqz warns of moving toward a quality-of-life ethic where persons are judged according to their social utility and refuses to believe that death is ever preferable to life, no matter what the conditions or quality of life are. The right to life as expressed by the most vocal opponents of abortion negates the concept of quality of life and forces the choice of life on the fetus. The resulting decision is the opposite of those who would abort the fetus in the interest of the mother or society, but again the fetus has no choice.

Only the cells in column 2 of the typology allow for the interests of the fetus in a life-death choice. In one case (II) the fetus is kept alive and in the other case (IV) the life of the fetus is terminated. The distinction between these two categories is dependent on the circumstances surrounding the health of the fetus. It is founded on the assumption that the choice of the fetus in each case would be that of a "reasonable" person under similar circumstances. Murphy, Chase, and Rodriguez (1978: 394) demonstrate how dangerous this is by pointing out that we have little knowledge of the attitudes of affected persons toward their own situation. We simply do not know whether it is better to suffer and live than not to live at all, despite Purdy's (1978) assertion that we do not harm possible children if we prevent them from existing. In other words, does the quality of life of this future person reflect the perception one has of "human" existence? Such an assumption of "reasonable choice" is obviously heavily value-based; still, most people would agree on basic minimal characteristics in defining what is human, at least at the extreme.

In cell II, the fetus's interests would lead to a decision to keep it alive. In this situation there would be a high probability of meaningful human existence. Based on medical knowledge of similar cases, we would expect individual happiness to outweigh pain and suffering, or at least that the affected person would have a reasonable chance to experience happiness. There might be a few individuals without physical or mental impairments who might desire never to be born, but the assumption here is that an overwhelming proportion of unaffected fetuses would choose to live.

In category IV the fetus is terminated, not because the mother or society deems it expedient or necessary, but because the fetus if given the opportunity would be assumed to decide not to live under the circumstances. It is expected that such a decision would follow if and only if there was little or no probability of meaningful human existence. This would be most apparent in a situation in which suffering would substantially outweigh the potential for happiness and in which the fetus, if carried to term, would be condemned to a life of pain. If the parents or society decide to force life under such circumstances, it is similar to allowing parents or society to condemn innocent children to a subhuman or nonhuman existence. Interestingly, often "mere animals" are given more consideration of their circumstances and treated more "humanely" than affected children. Although many humans with great physical disabilities have overcome them, there appears to be a consensus that severe mental retardation or grotesque physical impairment leads to a less-than-human existence. Again, the definition of "meaningful life" would vary somewhat and some would argue that any life is better than none at all, but there are many situations in which a substantial majority would agree that they would choose never to have lived at all.

A logical conclusion, based on this discussion of the interests of the fetus, is that healthy fetuses with potential for a reasonably happy existence would choose to live. On the other hand, fetuses with severe physical or mental disabilities, or both, which would lead to a life devoid of "human" experience, would be expected to choose not to live under those conditions. Does this then lead to the conclusion that abortion of healthy fetuses is morally wrong? Certainly such a conclusion challenges those who favor abortion not in the interests of the fetus but for the parents or society and could be translated as a modified right-to-life stand.

This typology, however, is not presented to suggest what decision will be made in each case, as the rights of the fetus can seldom be expected to predominate. Instead, the attempt is made to contend that, by including the interests of the fetus, the decision takes on an additional dimension. It is argued that the interests of the fetus are seldom a prime consideration, but that they should be. Abortion opponents maximize and abortion proponents discount the perception of the fetus as a person; both fail to take into account the type of existence that can be expected to follow if the fetus is carried to term. Neither basic approach accounts for the interests of the fetus other than in a peripheral manner.

Hypothetical Persons. The responsibility toward the yet unborn persons or more hypothetical potential persons that might result, for instance, from a union of two carriers, is even less clear and more of a dilemma. Certainly, there is a societal responsibility to reduce the probability of any one individual being genetically defective. Does this mean, however, that any fetus so diagnosed should be destroyed? From a societal standpoint such action eliminates the problem in that case, but for some this is equivalent to murder. Generally, American society would accept abortion under such circumstances—not out of responsibility to the affected fetus but on some parental or societal basis.

Responsibility to affected persons becomes even more ambivalent when discussing screening for carrier status. In this case, who is the affected person? Carriers of the sickle-cell trait, for instance, might suffer some trait-related problems, but certainly they do not have a disease. It is their potential or actual offspring who have a one-in-four chance of being affected. On this basis, does society have the duty to mandate the screening of carriers in order to protect potential affected persons? If it has the responsibility to make screening of carriers compulsory, does it then have the further duty to outlaw sexual unions between carriers based on the chance that some of their offspring might be affected, in order to protect these potentially affected persons? Implicit in such an argument would be the sacrifice that might result if the two carriers were not allowed to reproduce. In other words, probability dictates that any action taken to eliminate the union of two carriers will affect a larger number of potentially healthy than unhealthy children. On this basis alone, without taking into consideration the rights of the carriers, compulsory screening of carriers and its logical extension of prohibiting procreation in such instances would be illogical on public-health grounds. Obviously, this does not preclude the screening of carriers on a voluntary basis or even the justification of mandatory screening based on some broader responsibility.

Conflicts Among Affected Persons. The complexity of the rights of persons with genetic disease substantially increases when the factor of scarce resources is introduced and those affected compete for limited monies. Joseph Fletcher (1974: 160) illustrates this problem in his statement that "it is cruel and insane to deprive normal but disadvantaged children of the care we should give them with the $1.5 billion we spend in public costs for preventable retardees." It could be argued that the disadvantaged children do have a right to a minimally decent standard of living and that this right conflicts with the right of the retardees. This line of thinking has led some to suggest that the severity of the abnormality must be considered and that some sort of triage system should be established, simliar to that for neural tube defects in Great Britain. Harris (1975: 74) contends that "it is apparent that because of continuous gradations in severity . . . lines are going to be drawn."

Birch and Abrecht (1975: 206) conclude that no precise spectrum of severity of disorders, from most destructive to meaningful human life, can be defined, although some consensus might exist at least on the extremes. They warn that the decision to deprive a fetus of its life depends on a vast number of factors in addition to severity: impact on the family, availability of medical management, the predictability of expression of the particular disorder,[10] possible compensation in other respects, and so forth. In other words, even if one accepts the premise that quality of life should be the determining factor in selective abortion, there is at present no consensus on the criteria for such a decision.

In addition, there is a danger that widespread acceptance of selective abortion will reduce even further concern for the living affected.[11] Kass (1976: 317) expresses concern for abnormals who are viewed as having escaped the "net of detection and abortion" as attitudes toward such individuals are "progressively eroded." In this atmosphere, such individuals increasingly will be viewed as unfit to be alive, as second-class humans or lower, or as unnecessary persons who would not have been born if only someone had gotten to them in time. Parents are likely to resent such a child, especially if social pressures and stigma are directed against them. The right to be born healthy, according to Murphy, Chase, and Rodriguez (1978: 358), is misleading because it actually means that "only healthy persons have a right to be born." The choice of those affected is not between a healthy and unhealthy existence, but rather between an unhealthy existence and none at all. What might be seen as protecting the rights of the unborn, therefore, might result in degrading the rights of the affected.

Parental Rights

Although the rights of those affected by genetic disease are in a primitive stage of definition at best, parental rights in this area are clearly defined.[12] Except in rare instances, the parents' rights take precedence over the interests of the affected persons. In large part this reflects the premise that parents will use their best judgment in doing what they consider in the interests of their offspring. They might not always make the correct choice, but it is assumed they are in the best position to protect the welfare of their children. Freund (1977), for instance, would honor the wishes of the parents except when they fail to make the right decision as he defines it and are unwilling to bear total responsibility for the consequences.

Reinforcing this view in the United States is the Lockean emphasis on property rights, which still seems to underlie our perception of children. Although there are trends to the contrary developing, children generally are considered the property of their parents.[13] Unless they seriously mistreat their children, usually physically, little outside concern is manifested and seldom does the state intervene. In spite of the recent emphasis on "battered children" (child abuse) and suggestions of the need to screen prospective parents, American society is not disposed to governmental intervention in the parent-child relationship. Again, the presumption that parents will act in the interest of the child leads to a hesitancy on the part of society to interfere with parental rights.

Although individual rights include a broad range of civil and personal rights, there are some that relate most closely to this discussion of human genetic intervention. Most human genetic technology has a direct impact on rights regarding procreation, privacy, and self-determination—all dimensions of an integrated package of fundamental personal rights. Although none is discussed explicitly in the Constitution, the courts have dealt with specific cases involving each. The rapid advances in human genetic technology will, without doubt, intensify the questions relating to these rights.

Certainly the most basic and universally recognized rights in human terms relate to the freedom to marry, to bear children, and to raise them according to one's own values. Justice Goldberg, in a concurring opinion in *Griswold* v. *Connecticut* (1965), sees the marital relationship as a fundamental area of privacy protected by the Ninth Amendment. The state can interfere with marriage and procreation only upon proof of a "compelling state interest." This philosophy was reiterated in *Roe* v. *Wade* (1973), in which the Court ruled that a state cannot dictate to a pregnant woman whether or not she may have an abortion during the first trimester of pregnancy, and in *Eisenstadt* v. *Baird* (1972) where the court recognized "the right of the individual, married or single, to be free of unwarranted government intrusion into matters so fundamentally affecting a person as the decision whether to bear or beget a child."

The concept of "fundamental interests" as relating to procreation was first raised by Justice Douglas in *Skinner* v. *Oklahoma* (1942) when he placed eugenic sterilization within the confines of the Fourteenth Amendment: "We are dealing here with legislation which involves one of the basic civil rights of man. Marriage and procreation are fundamental to the very existence and survival of the race. The power to sterilize, if exercised, may have subtle, far reaching and devastating effects . . . there is no redemption for the individual whom the law touches. . . . He is forever deprived of a basic liberty." The technological developments in reversible sterilization techniques (see Largey, 1979) might take some of the impact from Douglas's statement, but the concept of fundamental interest has become central to state attempts to intervene in procreative decisions.

The relative nature of regard for procreative rights, however, can be seen vividly in comparing the statement of Douglas to the conclusion reached by Justice Holmes only fifteen years earlier in *Buck* v. *Bell* (1927), where the Court affirmed the right of the state to impose sterilization as an appropriate exercise of its police power. According to Holmes, "We have seen more than once that the public welfare may call upon the best citizens for their lives. It would be strange if it could not call upon those who already sap the strength of the state for these lesser sacrifices, often not felt to be such by those concerned, in order to prevent our being swamped with incompetence." These clashing views on the role of the state vis-à-vis the individual's right to procreation and self-determination were offered by two educated and rational men. There is nothing to guarantee that future courts will refrain from a return to the views of Holmes. Some observers fear that advances in genetic technology might make such a reversal easier than at present by providing new techniques of intervention viewed as less threatening than irreversible sterilization.

The Impact of Genetic Technology on Parental Rights. On the basis of this very brief review of several cases, the interaction among rights relating to privacy, procreation, and self-determination is obvious. But how are these fundamental rights affected by genetic technology? Almost every application of human genetic intervention requires redefinition of these rights. The goal of much genetic technology is to provide more information and more options, but the effective use of these techniques often requires some coercive mechanism. This is most clearly seen at present in genetic screening and prenatal diagnosis, in which the receipt of such information affects the context within which any decision is made. Just as Holmes's decision was made at the height of the eugenics movement and Douglas's decision was made at a time when the horrors of the Nazis were being revealed, so any individual making a procreative decision will be influenced by circumstances. Even voluntary intervention programs, therefore, are bound to influence the alternatives available and ultimately the choice made.

The impact of the technology of intervention need not be viewed as restricting fundamental rights, however. Some would view any screening and diagnostic programs conducted on a voluntary basis as an expansion of rights: provision of information that will result in healthy offspring. Certainly artificial insemination, in vitro fertilization, and genetic therapy can easily be viewed as furthering procreative freedom by allowing those otherwise unable to have children. Although genetic intervention techniques provide an opportunity for interference with privacy, procreation, and self-determination, it is a mistake to focus solely on negative aspects. Compulsory amniocentesis might represent an invasion of privacy, but the technique of amniocentesis is more often employed to expand the informed choice of the parents. Similarly, the impact of carrier screening and even sterilization depends upon the way in which programs are implemented.

What are fundamental rights, then, and how are they affected by human genetic technology? The answer to both questions is relative. The concept of rights is a shifting one, as shown by the disparate views of Holmes and Douglas.

> With regard to constitutional questions, one should recognize that the entire constitutional rights and protected interests analysis should be seen as a shell game the Court must play in adapting to the changing mores and demands of modern urban society, without violating certain rights, reserved in the people, which cannot be infringed upon by the government. The central issue is to determine which of these rights will remain beyond governmental control. [Gray, 1976: 192]

Similarly, the impact of these technologies cannot be generalized; it is dependent in large part on how the technologies are applied. The specific policies implementing these technologies will determine in which direction and to what extent rights are affected.

The Limits of Parental Rights. Despite the uncertainty over the long-term consequences of human genetic intervention on individual rights, there are many situations in which the fundamental rights of some people obviously are compromised. A recurring question is: how inviolate are these rights? What are the limits, if any, of reproductive privacy and the right to bear children? Social pressures for population control and quality of life are growing and are certain to accelerate in the future as world resources become more constrained. The extent to which these rights are open for redefinition is a question that increasingly will concern the courts. Past experience suggests that the courts are not immune to altering drastically their perception of rights in relation to the interests of the state, the public health, or some other broader interest.

No rights, including the most highly valued parental rights discussed here, are absolute. Not only are they bound by social and cultural constraints, they also are defined relative to the rights of others that might take precedence in a particular situation. For instance, a series of limitations on the "fundamental" rights of marriage have withstood judicial scrutiny: Age limits designed to discourage young childbearing have held despite the failure of their ostensible objective; certain consanguineous marriages are forbidden despite the questionable status of their genetic rationale; and finally, the administration of blood tests for syphilis prior to the issuance of marriage licenses has been supported as a proper function of the state in protecting the public health.

At some point, consensus must define if and when responsibility to the affected persons takes precedence over the rights of the parents to have or not have children. This question without doubt is a difficult and sensitive one and any determination of the boundary between parental rights and responsibility and concern for the affected person is bound to be controversial. The extent to which society is bound to overrule the right to procreate in order to protect those affected or potentially affected by genetic disease will be an even more crucial question as more is understood about genetic disease.

Societal Good

A third consideration in decisions concerning the application of various methods of human genetic intervention relates to the needs of society at large. In addition to the indirect influence of societal values on all policy decisions, there is the more direct impact of the costs society is willing to bear to care for those with genetic disease or to implement genetic intervention programs. This question is certain to become more critical as competition for ever scarcer resources becomes more intense. Recent moves to restrict the taxing powers of states indicate the movement toward less government spending. Programs with low visibility and narrow constituencies are most likely to suffer. Care of the mentally retarded at present is less than adequate, and it seems unlikely that the situation will improve.

Also, as the population increases and the proportion of the working members decreases, pressure to restrict support for the "genetically defective" might increase. One result might be increased efforts to reduce or eliminate the incidence of genetic disease by introducing mandatory screening and restrictions on procreation by carriers. Compulsory diagnosis of high-risk fetuses and implicit or explicit pressure to abort fetuses diagnosed as having genetic defects might also follow under such circumstances. There certainly will be pressures in the opposite direction, i.e., to protect the rights of parents and concerned others, but the rapid and pervasive proliferation and acceptance of cost-benefit analysis indicates a long and intense battle. Thus, although it appears unlikely that compulsory genetic intervention programs could be justified from an individualistic standpoint, societal pressures on the distribution of limited resources might preclude certain options in the future, especially as technology offers inexpensive, effective, and less-intrusive means of testing. A public-health justification might be projected under such circumstances, but at base would be a monetary decision.

The most common orientation for political decision making in the United States today is the public interest. Generally, "the public" has come to refer to either the majority or some subset of it; the public interest on any issue is at most the interest of a majority of those involved in that specific issue and seldom if ever an objective good for society at large. As various "publics" conflict, it becomes difficult to demonstrate the existence of benefits that would accrue to all members of society. The concept of public interest, then, is much more restrictive than the traditional concept of the common good. As a moral justification for public policy, especially on the issues described in this study, the public interest appears to be quite limited.

The liberal concept of special or attentive publics further confuses decisions in the area of genetic research. Much of the current pluralist theory accepts the notion of intense minorities-and their rights to protect their interests despite the implications for society as a whole. In terms of genetics, interest-group pluralism might limit the public to the small proportion most directly affected by various techniques under consideration, i.e., those with genetic diseases. Does society have the right to limit certain research that might benefit only a minute fraction of the population? Does that minority have the right to lobby for such research? In many states, primary impetus for genetic screening programs for PKU, Tay-Sachs, and sickle-cell anemia came from the organized interests of those directly affected (see Chapter 4). They functioned not as common-good advocates but as special interest groups with specific demands for aid in preventing small numbers of future citizens from sharing their experience.

Etzioni (1974: 39) notes that society eludes clear definition and is an even more abstract concept than the individual. He warns that it is misleading to refer to society as a biological entity apart from the individuals who constitute it; rather, it is more accurate to view society as a set of interests, either individuals or groups, that attempt to achieve particular goals. The apparent dichotomy of individual rights versus societal good in actuality is nothing more than conflict between the rights of some individuals and those of other individuals. In a democracy, mechanisms are established to mediate disputes over rights (courts), set priorities and distribute resources (legislatures), and implement and enforce these programs (bureaucracy).

Despite the difficulty of dealing with society in other than an individualistic orientation, several authors have argued for the need to nurture a collective approach to the issues raised by genetic technology. Bevan (1977: 539) sees the need to develop a "culture of restraint" to "provide ways of changing the deeply ingrained human preoccupation with doing things primarily for individual advantage, come what may, rather than with meeting the needs of humankind as a whole." Kieffer (1975: 3) agrees that a shift from individual to collective goals is necessary: "the nature of modern society and technology poses serious obstacles to private solutions." It is not enough to require only that a person act according to his or her own conscience or be allowed a free choice on that basis; decisions must be right, not simply conscientious, since they may well affect the lives of many, in the present and the future. According to Kieffer, a "live and let live" tolerance does not serve societal good. Callahan (1973: 265) agrees that neither rugged individualism nor single-minded crusades for personal self-realization can lead to genuine human community. Still, he contends, the community cannot be given "moral preeminence" without the potential of persecution in the name of the common good. Tyranny of survival is just as dangerous as tyranny of individualism. The only "viable public morality" is one that sets limits on the government as well as on individuals. He sees an urgent need to recognize the valid claims of the community, which, although necessarily repressive, also provide their own measure of satisfaction.

Responsibility to Future Generations

Considering all the difficulties in balancing out the rights and obligations of people in the present, it is not surprising that concern for generations of the remote future is constrained. Despite this, recent emphasis on environmental pollution and depletion of natural resources has created an awareness of our responsibility to future generations to pass on a world where there is at least a reasonable chance of confronting successfully the problems left by twentieth-century humans. Some have argued that this concern should be directed not only to the obvious cases of population size and the environment but also to medical and genetic technology.

A central question, then, is the extent to which future generations must be considered in setting priorities for the use of genetic technologies. How much effort should be made to include the interests of those yet unborn? Who should speak for the future? Do we have a moral obligation to deny ourselves certain advantages now in order to provide better lives to those who are not yet born (Kieffer, 1975: 180)? In the area of genetic technology, the questions are more complex, the goals are less clear, and the implications are more complicated than in the areas of environment and population. For instance, certain types of genetic engineering might indeed reduce the suffering of parents and the children who would otherwise have been born with birth defects, but even if this potential is successfully met, there is the possibility that mutations formed by such a process might have adverse effects on generations of the distant future. Do we ban research on this basis or simply minimize the possibility of adverse long-range consequences?

There is disagreement as to how obligations toward future generations figure in the choices we make in the present. Kieffer (1975: 86) argues that, at a minimum, the living have an obligation to refrain from actions that endanger future generations' enjoyment of the same rights now assumed. Proper moral concern is not limited to the near neighbor, but extends to distant neighbors in space and time. We must be aware of any process that might be irreversibly harmful for future human life. In discussing claims on behalf of future generations, Twiss (1976: 39) concludes that such obligations do exist and that they can affect the priority ranking of genetic technologies. According to Feinberg (1974), we have a strong obligation to future generations out of respect for their rights as humans. In his view, we do not have a right to deprive future generations of the necessary conditions for life as we know it, even if this requires restrictions on certain freedoms of those now living.

Although Rawls (1971) does not speak directly to eugenic matters, he does state that persons "under the veil of ignorance" would be expected to have concern for future generations as in the original position they do not know into which generation they will be born.[14] The "principle of just savings" does not require heroic sacrifice on the part of any generation for the sake of posterity, but it does imply minimal obligations to the remote future. Barry (1978: 12), however, contends that neither the utilitarian nor the contract theory is adequate for justifying such obligations. Instead, he suggests that two prinicples that might be accepted provisionally in dealing with contemporaries have reasonable application to future generations: (1) not harming others is obligatory and (2) beneficence is not in general obligatory except to provide some minimal level of well-being. Callahan

(1971) agrees that there is no overarching obligation to promote the good life for future generations; still, we ought not consciously harm them through our actions.

Another position is that our first obligation is to immediate generations and not to some potential populations. Just as the present generation has had to adjust to the effects of decisions made in the past, so future generations must adapt to decisions made now. Although most would agree that no decisions should be made consciously that would endanger the rights and survival of future humans, it is argued that primary responsibility lies in those now living and their immediate offspring. This position encourages only minimal restraints upon actions based solely on the fate of those in the distant future. According to Golding (1968: 457), for instance, "It is highly doubtful that we have an obligation to establish social programs that would secure a 'good life' (prevent the undesirable, promote the desirable) for the community of the 'remote' future. The conditions of life then are likely to be so different from any that we can now imagine that we do not know what to desire for them." As a result, conflicts between the good of nearby generations and the good of remote generations should be resolved in favor of the former (Golding, 1972).

This second position seems to be less tenable under conditions faced in the 1980s simply because today's actions more than ever before might constrain greatly the alternatives open in the future. Decisions made now might inalterably limit or expand the decisions of all who follow. This possibility of irreversibility should make us more aware of the potential of current technology to affect the future. Also, contemporary knowledge of genetics has greatly enlarged responsibility, according to Gustafson (1974: 213): "Present generations are 'causally' responsible to some extent for the genetic health of future generations, and thus it can be argued that they also have a 'moral' responsibility to them."

In terms of genetic intervention techniques, it seems that responsibility to future generations must become an integral aspect of any policy decision. The decisions made in the next decade are likely not only to modify our conceptions of humanhood but also potentially to alter future individuals and the prospects of continued survival of the human race. We cannot afford either to ignore the opportunities presented by genetic technology or to actively pursue human genetic intervention without including futuristic considerations. Many of the recipients of the benefits of today's research are tomorrow's citizens; unfortunately, any harmful effects of such research might irreversibly affect those same generations. Policy decisions made now, therefore, must consider such concerns to the maximum extent possible. We should not make decisions based solely on concepts of obligation to future generations, but we must be aware that each innovation has broad ramifications on future alternatives.

Reproductive Rights Versus Societal Good

This summary of rights and responsibilities in each of four categories of interests relating to genetic technology demonstrates the multifaceted concerns central to each policy decision. Ultimately, the question reduces the extent of the government's responsibility to act as the primary agent for balancing the genetic rights and needs of these often conflicting interests. At what point is societal intervention into individual reproductive decisions justified? The answer depends on the observer's orientation toward the rights of parents. If the notion of inalienable rights as applied to procreation is accepted, then state interference can never be justified. On the other hand, if one agrees that no rights are absolute, including that of reproductive self-determination, then such intervention might be justified for a variety of reasons including the public health, paternalism, or protection of the rights of the affected. Finally, a utilitarian approach, such as Joseph Fletcher's (1974) situational ethics, would give society wide discretion in genetic matters if circumstances warranted intrusion in order to achieve the greatest good. In order to explicate the direct tension between parental rights and societal good, a variety of viewpoints is reviewed here.

Gustafson (1973: 102) argues that the "major persisting matter of moral choice is whether preference should be given to the individual or to a community." In agreement is Duncan (1974: 31), who observes, "The argument of the Common Good versus individual human rights is ever with us." Lipkin and Rowley (1974: 163) contend that genetic decisions involve major conflicts between the rights and needs of individuals and those of other individuals called "society." However stated, most resolutions of genetic dilemmas center on this conflict between the individual and the good of the community. Rights of individuals must be weighed against the needs of society. Callahan (1973: 24) sees little chance of a happy balance and claims that all solutions are bound to be temporary.

Societal Good. Joseph Fletcher (1974) sees this conflict reduced basically to a sanctity-of-life versus quality-of-life ethic, and he opts for the latter. His "situational ethics" places emphasis on the utilitarian principle of proportionate good. He contends that one must compute the gains and losses following several courses of action or nonaction and then select the alternative that offers the most good despite its implication for individual rights. The common welfare must be safeguarded, by compulsory state control if necessary, according to Fletcher (1974: 180): "Ideally it is better to do the moral thing freely, but sometimes it is more compassionate to force it to be done than to sacrifice the well-being of many to the egocentric 'rights' of the few." Fletcher favors mandatory controls on reproduction if they are needed to promote the greatest good for the largest number. Elsewhere (1971: 782) he states: "The right to conceive and bear children has to stop short of knowingly making crippled children."

Glass (1975: 56–57) suggests that in the near future advances in human genetics will result in a reordered priority of rights. These changes in technology will demand that the right of individuals to procreate must give way to a more "paramount" right—"the right of every child to enter life with an adequate physical and mental endowment." Not surprisingly, Muller (1959: 590) argues that those who are "loaded with more than the average share of defects" must refrain from engaging in reproduction "to the average extent." Finally, Heim (1975: 263) rhetorically asks whether an eleventh commandment, "Breed not, ye who carry defects," ought to be promulgated.

Several other authors have strongly supported intervention in procreative freedom but only under conditions that would otherwise lead to severe disorders. For Huntington's disease, Purdy (1978: 25) emphasizes the importance of knowledge of risk and concludes that "it is wrong to reproduce when we know there is a high risk of transmitting a serious disease or defect." He argues that it is the parents' responsibility to provide every child with a "normal" opportunity for health.[15] Although he stops short of recommending state intervention, he asserts that such a duty may require one to refrain from bearing children.

According to Ulrich (1976: 359), human rights are always negotiable and include an obligation to pursue actions that foster and protect the "right of species survival." He goes further than Purdy and argues that "those who are at high risk for passing on clearly identifiable, seriously deleterious genes and debilitating genetic disease *should not be allowed* to exercise their reproductive prerogative." Similarly, Bayles (1976: 301) explains that it is not implausible to suggest that it is justifiable to limit the procreative liberty of some persons if that increases the quality of life for those who live. "If it could be shown, for example that most persons with a certain genetic defect such as Tay-Sachs did not have a quality of life of level 'n', then there would be sufficient grounds for the principle to support a law to prevent their birth."

Procreative Rights. Taking the opposite position, Beecher (1968: 133) argues that society exists to serve humans and not vice versa. Therefore, individuals have certain inalienable rights that cannot be taken from them by the state. Paul Ramsey (1975: 238) contends that "parenthood is certainly one of those 'courses of action' natural to man, which cannot without violation be dissembled and put together again." He also defends vigorously the rights of individuals to unique genotypes and sees germinal engineering as immoral (1975: 235). Murphy, Chase, and Rodriguez (1978: 367) argue that there must be a "presumption in favor of the parents to reproduce" as they desire. The state may interfere only if parents abuse their privileges, but at present there is no "justification for restricting this right by law on even social pressure."

In examining the societal and individual costs of genetic disease, Lappé (1972: 425) minimizes the social costs. He sees the burden resting mainly on the family, not on society. He also dismisses the genetic load or genetic burden concept as well as Muller's (1959) theory of social cost and is disturbed by the current advocacy of societal intervention in childbearing decisions, denial of medical care to the congenitally damaged, and sterilization of carriers (p. 420). He contends that society has no right to intervene in childbearing decisions except in very rare cases. Despite acknowledgement of statistics on social costs, Lappé (1972: 425) states: "I know of no such decision . . . where the decision to procreate or bear children should be the choice of other than the parents." It is they, not society, who bear the burden of deleterious genes.

Callahan (1973) agrees that an affluent society should be able to absorb the costs. Parents should have the right to bear defective children even if the social costs of this freedom are high. He contends that it is difficult enough to resolve conflicts among individual rights, much less between individual rights and some nebulous greater social good. On the other hand, parents should not be forced to bear defective children. Milunsky (1977: 185) reiterates that a child has a right to begin life with a sound mind and body, but ultimately the parents should have the right to make the final decision. In proposing guidelines for genetic screening, Lappé et al. (1972: 214) reject any screening program that in any way imposes constraints on childbearing by individuals of any specific genetic constitution or that might stigmatize couples who, despite knowledge of the risks, still desire children of their own.

Balance of Society and Individual Interests. Somewhere between those who view societal good as predominant and those who view procreation as a fundamental right reserved for the parents' decision are many observers who stress the need for a balance. Most persons with this perspective agree that procreation is a fundamental human right that must be weighed against broader social concerns. State intervention might be justified under certain circumstances, although each case must be addressed with caution.[16] For instance, although Etzioni (1974: 51) expresses concern for individual rights, he sees the tendency to give the individual "unlimited priority" over society as counterproductive, as "the individual is part of society and needs it for his or her survival and well-being."

Reilly (1977: 132) asserts that no rights are absolute and that it is erroneous to conclude that state action to control reproduction on genetic grounds could never survive a constitutional challenge. Nevertheless, he concludes (1977: 148) on a cautious note:

> The right to marry and the right to bear children are so fundamental that a heavy burden of proof should be placed on those who claim that society should give special priority to the reduction of genetic disease — even through programs that envisage minimal compromise of these freedoms. . . . I would demand a convincing demonstration that a really impressive societal benefit could be derived from more intrusive programs.

Similarly, Twiss (1974: 259ff) concedes that as procreation is not an absolute right, parents may have a duty to avoid bearing children with serious genetic defects, especially when it would "affect adversely the welfare of other extant children for whom the parents bear a prior responsibility." Still, he concludes that "considerations against recognizing a societal right to intervene in parenthood and reproductive behavior seem eminently more persuasive than the utilitarian-based affirmative considerations." In other words, society does not have an unmitigated right to preclude fundamental procreative rights.

Several authors have noted that the conflict between the rights of parents, affected offspring, and society have been exaggerated and that they will be congruent in most cases. Morison (1976: 208) notes that most decisions concerning the use of human genetic technology reflect what "individuals are likely to want to do for themselves and at the same time will be of benefit to society." As most people greatly desire not to have defective or abnormal children, Sonneborn (1973: 5) believes that we will decide eventually that it is right and good to use genetic knowledge and reproductive technology for that end. Milunsky (1977: 171), too, sees prenatal diagnosis of benefit to all parties concerned and minimizes the conflicts among interests. Most couples who know they will have an affected child, for instance, decide to abort for personal reasons, though in the end societal interests are also served.

In sum, there is much disagreement as to whether state intervention in reproductive decisions is ever justifiable and, if it is, under what conditions it is warranted. Most of the attention recently has focused on the second question, although the first has yet to be resolved. The three sets of positions summarized here provide alternative frameworks with which to analyze human genetic intervention policy. Their conflicting assumptions, however, result in a stand-off. Those emphasizing societal rights fail to account for the rights of individuals and for future extensions of the present population. Those who focus on the individual rights of the parents overlook or minimize the corresponding rights of potentially or actually affected persons and of others in the community. When examining specific applications of screening and prenatal diagnosis, one must keep in mind the complex interrelationships between the affected individuals, the parents, society, and future generations. Initiation of any genetic intervention program rests on full consideration of all four dimensions of responsibility.

Justifying Limitations on Rights

This ongoing debate over what constitutes the social good and when, if ever, it takes precedence over fundamental individual rights might lead to the conclusion that rational discussion of these issues is impossible. Although no consensus is apparent, it appears that most observers are willing to permit genetic intervention when particular conditions are met. All but the most adamant opponents to state interference would consider such action appropriate within limits. The problem, then, is one of defining justifiable boundaries.

As usual, there is great disagreement as to what conditions justify state genetic intervention. According to Beauchamp (1976: 361), "the acceptability of these liberty-limiting laws ultimately depends on the adequacy of the justification offered for them." Although the "general welfare" or "societal good" are too abstract to be of any aid in clarifying this problem, several other principles have been used to justify state interference and establish conditions for it. Among the most widespread justifications are paternalism, the public health, social justice, and utilitarian criteria for costs and benefits.

Paternalism

According to Gerald Dworkin (1972: 65), paternalism is "the interference with a person's liberty of action justified by reasons referring exclusively to the welfare, good, happiness, needs, interests or values of the person being coerced." Under this principle, restriction of individual liberty is justified if it is for that person's "own good." State imposition of speeding limits, helmet safety laws, and drug usage laws are often justified on paternalistic grounds. Rawls (1971: 249) sees paternalism as a protection against our own irrationality: "Others are authorized and sometimes required to act on our own behalf and to do what we would do for ourselves if we were rational, this authorization coming into effect only when we cannot look after our own good." The obvious problems with this justification relate to who determines what is best for others and how irrationality is defined.

Beauchamp (1976: 362) rejects the paternalistic principle as good grounds for "coercive genetic intervention," but Dworkin (1972: 84) suggests that it might be appropriate in some situations. He argues, however, that such intervention should be kept to a minimum and that the least restrictive alternative in each case must be adopted. Furthermore, in all cases of paternalistic legislation, a heavy burden of proof to demonstrate that the action is in fact to the benefit of those restricted is placed on the authorities. It appears that many types of genetic intervention would have difficulty in meeting Dworkin's criteria. Compulsory PKU screening and even some types of carrier screening might be justified on paternalistic grounds, but it would be difficult to demonstrate that conclusively. Due to the uncertain status of fetus rights and the improbability of demonstrating that death is preferable, for the fetus, to a life of abnormality, it is even more difficult to defend procedures that result in the abortion of a defective fetus. Most nontherapeutic forms of genetic and reproductive research must be justified on other than paternalistic grounds.

Public Health

The public-health argument usually justifies restrictions on the liberty of some individuals by demonstrating that such restrictions help protect the health of others in the community. Beauchamp (1976: 361) cites the "moral" force behind this argument as being generated by the "harm principle." Even though he agrees that the harm principle is an acceptable justifying principle, Beauchamp concludes that "those who invoke it for purposes of genetic intervention . . . have not shown that the potential of harm to others . . . is sufficient to warrant the loss of liberties which would accompany the adoption of coercive genetic laws." It is yet to be determined whether the genetic health of the population would be substantially improved through enforced intervention in the procreative process.

Despite this, genetic legislation has often been justified by the need to protect the public health. Reilly (1978: 31), for instance, notes that mass neonatal screening is "rapidly becoming established as a valid public health enterprise." There are oft-cited precedents for state intervention into the reproductive activities of its citizens, for example, compulsory rubella vaccination and premarital tests for syphilis. Compulsory immunization for highly contagious diseases has been accepted on public-health grounds, but mandated genetic screening is a less immediate and viable concern for many observers as genetic disease is not contagious and there is no danger it will become epidemic. In addition, the lack of treatment in most cases of genetic disease suggests a qualitative difference between genetic intervention and other conditions or diseases. Although the long-term impact on the gene pool might be a threat to the health of those in the remote future, we have seen that obligations to those generations are seldom given much weight and play little role in our perceptions of public health. For those reasons, Lappé (1973: 154) minimizes the public-health aspects of genetic disease. Any consideration of the harm principle must balance the risks to individual rights with the health benefits gained.

Social Justice

There are innumerable theories of social justice that have implications for a discussion of genetic intervention by the state.[17] Rawls's theory, with its impact on political thought in the 1970s, seems the most appropriate example. Rawls appears to be favorably inclined toward genetic intervention, in principle at least, from two directions. First, he contends that in the original position (the hypothetical situation prior to the etsablishment of a society), "the parties want to insure for their descendants the best genetic endowment," assuming their own to be fixed (1971: 108). Although an open society encourages the widest genetic diversity, the pursuit of "reasonable" eugenic policies is something earlier generations owe later ones. Society, therefore, appears to have a responsibility over time to take steps necessary "at least to preserve the general level of natural abilities and to prevent the diffusion of serious defects." He justifies this with his first principle, that "if there is an upward bound on ability, we would eventually reach a society with the greatest equal liberty the members of which enjoy the greatest equal talent." Furthermore, it is not to the advantage of those worst off to propose policies that reduce the talents of others. The greater abilities, which would be lost under such a policy, are viewed as a social asset to be used for the common advantage. It would seem, then, that a just society according to Rawls would utilize eugenic policies to raise the abilities and talents of the members, presumably in the process providing more equality by raising those at the bottom (the difference principle).

This leads to the second aspect of Rawls's support for intervention in the genetic composition of society, which relates directly to his second principle. The emphasis in critiques of the difference principle have revolved around economic concerns and advantages found in inherited wealth. Rawls also sees genetic endowment and superior character as undeserved social advantages. As he is unwilling to permit genetic superiority to be converted into an unfair competitive edge, Rawls appears supportive of attempts to mitigate these "accidents of birth" and reduce the scope of such undeserved advantages. Strict application of the difference principle to genetic heritage implies that any attempt to intervene in the evolutionary process could be justified only if the resultant condition maximized the prospects of the least advantaged. Given the present views toward genetic characteristics and the nature of the institutional structures, however, it is unlikely that any eugenic attempt would be designed primarily to improve the lot of the worst off.[18] In fact, in translating the difference principle from economic to genetic concerns, it is unlikely that the terms of this second principle could be met unless it can be assumed that the least advantaged genetically (presumably those with the weakest genotypes) would be better off having not lived at all. Darlington has been quoted (in Chapman, 1975: 590) as stating that every technological advance worsens the competitive position of the genetically disadvantaged. Only when one discusses the theoretical possibilities of genetic therapy and surgery can the intent of the difference principle be attained, that is, when and if changes in specific genes of an individual can be made directly.

Rawls explicitly supports the concept of eugenics through both the original position and the difference principle, but this perception of genetic engineering as an equalizer of genetic traits is not realistic, at least in the near future. Rawls would like all persons to have approximately equal chances to pursue their "preferred plan of life." He fails to note, however, that genetic diversity itself might lead to different preferred life plans, only some of which could be approached through eugenic programs.

In addition to Rawls's explicit reference to eugenics as a potential means of maximizing his two principles of justice, other aspects of his theory have broad implications for such policies. For instance, the impact of various genetic technologies on primary social goods is substantial. Although Rawls's concern for eugenics is directed toward succeeding generations and in the reduction of undeserved social advantage, the implementation of any genetic intervention program would certainly challenge many of the primary goods that he emphasizes. As expressed elsewhere in this book, the initiation of genetic screening and other eugenic techniques, even if conducted on a purely voluntary basis, redefines rights and liberties as reflected in social values and conventions. The tension between the rights of various agents (e.g., the right of the mother versus the right of the fetus) becomes most crucial in the life decisions posed by genetic technology.

One primary social good that is affected is self-respect (Rawls, 1971: 440): "the person's sense of his own value, his secure conviction that his conception of the good, his plan of life is worth carrying out." In fact, Rawls suggests that self-respect or self-esteem is the most crucial of the primary goods. Without it our life plans will appear worthless and other goods will have little value. Eugenic policy certainly has the potential to increase the level of self-respect by improving the genetic potential of the population as a whole. However, not only is it less likely than Rawls appears to believe that the distribution of these benefits will be "just" according to the difference principle, it is also possible that self-respect is undermined by eugenic attempts. As we shall see later, potential stigmatization, social pressures, and coercive measures weaken the concept of self-respect considerably. Genetic intervention on grounds of social justice appears to have problems not envisioned by Rawls. Again, it depends heavily on the manner in which these policies are implemented.

Utilitarian Criteria

As noted earlier, most policy decisions in the United States are based upon utilitarian criteria. While paternalistic, public-health, and social-justice principles are often given as the rationale for particular programs, ultimately pragmatic political reasons are at the core. Within this framework, justification often rests on cost-benefit criteria: what alternative action will maximize benefits and minimize costs to those able to influence the decision? The policy that decreases the costs to society normally will be adopted; if at the same time it serves humanitarian or other goals, so much the better. The costs and benefits are not always monetary. For instance, one political cost to be weighted heavily is that involved in abrogating fundamental individual rights. In a society where such rights are jealously guarded, they become an integral element in the decision-making context and, therefore, must be reflected in resulting policy decisions.

Human Genetic Intervention:
Individual Choice or Social Control?

In many discussions of human genetic intervention there is little reference made to differentiation of motive. Instead, there is a tendency to either favor or condemn intervention in principle or to accept or reject particular techniques on the basis of their perceived use in society. It is seldom made clear that each application has at least two dimensions that must be clearly distinguished. The first is the individualistic orientation reflected in each technique. This centers on the use of genetic technology to reduce genetic disease or its debilitating effects through such means as neonatal and carrier screening, prenatal diagnosis, and therapy for some genetic diseases. Also included here would be the voluntary use of various reproductive technologies such as in vitro fertilization and artificial insemination to overcome problems of infertility. Intervention here is for the benefit of the affected person, although the term "benefit" in some cases (e.g., abortion of an identified defective fetus) is debatable. The balancing of the various interests, for instance, the parents versus the affected child, causes ethical dilemmas, but the use of human genetic intervention to help people on an individual basis presents relatively few problems.

The issue often becomes complicated, however, with the introduction of the societal dimension. The motivation shifts from helping individuals, or doing what one feels is best for them, to providing a stronger genetic base for society or for survival of the species. This "eugenic" dimension is the cause of much confusion and the most heated debate over genetic intervention. Techniques that can give prospective parents valuable information concerning the risks involved in procreation or the status of their fetus and allow otherwise infertile couples to have children can just as easily be used to control reproduction for eugenic or economic purposes. It appears that much of the opposition to human genetic intervention is derived from fear of the latter motivation. Even Lederberg (1972: 14), who is an outspoken proponent of eugenics, admits that "the remaking of man is an illusionary goal for the application of genetics in a liberal society. . . . The principal target for its applications to man is the alleviation of individual distress." A common concern is that once these techniques become widely accepted for whatever reason, they will be an invidious means of eugenic control. Conversely, many of the proponents of genetic intervention (Joseph Fletcher, 1974; Pauling, 1968) do emphasize the eugenic needs of society and thus fuel the debate over genetic intervention.

What is necessary, therefore, is a clearer distinction between public policy that emphasizes the individual prerogative and policy directed toward eugenic objectives. Then, a choice can be made between alternative policies, not simply on "all-or-nothing" terms, and the impasse can be moderated and the technology applied where acceptable and feasible on individualistic grounds. To put it differently, the manner of implementation and the motivation behind it, not the acceptance or rejection of a technology per se, are the crucial issues. So far in the debate over intervention, this mode of thinking has not emerged and the bulk of the policy decisions appear to be made in a confused and haphazard manner with no clear-cut priorities. In order to achieve a more realistic ground for making these decisions, we must move to a two-dimensional level of analysis.

What appears to be one policy question, then, is in actuality a series of questions. Consider prenatal diagnosis, for example, in the following set of questions:

Should the government support through tax revenues prenatal diagnosis of any type?
        a. Yes.
        b. No
If yes:
    1. Should it support on the basis of individual prerogative?
        a. Yes
        b. No
    2. Should it support on eugenic grounds?
        a. Yes
        b. No

3. Should it support on economic (cost/benefit) grounds?
   a. Yes
   b. No

A positive answer to the general question does not preclude a positive answer in any single subcategory, nor does a positive response to 1 preclude a positive or negative response to 2, and so forth. Obviously, the means of implementing a prenatal diagnostic program under 1 would differ substantially from a program justified on eugenic or economic grounds. The 1a response would require vast expenditures on education programs and offer voluntary testing to provide individuals with the broadest possible informed choice. A eugenic rationale (2a) would require a mandatory program, or at least one with some coercive mechanisms available, to meet its objectives. The entire context of a program conducted under a eugenic approach would be drastically different from one aimed at furthering individual choice, in which emphasis would center on the good of the individuals concerned. There would still be conflict in the latter approach and it would be less cost–effective from a eugenic standpoint, but it would neutralize the concerns of those fearful of social control over genetic factors. Although the distinction between the individualistic and the societal (eugenic or economic) model is not great, the thrust of programs based on each would vary substantially.

Despite opposition to the individualistic orientation from those against any form of genetic intervention, the individualistic approach is more readily defended than the eugenic approach. With that assumption in mind, it appears likely that any successful intervention program must be carried out with emphasis on individual prerogative rather than eugenic objectives. In order to keep the discussion of the characteristics of an individualistic program manageable, it focuses on genetic screening.

Genetic Intervention: Compulsory or Voluntary?

An issue central to all genetic intervention programs is whether society should mandate a particular action, for reasons of public health or some other societal goal, or whether all actions should remain voluntary. This is commonly presented in strict "compulsory versus voluntary" terms, but it is misleading to discuss the implementation of such programs as a dichotomy, as even a voluntary program has an inherent coercive aspect if accepted by society. The choice of policy options is better represented by a series of approaches ranging from purely informative to compulsory, depending on how compliance is effected. The most coercive approach is to compel screening by law. This could apply to the entire population or to certain high-risk groups as determined by lawmakers. The severity of the compulsory aspect depends on the penalties for noncompliance. Obviously, if criminal penalties are processed, compliance will increase although public acceptance will be difficult to achieve except in extreme circumstances.

Although some theorists (Vukowich, 1971; Hardin, 1974) claim that voluntary programs are bound to fail, Powledge (1974) contends that voluntary programs are capable of achieving as high a level of compliance as mandatory ones, if they are properly planned: "One inescapable conclusion is that participation is clearly far more a function of desire, organization and the availability of testing facilities than of legal sanctions." Conversely, Vukowich (1971) and Green and Capron (1974) suggest that although voluntary programs do not seem to involve "insurmountable constitutional problems," compulsory programs do. Given the current emphasis on individual choice in reproductive decisions and the need to demonstrate "compelling state interest" in order to intervene, mandated genetic intervention appears to be difficult to implement, at best. There are, however, other means falling short of legal coercion that might achieve similar goals.

An intermediate approach to genetic screening or eugenic attempts is to construct incentive programs of greater or lesser intensity. Positive tax incentive programs have long rewarded marriage, encouraged home ownership, and influenced family size. Although negative financial incentives are less obvious, limits on the number of children eligible for Aid to Financially Dependent Children (AFDC) payments and restrictions on the distribution of federal funds for prenatal diagnosis and abortion might have a direct influence on genetic screening programs. Another type of incentive program could be the provision of particular services without cost. Attempts to provide broad access to family planning services and genetic counseling clinics are prime examples of the incentive approach to implementation of specific principles. Such programs are less directly coercive in nature, but they might be used to achieve the same objectives as legislation. Their success largely depends on the extent to which they increase compliance to the predetermined goal.

A last approach to implementation of genetic programs is simply to provide citizens, or those in high-risk groups, with specific information upon which to make an informed choice. Experience demonstrates that this approach is the most difficult with which to achieve broad compliance, but the lack of direct coercion and the resulting impression of free choice makes it most appealing in cases in which there is no serious and direct threat to the health and public. Despite its appearance as unobtrusive and the assumption that it guarantees free and informed consent, this approach does include a degree of coercion. The mere dissemination of available information carries with it at least implied pressure to conform with some standard defined by society. It would be misleading to state that any approach is totally objective; the choice, then, becomes one of the degree and type of coercion utilized to assure compliance and the means employed to achieve the policy goals.

Genetic Screening Programs

Due to the recency of genetic screening and diagnosis programs and the lack of standard legislation across the states, implementation of these programs tends to be fragmented and varied from state to state and program to program. Most attempts currently are based on incentives and voluntary compliance. In addition, two types of laws mandating particular screening procedures have been established. The first is aimed at detection of affected individuals so that treatment can be offered; for example, PKU screening of newborns and similar programs for detecting metabolic disorders. The second type of mandatory screening program is designed to identify carriers of recessive deleterious genes and inform them of the risk of bearing children with genetic diseases if their mate is also so identified. The most obvious example of this second type is compulsory screening for sickle-cell anemia.

Screening of the first type, when combined with treatment of affected individuals, might be justified as a public-health measure or as a means of saving public funds. The compulsory screening element might be supported by the "parens patriae" doctrine that the state can act to protect those that cannot protect themselves (National Academy of Sciences [NAS], 1975: 189). Specific conflicts with religious freedom must be resolved by the courts, but mandatory screening of this type is much less controversial than compulsory screening for carriers. There is little evidence that the latter can meet either public-health or paternalistic grounds of justification: "We have been impressed with the effectiveness of the voluntary approach and we believe that the psychologic, political, and moral dangers of legislating human genetic testing far outweigh the potential medical benefits. . . . As a practical matter, legislation alone cannot solve genetic problems" (Kaback and O'Brien, 1973: 262). As this type of screening contains implications for influencing reproductive decisions, it is effective only if the carriers refrain from having children or make use of prenatal diagnosis followed by selective abortion when indicated. Each of these steps is controversial and ethically and legally questionable, at best. There appear to be few benefits and many costs of mandatory screening of carriers. Any screening programs for carriers of autosomal recessive diseases should be predicated on the assumption of voluntary compliance, and an adequate education program and the availability of services to all citizens is a solid base from which to proceed.

Although screening for PKU and related diseases appears to be less troublesome, a basic objection to all mandatory screening is its potential interference in "respect for individual choice in child-rearing matters" (NAS, 1975: 189). Screening is intended to provide accurate information upon which informed choices can be based, but there is some concern that the seeking of information should be up to the individual. The knowledge of adverse information might be a "powerful impetus toward action" — in effect, offering very little choice. Callahan's (1973) concern for the causal logic of information is most appropriate in mandatory screening, as once the information is available, free choice is constrained. In other words, the only stage at which free choice can be assured is if the decision to screen is voluntary. If not, all succeeding choices are at least in part bound by the knowledge of the screening result.

Although it might be assumed that it is preferable to know that a fetus is affected with Down's syndrome early in pregnancy, it might be argued that only the woman should be able to make that decision because the pressures for an abortion in case of a positive diagnosis might be counter to her sense of personal morality. As one source (NAS, 1975: 49) notes: "Compulsory screening of prospective parents before conception or directly of the fetus prenatally forces information on the parents that they may take into account in their childbearing decisions." Such intrusion into private childbearing decisions is much less drastic than sterilization; still, the constitutional questions of mandatory screening are yet to be answered. It is probable that screening in cases of treatable diseases, which does not directly infringe on the right to bear the child, is on a more solid ethical foundation than prenatal diagnosis and screening of carriers when alternatives are limited even with the screening information.

The extent to which mandatory screening programs can withstand legal and social challenges, then, will most likely depend on the procedures and objectives of each program. Screening conducted with minimal risk to those being screened, and which results in treatment, is more easily defended than that for untreatable metabolic disorders. Screening for recessive gene carriers, although offering more informed decisions about marriage and reproduction, should remain voluntary for now. At the same time, however, it seems reasonable that screening services and facilities, combined with broad educational programs, should be made widely available to those who desire them.

The Need for Public Education

Despite an increased interest in genetic technology by the press and concerned segments of the public, genetic disease continues to be an area of ignorance for a major portion of the public (Levin, 1976). In spite of new screening legislation and awareness of the rapid advances in genetic technology, most lawmakers, under the pressure of a heavy workload and more immediate matters, tend to be uninformed and only marginally concerned (Jasper, 1974: 149). It is difficult under such circumstances to convince lawmakers to provide public funds for education concerning genetic problems and programs. Even in states with energetic screening programs, money for educating the public constitutes only a minor fraction, if any, of the program cost (see Reilly, 1977). Instead, the funds go almost exclusively to the actual cost of administering the tests. As this is more visible and easily measured, the funds appear to be well spent.

As the advances in genetic technology continue to accelerate and the technical possibilities for human genetic intervention multiply, it is imperative that public education be made an integral part of any attempts to apply the technology. This need centers on two aspects of education. First, there must be more general information on what genetic disease entails and a clarification of misunderstood concepts such as inheritance, carrier status, and the chance nature of chromosomal abnormalities. The guilt associated with genetic disease must be dispelled, and people should be encouraged to discuss openly the ramifications of genetic disease for the affected person and the family as well as society. This is best accomplished through counseling and public education programs.

Education is essential in every effort to minimize the stigmatization raised by genetic intervention. No matter how elevated the objectives of a genetic program are, the program is likely to accentuate the notion of "abnormality," whether represented by a person diagnosed as a "carrier" or a fetus diagnosed as "defective." Sorenson (1974: 172) contends that the amount of prejudice expressed toward mentally and physically disabled persons is "generally more than that expressed toward various minority groups." Annas (1979: 20) terms the mentally retarded "an oppressed minority group." Gustafson (1974: 210) sees a real danger in establishing "genetic profiles" of individuals. When the stigma of genetic disease is directed toward groups already the target of social discrimination, the problem is even more severe. Education alone cannot eliminate the stigma and resulting social pressures attached to people with particular genetic disorders or to the parents of such persons, but it can help reduce the belief that genetic disease is the fault of the parents or that those affected are less human because of their misfortune in the "reproductive roulette."

Second, in addition to educating the public on genetic disease in general, specific education programs relating to screening, counseling, or other programs designed to reduce the incidence of genetic disease must be included in all legislation. The public, and especially certain high-risk groups, not only must be made aware of the services available, but also must be educated on the scope and limitations of each program. The importance of specific intervention techniques should be presented in a balanced and objective manner so that informed consent is possible. Education concerning these programs should be most intensive among those at risk, but as broadbased as possible. The disastrous attempts at sickle-cell screening in some states, when carriers were led to believe they suffered from the disease, should serve as examples of how not to conduct a program. The well-organized and community-controlled education procedures used in various Tay-Sachs screening efforts, on the other hand, serve as models for successful programs.

In analyzing any attempt to intervene in human genetics, it is crucial to include the needs and interests of a wide variety of elements in society. As noted in this chapter, there are numerous normative conceptions of what a democracy ought to be, each with its own assumptions as to which interest should be uppermost in making public decisions. Although the history of genetic policy in the United States demonstrates a propensity to support state intervention to prevent society from being "swamped with incompetence,"[19] priority recently has been given to the rights of parents to bear children. Procreation is perceived by many as an interest so fundamental that society has no right to intervene. Both of these absolutist positions neglect the primary responsibility to those who would be affected by genetic disease if born and to future generations. Too often the policy choice is based solely on either the rights of the parents to reproduce at will or certain inherent powers of the state to protect the health of its citizens.

Again, it must be noted that all rights are relative to other rights, not absolute. Society cannot indiscriminately violate the rights of parents and their reproductive autonomy, but society also has a responsibility to those directly affected by the broad range of genetic diseases. It is unfair to concentrate on the rights of today's parents without accounting for the concerns of those potentially or actually afflicted or to some broader societal needs. Certainly, the fundamental right to bear children, although at the core of any genuine democratic society, has limits. Whether or not the imposition of any specific genetic intervention on this right is justifiable within a broader social context depends on the characteristics of each particular program.

4
The Public Policy Context of Human Genetic Intervention

Thus far this study has attempted to demonstrate why human genetic technology is so controversial. It has reviewed the traditional relationship between technology and society, summarized the current state of and possible future developments in human genetic technology, and discussed the political and social issues raised by such innovations and applications. The impact of human genetic technology on Western culture, which emphasizes individual responsibility and freedom, is substantial as many previously assumed values are challenged by the technological developments. The clash between individual rights and societal good is perceived as central to the debate over human genetic intervention.

At a more abstract level, these techniques raise questions concerning the role of humans vis-à-vis nature or God. To what extent should humans tamper with human nature and modify heretofore unalterable genetic features? Although there is much support for social and environmental intervention to improve the quality of life, there is no agreement as to whether direct genetic intervention is desirable. Such intervention in humans has been shown to have many potential benefits (for instance, reducing genetic disease, improving the human condition, and reducing costs to society in a time of diminishing resources). But questions concerning possibly unintended and unanticipated consequences (ethical and social as well as biological), the irreversibility of the procedures, and the costs to society are increasingly evident and will become more difficult and demanding as the technical possibilities of human genetic intervention are broadened.

Ultimately, these questions must be resolved within the realm of public policy. As stated in a current national commission report (Department of Health, Education, and Welfare [DHEW], 1978: 105), "it should be clear that all such decisions finally rest on a political basis and that the entire American electorate has a legitimate stake both in the procedures by which the decisions are made, and in the steps that are taken to monitor and control the consequences." Tribe (1973: 593) notes the growing significance of federal programs and policies in the evolution of technology and foresees even more dependency on future federal action. Although biomedical issues are not at present the nation's "most important problems," they are emerging as major political issues and are of growing significance in the public consciousness (Ostheimer and Ritt, 1976: 283).

As these issues become more salient, it is inevitable that pressure for "legislation designed to prevent or control aspects of scientific research will . . . increase at all levels of government" (Stine 1977: 427). Many observers see this trend toward government involvement as dangerous or unfortunate; others feel that these questions must be part of the public debate (Kindig and Sidel, 1973). History has shown that American society has always experienced difficulty in making acceptable policies on moral issues, so it is crucial to monitor the policymaking process and the public's reactions to determine what institutions might best assure fair and comprehensive consideration of these issues.

Furthermore, the policy issues raised by biomedical technology are among the most difficult and divisive issues imaginable. They do not fit the traditional mold of political issues that are resolved through a bargaining and compromise process. Instead, they are reflections of the most basic value conflicts over the meanings of human life and death and are bound in a variety of religious and secular ethical frameworks. Furthermore, the rapid pace of technological change has created these value conflicts in a very short time span whereas values themselves normally change gradually through the socialization process.[1] Public involvement in such issues not only broadens the scope of the political system but also threatens to disrupt most basic distinctions between the private and the public (for instance, privacy in procreative decisions). There is no doubt that these issues are difficult to deal with politically, which explains the tendency of many officials to ignore them or wish them away, but the rapid advances in technology make it mandatory that action be taken, at least to discuss the issues within the political context.

Another tendency in the political system is that of postponing action until a situation reaches crisis proportions. Although it is doubtful that human genetic technology at present represents a crisis (Green, 1973), it is clear that we cannot afford to wait until such a situation develops, because at that point it might be too late to establish a groundwork for the rational discussion and deliberation of the issues. Also, the extent to which the political institutions deal with these issues now, when the technology itself is relatively limited, will determine their ability to react to future innovations that are bound to be even more controversial. We must begin now to establish mechanisms by which decisions on these issues can be made in the near future.

Defining the Role of Government in Genetic Technology

A major factor contributing to the confusion and fueling the controversy over government involvement in genetic technology is the inability or unwillingness to define clearly what such involvement entails. Both proponents and opponents of these technologies often intentionally emphasize the dangers of the form of state control they most fear without clarifying the distinctions among the various types of governmental action possible. Proponents stress the need for the imposition of government controls on the development and application of genetic technology, while those opposed most often point to potentially coercive eugenic programs mandated by the state. Seldom is an attempt made to discuss rationally the broad range of government intervention schemes that are possible. Given these disparate definitions of government or "public" involvement, it is not surprising that much fear is expressed by those of all persuasions.

Government intervention can take at least five forms,[2] each with a distinctive impact on genetic technology. The continuum in Figure 4.1 illustrates the range of government involvement that can occur from the earliest stages of research to the application of specific techniques.

Prohibition

Some have proposed that the government actively preclude certain types of genetic research and application. The 1974 Massachusetts moratorium on fetal research (see Stine, 1977: 426) and current attempts to prohibit reproductive research in which human embryos are destroyed (such as in vitro and cloning research) are examples of this form of social control. Obviously, those favoring the research and the use of such technologies are most fearful of state bans and attack such attempts as infringements on freedom of scientific inquiry or impediments to important research. Although there have been many calls for the imposition of governmental prohibitions on genetic research, most recently in recombinant DNA research, it seems unlikely that the U.S. government will completely ban specific areas of technology in the near future.

Regulation

A more likely government activity and one now present to a large degree is the regulation of genetic technology by various agents of the government. Stine (1977: 425) asserts that increased "regulation, including enforcement strategies from outside of science, is probably inevitable and may be necessary." Safety regulations, research priorities, and proper procedures, which until recently were viewed as problems of self-regulation by the scientific community, are increasingly coming under the purview of public institutions. From the basic research stage to widespread application,

FIGURE 4.1
Types of Government Involvement in Genetic Technology

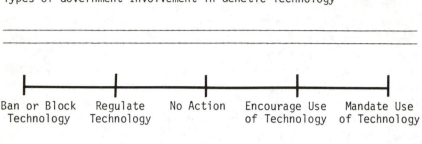

Ban or Block   Regulate   No Action   Encourage Use   Mandate Use
 Technology   Technology   of Technology   of Technology

genetic innovations are covered by numerous federal regulations. The increased public funding of genetic research has given the federal government a lever for increased regulatory activity. Although nonaction is still the practiced national policy in some areas of genetics, the 1976 National Genetic Disease Act, which combines federal funding and regulation for several genetic screening programs, is one example of this new governmental activity. Despite criticisms from the scientific community that such action results in cumbersome and unnecessary bureaucratic impediments to research, regulation is bound to increase as these technologies become more prominent and opposition groups are mobilized.

Encouragement

State intervention could also be designed to encourage the use of genetic and reproductive technologies by its citizens. As seen in Chapter 3, the government has at its disposal many discretionary measures to facilitate research as well as apply specific technologies. Continued federal funding of genetic research, for instance, is crucial to the expansion of future genetic applications. The government can, through increased funding, make current technologies available to all citizens on a voluntary compliance basis. Provision of amniocentesis and abortion to those who cannot afford these procedures on their own, adequate funding of voluntary neonatal and carrier screening programs, and the establishment of genetic education programs are several methods of encouraging the use of current genetic knowledge. Although there have been many attempts in these directions, especially in neonatal and, to a lesser extent, carrier screening programs, other policies have had the opposite effect. For instance, in the Hyde Amendment to the 1977 DHEW appropriations Congress decided that a pregnant woman carrying a defective fetus does not qualify for a federally funded abortion if she cannot pay for one.[3] This precludes many poor women as well as those at military installations from obtaining the necessary prenatal diagnosis and discourages use of related technologies.

Mandate

A final form of governmental action, most condemned by those opposed to human genetic intervention, is the establishment of compulsory screening or eugenic policies, generally defended on public-health or economic grounds. The compulsory sickle-cell legislation of the 1970s in some states and compulsory PKU testing programs in most of the states are examples of such public intervention. Eugenic sterilization laws still on the books in some states represent more direct intervention in procreation. Although it is not inconceivable, given some of the value trends outlined in Chapter 1, that there might soon be pressures on the government to take an active role in promulgating eugenic programs, it is more probable that most efforts will be directed toward broadening accessibility to screening, diagnostic, and eventually therapeutic technologies. Recent moves, such as the Chicago Bar Association's 1974 attempt (Beckwith, 1976: 53) to require all applicants for marriage licenses to be tested for carrier status as well as venereal disease, indicate that state involvement of a compulsory nature cannot be ruled out, however, and that it is attractive to many segments of society (see Stine, 1977: 508–509).

Obviously, each of these types of government involvement in genetic policy deeply worries various interests in society. Seldom, however, is the role of government defined clearly, and frequently public involvement is attacked without clarifying exactly what it constitutes. Those opposed to government intervention usually view it as an "intrusion" and emphasize either government prohibition or mandated eugenic policy. Those supporting government involvement, on the other hand, usually refer to the more moderate forms of control represented by regulation or encouragement or both. Despite the warnings of those fearful of government intervention at either extreme on the continuum, most activity appears to be directed toward moderate involvement.

Another factor contributing to the confusion over governmental intervention is the inability or unwillingness to distinguish between the technologies themselves and the uses to which they are put. Often the debate becomes confused because the participants fail to clarify that they are in fact discussing uses of the technology rather than the techniques. Any of the reproductive technologies discussed in Chapter 2 can be applied either to allow couples who are otherwise unable to have children or to serve as a means of implementing a eugenic program. For example, sterilization, when conducted on a voluntary basis, expands reproductive freedom, while involuntary sterilization might violate parental rights.

Those who oppose genetic technologies often focus on potential eugenic extensions, while those who support them usually deal exclusively with clinically indicated applications and minimize the possible eugenic applications. The controversy over these technologies would not be eliminated if this distinction were clearly defined, but it is unfortunate that at least a part of the debate centers on this lack of conceptual clarity. It is not surprising, considering the lack of agreement on basic assumptions, that the public debate over these technologies is intense.

Formal Political Institutions and Genetic Issues

There currently are numerous formal and informal mechanisms available for making decisions relating to genetic technology. Baram (1971: 536) lists approximately 20 forms of social control over technology ranging from peer groups to torts. A more complete list of channeling mechanisms is presented in Table 4.1. A key question that arises from the review of such lists is: What type of control is most conducive to protection of the variety of interests discussed in Chapter 3? Given the complexity of issues and the critical implications of genetic technology for society, it is unlikely that any single mechanism is adequate. What combination, then, offers the most reasonable means of making these difficult decisions? Ultimately, the answer depends upon whom we want to entrust with this decision-making responsibility. It is assumed that the individual value and belief system underlies decisions at each level. In other words, no matter which mechanism is chosen, decisions will be conditioned to some extent by the broader social/cultural context. Beyond that, however, decisions might vary substantially depending upon how and by whom they are made.

Although professional (Table 4.1: II; A,B,C) and private (III; A,B) mechanisms have important roles in more narrow technical or clinical choices, they are less adequate to handle broad questions of social priorities, distribution, and accountability. Nelkin (1977: 404), for instance, concludes that the scientific community is ill equipped to deal with broader political issues. Baram (1971: 537) dismisses scientific peer groups as inadequate means of social control over technology. They have neither the objectivity nor the capability to reflect social goals because of their personal stake in the outcome and their narrow disciplinary backgrounds. Baram (1971: 536) also contends that industrial decisions and insurance controls do not include full consideration of the public interest.

Despite the ongoing debate over the appropriateness and effectiveness of self-regulation by the scientific community, the expanded role of the public agencies in genetic policymaking is genuine. The public mechanisms in Table 4.1 include both formal political institutions (III: C,D,E) and

TABLE 4.1
Channeling Mechanisms for Biomedical Technology*

I.   Individual: person's value and belief system as shaped by
     culture, society, family, education, and so forth.

II. Professional: self-regulation, internal controls.

     A.   Scientist's own background and values

     B.   Peer Mechanisms: both formal and informal, including
          professional certification; professional collaborative
          efforts; professional organizations; codes of ethics;
          and informal communication networks.

     C.   Institutional Mechanisms: staff meetings and clinical
          rounds; peer review committees; ethical/legal research
          and advisory bodies.

III. External Controls

     A.   Institutional: budgetary allocations; policies for
          hiring and promotion; administrative decisions.

     B.   Private Funding Mechanisms: universities and foundations;
          industrial funding; insurance companies and other third-
          party payers.

     C.   Legal: professional licensure; licensure of research
          facilities; malpractice decisions; decisions on consent,
          privacy, occupational health standards; and tort law.

     D.   State and Federal Legislative Acts: establish regulatory
          agencies; appropriation of public funds for research and
          application; Office of Technology Assessment; etc.

     E.   Administrative Agencies: peer review process for awarding
          funds; agency regulations and guidelines; technology
          assessment.

     F.   The Public: mass media; elections; religious groups;
          political parties; interest groups.

*Extracted from Adjunct to Special Report: DHEW, 1978: 80-83.

numerous informal linkages between the public and the decision makers (III: F). Of the many public-policy mechanisms available at each stage of scientific and technological development, none is adequate to resolve these complex and emotional issues. The rapid advances in genetic technology, with their substantial moral and political implications, have produced problems of a different nature from those traditionally part of the public-policy spectrum. According to Schoenberg (1979: 90), "To a considerable extent, the shortcomings that have created the crisis of modern science spring from defects in the present political system. Indeed, our political system and institutions have not kept up with scientific and technological change." Joseph Coates (1978: 33) agrees that "mechanisms of government and their organization and structure are obsolete to a degree that has engendered a fundamental built-in incompetence to deal with many of the new issues which the nation faces."

Although the political system has proved itself quite persistent and adaptable in times of stress in the past, it may not be capable of adjusting to these sensitive genetic issues of the present and future. In order to assess this capability, the characteristics of the major political institutions that limit the latter's ability to make policy decisions relating to the development and use of human genetic technology are summarized here. Among the major problem areas examined are: the fragmented nature of decision making, the influence of special interests throughout the process, the slow reaction to change, and the tendency to act only on immediate problems.

Congress

The most obvious lawmaking body in the United States is Congress. Traditionally it enjoys a central symbolic role of representing the interests of the public. Although the Constitution does not give Congress powers with respect to public health and welfare, it has enjoyed liberal interpretation of its implied powers by the Supreme Court, especially in recent years. Tribe (1973: 609) sees Congress as the best means of reflecting public concern and asserts that congressional involvement in biomedical issues is indispensable. Green (1976) also places much faith in Congress as the primary means of ensuring public involvement in the policy process for genetic issues.

Despite the importance of Congress in making public policy, the congressional process as now constituted is not designed for the kind of issues raised by genetic technology. As a deliberative institution, Congress is extremely slow both in recognizing policy problems and in acting upon them. The multistage process is designed to provide multiple points of access, but it results in numerous occasions for legislation to be delayed or vetoed. To become policy, a bill must be successful at every stage in both houses.

Therefore, "the legislative process is weighted against quick and comprehensive responses," and encourages bargaining and compromise in order to build majorities at each stage (Shick, 1977: 10). The broad moral issues raised by genetic technology, however, are not conducive to compromise.[4] Furthermore, most decisions in the field are incremental; they build upon past decisions instead of representing major innovations (Van Der Slik, 1977: 269). As a result, it is improbable that Congress is capable of keeping up with the rapid advances in new areas of genetic technology.

The tendency of legislatures to "refrain from enacting regulatory laws until there is an obvious need for legislation" (Green, 1973: 388) reinforces this inherent bias against quick and comprehensive congressional response to new problems. Congress is slow enough to react even in crisis situations; it is not likely to consider seriously more remote problems. Green (1976: 172) suggests that Congress fails to direct attention to issues that are not pressing because it is too busy with urgent problems. This seems to result in a circular pattern of priority setting that is difficult to alter. It is improbable that Congress as presently structured can be depended upon to assess and evaluate policy issues that are less immediate.

Nowhere is the fragmentation of political power more clearly illustrated than in the U.S. Congress. Power is divided not only between the two houses, but also among numerous committees and subcommittees, where most of the actual lawmaking takes place. One product of the 1946 Legislative Reorganization Act was the proliferation of subcommittees, which now number over 250. When added to the 40 or so standing committees and other ad hoc committees, it is apparent how widely dispersed policymaking has become. The rationale behind the committee system is to divide the labor to maximize skill and minimize the overall workload. Tribe (1973: 609), however, concludes that "the existing system of specialized committees, riddled with rivalries and fragmented by jurisdictional division, cannot be relied upon to provide the focus without which public concern is just so much undirected energy."

In addition to this intercommittee strife over jurisdiction, the present committee system fails to reflect the crosscutting issues and has increased duplication as numerous committees stake claims to jurisdiction on important issues. This results in a "jumble of often unrelated jurisdictions," which further slows the process without assuring that relevant policy interdependencies will be considered (Shick, 1977: 14). Although the present clientele-directed and functionally oriented committees provide some advantages where legislation can be readily segmented, problems have become more interrelated and it has become increasingly difficult to isolate particular issues without spilling over into other policy areas. As a result new, more complex issues are less amenable to congressional action.

Shick (1977: 8) contends that the policy questions raised by these complex issues are more difficult to resolve because they combine what in the past were perceived as separate issues and they have increased the number of interests that must be taken into account. Obtaining the requisite majorities needed at each stage becomes more difficult, thereby further frustrating the process. As these inputs into the congressional process increase, each bill requires more hearings, staff consultations, committee meetings, and floor debate on amendments. With this increased clash and disarray of interests and competing committees, Congress has a difficult time accomplishing anything. Shick (1977) argues that Congress must reorganize in order to handle these complex policy questions. New committee-based specialties sensitive to major policy interdependencies must be established in which policy issues that complement each other are placed on the same committee. Given the stake that many members of Congress have in the current committee system, especially those with power, such a massive reorganization does not appear imminent. There is no strong coordinating mechanism or single position of power in either house capable of initiating the necessary changes, except perhaps in an incremental manner, which might prove too slow.

The specialization in Congress has also led to a situation in which few members are well informed about any specific issue. Voting is often the product of cue giving by colleagues considered substantive experts (Matthews and Stimson, 1975) or the result of logrolling or vote tradeoffs. Seldom is more than a handful of members familiar with any piece of legislation. Not surprisingly, Jasper (1974: 152) concludes that members of Congress are not any better informed about genetic technology than the public at large. "So in the Congress there is a very thin base of knowledge and very limited resources for solving these problems in an intelligent and thoughtful fashion." Schoenberg (1979: 93) adds that "legislators are frequently unsophisticated about science and do not understand the fundamental issues involved in the application of new discoveries." He notes that hearings are characterized by low attendance and that congresspeople are dependent on selective testimony, often from those with a high stake on either side of the issue.

Another outgrowth of the current system, accentuated by the growing technical complexity of the issues facing Congress, is a heavy dependence on professional staff members. Many of the more than 17,000 staff members are intricately involved in the policy process, especially on highly technical legislation. They conduct basic research, monitor hearings, and, increasingly, write the legislation. As Boggs (1976: 153) asserts, "It is only realistic to recognize that the principal assimilators of this kind of information are not the elected officials but their numerous 'staffers.'" This dependence on professional committee staffs might help open access somewhat, or at least shift lobbying efforts from the elected officials to key staff members. So far, it has further dispersed influence and created a dependency among elected officials on internal expertise. Although legislation is voted on by elected representatives, it often reflects clearly the work and perceptions of staff members. These individuals have a near monopoly on expertise within Congress but are insulated from the public, which this body supposedly represents.

Congress has not been oblivious to these problems, especially as they relate to data gathering and information processing. Since the mid-1960s several congressionally controlled offices have been created in an attempt to carve out an independent role in policy formulation (Boggs, 1976: 153). The establishment of the Congressional Budget Office (CBO) and the expansion of the function of the General Accounting Office (GAO) to conduct program audits have given Congress a more adequate oversight capacity in evaluating administrative compliance to congressional intent.

Most important to this study was the creation of the Office of Technology Assessment (OTA) in 1972 to increase the analytical capabilities of Congress as they relate to technological developments. Despite this intention, OTA was criticized by the Technology Assessment Advisory Council in 1976 for dissipating its energies on routine tasks for congressional committees while failing in its ostensible goal of providing "an early warning system for Congress, so that Congress can consider the social . . . impacts of technological advances . . . before these effects are upon us" (Boffey, 1976: 213). This assessment reinforces the feeling that the congressional process is dominated by short-run parochial concerns and that it is difficult to establish a prospective orientation in that body.

State Legislatures

Traditionally, state legislatures have been responsible for making laws relating to public health. It is not surprising, therefore, that genetic screening legislation and laws regulating most other aspects of human genetic intervention have been initiated in the states. When Congress has acted, for example in the National Sickle Cell Disease Control Act (1972), it has been in response to already existing state legislation and has served to standardize procedures and/or provide federal funding. Supreme Court decisions also have been in response to state laws and have generally either declared the particular legislation unconstitutional or resulted in liberalizing and standardizing the laws. Overall, the role of federal action has been limited and most public-health legislation continues to be the product of the 50 state legislatures. Certainly the current status of PKU and sickle-cell anemia laws reflects this emphasis. One result of this lack of unified action has been to further fragmentize genetic policy.

Although the state legislatures suffer from the same problems demonstrated by Congress, they also exhibit further limitations for dealing with the difficult issues raised by genetic technology. Most state legislatures continue to be part-time vocations with low compensation and relatively short tenure of members. According to Rosenthal (1974), it is not uncommon to find one-third to one-half of a state legislative body composed of freshman members, although Ray (1974) suggests that stability is increasing.[5] The high turnover rate implies that power in the states is more likely concentrated in the hands of a few legislators who return on a regular basis and in interest groups whose lobbyists usually enjoy a long tenure.

In addition to the amateur nature of many state legislatures, the sessions of most are limited in length, often by the state constitution. About 35 legislatures now meet annually and at least several states have removed restrictions on length (Berman, 1978: 108), but most continue to limit sessions to 60 or 90 days.[6] Usually most of this time is spent on budgetary and revenue matters, leaving little time to consider substantive legislation. Contributing to the inability of state legislatures to draft adequate and well-designed legislation on substantive matters, especially that of a highly technical nature, is the paucity of professional staff in the states. While members of Congress rely heavily on professional staff members to research and write legislation, corresponding legislators rarely enjoy such a luxury. There is a trend in the larger states toward increased staffing, but most states lack even minimal levels of professional staffs.

Some states have established joint standing committees and interim committees that meet when the whole body is out of session. Despite this, committees in state legislatures do not play as important a role as those in Congress. Most lack adequate staffing, time, and experience (Berman, 1978: 110) and are clearly dominated by the legislative leadership. This reinforces the ability of lobbyists to gain strong influence over specific legislation if they can assure the leadership of its importance. It also permits the governor's office more flexibility and influence in drafting legislation in many states.

These characteristics of state legislatures represent a general pattern, although there is much variation from state to state. This, in itself, leads to inconsistency in the quality and content of legislature and contributes further to the fragmented and at times confusing policymaking process in the United States. It also leads to the practice of virtually copying the legislation of other states rather than putting it through a deliberative process within each state. For example, the rapid acceptance of PKU legislation was accomplished largely through passage of statutes borrowed from other states. Although the state legislatures do allow for experimentation and theoretically produce more thoughtful lawmaking by distributing policymaking among 50 political units, their ability to handle the highly technical and controversial problems offered by human genetic applications is questionable given the limitations summarized here.

The Court System

The impact of the judicial system on perceptions of rights and on defining responsibilities for action was readily apparent in the discussion of rights in a democracy in Chapter 3. The concept of fundamental rights, especially as they relate to privacy and self-determination in reproductive matters, and the notion of "compelling state interest" clearly demonstrate the influence of the courts on the application of genetic technology. A problem in attempts to address constitutional and legal principles, however, is that they are vague and therefore open to a variety of interpretations. At the basic level, definitions of legality are bound to be ambiguous and subject to change, temporally and spatially. The conflicting interpretations of the Constitution by Justices Holmes and Douglas, noted in Chapter 3, concerning involuntary sterilization is an excellent example of this inconsistency over time.

Tribe (1973: 98) contends that at the expressive and symbolic levels the law has a potential role as a catalyst for needed changes in the system. The law dramatizes injustices and channels executive and legislative attention toward areas needing more systematic reform or comprehensive regulation. It does reflect public values, but it also induces cultural and moral change through alterations in legal doctrine. One need only observe the recent "wrongful life" torts and the pressures they exert on physicians to utilize prenatal diagnostic techniques to see the professional and ultimately social consequences extending beyond the original litigation.[7] Regardless of the symbolic impact of the law, U.S. legal institutions are not designed to serve, nor have they traditionally served, a social planning and assessment function (Schoenberg, 1979: 93).

The primary function of the court is to resolve conflicts centering on the rights and obligations of the parties before it in a particular case. As it is imperative that individual cases be decided on evidence produced by the parties to each case and not on the basis of public-policy considerations, decisions are episodic, unpredictable, and often inconsistent. Case-by-case adjudication by a wide variety of state and federal courts adds to the confusion. Most of the crucial issues discussed here ultimately will be tested in the Supreme Court, which usually can act only after a series of lower-court channels have been exhausted. Due to the slowness of this process, Green (1967) concludes that we cannot rely on the courts to protect society against fast-moving technological developments. "Judgemade rules of law always come after, and usually long after, the potential for injury has been demonstrated."

This delayed reaction time of the courts is accentuated as they are essentially a passive or "reactive" institution: The rule of law is not self-executing, but instead must be initiated from outside before the court can take action. As court decisions are retroactive,[8] the conflicts they resolve are based on facts from the past. As a result, many observers feel that the judicial system is too slow to provide a basis for effective controls. Portnoy (1970: 861), for instance, notes that the passive nature of the courts makes it clear that they "cannot serve as society's primary instrument for technology assessment." Similarly, Baram (1971: 535) explains that the retrospective nature of the legal system "limits its ability to respond to many social problems today." Nelkin (1977a: 71) adds that new technological developments, such as fetal research or genetic experimentation, "continually raise problems that require reanalysis of legal principles."

Although particular decisions might serve as precedents with important policy implications, "The courts generally refrain from deciding individual cases on the bases of deliberately establishing public-policy controls" (Green, 1976: 171). As a result, it is unlikely that the courts could act to place injunctions on cloning research, gene therapy, or any other aspect of genetic technology before they take place. It appears more probable that the courts will act only after a technical application takes place and then only relating to the proper use or negligence of the technique and not the technique itself. Baram (1971: 536) adds that the courts are reluctant to impose controls and rarely intrude on substantive aspects of decisions of public agencies.

Even more so than Congress, the courts must rely on outside expertise in technical matters. According to Green (1976: 171), the very nature of the judicial occupation insulates judges from an appreciation of public values. Although they supposedly are experts in applying wisdom and values of the past, judges lack technical knowledge and must depend on "expert" testimony. Certainly, the role of expert testimony merits clarification as the technical questions become more complex. The fact that both sides in most cases can find experts to support them implies a danger that judicial decisions might be influenced by the side that employs the most eloquent and convincing testimony. The contradictory decisions in criminal cases involving defendants with the XYY complement demonstrate the role of technical experts in court action.[9]

In spite of the importance of courts in defining rights and their symbolic influence on values and attitudes, there appears to be a consensus that the legal system is ill equipped to respond to the social problems raised by human genetic technology. Ellul (1964: 251) sums up the argument: "The judicial regime is simply not adapted to technical civilization, and this is one of the causes of its inefficiency. . . . It has not registered the essential transformation of the times. Its content is exactly what it was three centuries ago. Judicial technique has been little affected by the techniques that surround us today; had it been, it might have gained much in speed and flexibility." As a result of these deficiencies, the administration has continued to enlarge its sphere of influence at the expense of the courts. Regulatory law appears more suited from a technical point of view than the traditional law outlined by Ellul. The court system does influence technology and vice versa, but this is tangential to the function of the law. Due to the unique legal tradition and the current role assigned the courts in the United States, "it is doubtful that the courts will contribute very much to the resolution" of issues raised by human genetic technology (Green, 1976: 170).

Bureaucracy

There is no need to detail the problems inherent in a bureaucracy as anyone who has ever dealt with any agency of government can only be impressed by the vast and cumbersome rules and procedures that are often ambiguous, jargon cluttered, and internally inconsistent. Accounts of bureaucratic "red tape" may be exaggerated often, but the large and unwieldy federal bureaucracy does have several characteristics that limit its appropriateness for making policy decisions on genetic issues. First, its very size and complexity, combined with a fragmented distribution of jurisdictional boundaries, result in overlapping lines of authority. Given the historical development of the various agencies and the competitiveness of these agencies for power and influence, there is nothing approaching a single locus of power for biomedical policymaking. There is no single coordinating mechanism to ensure that policy is consistent or to eliminate duplication and confusion that results when more than one agency makes policy in the same general area. Another unfortunate by-product of these overlapping jurisdictions is that agencies do not always cooperate fully with each other (Funke, 1979). Each agency is jealous of the influence it has and suspicious of those who might wish to cooperate in a joint effort and thereby dilute this influence. Comprehensive and future-oriented policy is unlikely to result as long as this competition exists. Again, emphasis in the decision-making process is on short-term planning and response to immediate problems.

A second characteristic that limits the capability of the federal bureaucracy to produce adequate policy, on complex issues especially, is the information-processing system within each agency. According to Boggs (1976), public policy is strongly influenced by little-known career officials at the bottom levels of the bureaucracy. Staffers, who are there because of their generic skills rather than for their in-depth grasp of the issues, are responsible for analyzing and interpreting the data, which ultimately determines the policy. As the information moves from those doing the research to those making the decision, the hard data is passed through a series of successive filters that simplify, weaken, or distort the original information, thus resulting in a "loss of specificity" (Boggs, 1976: 151). At the same time, those ultimately responsible for making the decision are often unaware of what has happened at the preceding steps in the bureaucratic process.

An incredible example of the problem of the agency head not knowing what is happening within the agency itself is a case involving genetic screening in 1980. In the process of publishing a series of articles critical of genetic screening programs established by large industries before hiring or assignment of individuals to certain tasks, the *New York Times* (Severo, 1980) uncovered a government regulation that could be interpreted as mandating such screening programs. This regulation had been in effect for six years as part of the Occupational Safety and Health Administration (OSHA) regulations, yet no key government officials or their advisors were aware of its presence. Upon being informed of this regulation in this highly controversial area of genetic screening, especially regarding the widespread testing of blacks for sickle-cell trait, Eula Bingham, the director of OSHA since 1977, could respond only that she was "astonished" that it was there. "I will ask our lawyers to study it. We'll either have to interpret it so that we can issue field directives, or take it out of the regulations altogether. In any event, it should not be used as an exclusionary tool against any group of people by industry" (Severo, 1980: 1). According to Severo, this situation provides an illustration of the "tangled" state of genetic screening. It also demonstrates the confusion inherent within the bureaucracy, when those responsible for policy have no awareness of the policy within their own agency. In addition, this case illustrates the problem of overlapping lines of authority as the Equal Employment Opportunity Commission has indicated that such screening mandated or at least condoned by OSHA is in violation of the Civil Rights Act of 1964. Such situations do not offer encouragement to those who would depend on administrative regulation to control genetic technology.

A final problem inherent to bureaucracies, and which minimizes their objectivity and causes them to lose sight of broader public responsibilities, is their dependence on special interest group support. "The larger diffuse goals of public interest easily become contracted to mean the goals of self-interested clients who are organized, constantly on the job defining problems, providing information and seeking advantage" (Freeman, 1974: 160). According to Downs (1967), the growth and survival of a public agency depends upon its success in establishing routinized relationships with its major clients. Because agencies are highly competitive, the "source of funds and political power is rooted in their ability to build and serve a clientele . . . which provides political support" (Freeman 1974: 159).

Lowi (1969) argues that this system of interest-group dominance results in a situation in which decisions are made by independent bureaucratic agencies rather than elected representatives. The ostensible purpose of these agencies is to regulate, but due to their need for clientele support, they largely reflect the needs and perspectives of the interests they are designed to regulate. It is not surprising that the government frequently is powerless to deal adequately with significant problems, as the process is dominated by interest groups having a stake in the outcome.

It appears that if the government is to make objective and comprehensive genetic policy decisions, an agency must be created that is free from dominance by interest groups yet allows for widespread public access. The theories of several observers of bureaucratic development, however, demonstrate the futility of that possibility within the current institutional context. Although their theories differ in detail, both Bernstein (1955) and Downs (1967) see interest-group dominance as a product of the pattern of development of regulatory agencies as they pass through various life stages. Although these agencies are created out of conflict between political forces that support or oppose regulation, once in place the agency finds itself in competition with other agencies for influence and funding. In order to survive in this hostile and competitive political environment, the agency seeks support from the very interests it was established to regulate. Gradually, the regulated and the regulator arrive at rapprochement, where the agency lessens its vigor and the interest supports the self-perpetuation of the agency (Bernstein, 1955: 76). As the agency ages, the personnel become less aggressive, more entrenched, and more isolated from broader political pressures. The agency and the interests find it to their mutual advantage to support ambiguous and largely symbolic legislation that results in policies greatly benefiting established interest groups while symbolically protecting the public interest (Edelman, 1964). As a result, organized private groups exert primary influence in drafting legislation. If these same groups are able to influence the congressional committees or subcommittees that process the legislation, as Lowi (1969) contends, they are able to protect their interests, often at the expense of the broader public.

As with Congress and the courts, the bureaucracy, at least as it now operates, appears incapable of dealing with the complex and controversial problems raised by human genetic technologies. In the words of Breyer and Zeckhauser (1974: 141), "The view that an 'agency' of wise men or experts can determine the social interest and then enforce its decision is naive.

Agencies have proved inept at regulating in areas where values conflict, particularly if they lack precise Congressional instruction." Although all three institutions have made attempts at genetic policy, these issues require more comprehensive, timely, and objective consideration than is available through the current process. For instance, the National Institutes of Health (NIH), in spite of its office for assessing medical technology, continues to be criticized for its medical-elite–dominated decision-making process. Due to these inherent institutional problems, recent attempts to examine the ethical and social as well as the technical aspects of technology have been concentrated in national commissions or panels designed to produce policy recommendations in specific problem areas.

Ad Hoc Mechanisms

National commissions, advisory councils, and other temporary mechanisms traditionally have been created when specific problems have reached national attention or when public officials feel they are politically warranted. According to Best (1973: 238), these mechanisms often serve to buy time for the officials until the problem becomes less salient. By calling for and establishing a commission in response to a crisis, instead of demanding legislation directly, the decision maker might defuse an otherwise explosive situation. Recent commissions on violence and crime, while collecting much valuable information, have largely served as a safety valve to reduce public pressure for action. Commissions have the capability of functioning outside the glare of publicity when that is desirable and they present an image of impartiality.

Despite the impression of being above politics, most presidential commissions and councils display obvious political aspects. Selection of commission members, for example, often represents a form of elite patronage: political considerations in commission appointments are obvious rewards for past service. The selection of the executive director and staff of these ad hoc bodies is also politically motivated. This is crucial as the findings to some extent are a reflection of the methodology and means of information collection employed in the study, and this is largely determined by the staff. According to Stine (1977: 428), "The basic defect of such agencies presently in existence is just this: In practice their primary allegiance is to the parent agency." Furthermore, the reception and dissemination of the final report depends not on the quality of the report but on how it corresponds to the perceptions of the officials who commissioned it. In other words, the ultimate influence of the product of these mechanisms depends on how well it is received by those in authority.

As all findings of commissions are advisory only, they are in no way binding at any stage in the policy process. Unlike the permanent institutions, ad hoc bodies have no policymaking capability; they can only recommend. Also, as their tenure is specified by statute and usually limited to four years or less, they provide no continuous review and evaluation. These mechanisms might provide important contributions by raising issues, demonstrating complex interrelationships, and setting the boundaries for debate, but they seldom have the means to offer continued scrutiny of the issue. Continuous evaluation is essential in the rapidly advancing area of biomedical technology; even the definitions of problems will be temporary and subject to change with the next technological development. Although commissions often give the impression of producing final, comprehensive studies of a problem, "truly effective control of the awesome capabilities of . . . eugenics must come from permanent bodies," according to Bass (1974: 625). Despite these limitations, we will see later that much of the effort to deal with recent genetic innovations so far has been delegated to ad hoc commissions.

Public Involvement in the Policy Process

Central to the concept of democracy is the principle that the public interest somehow be reflected in public policy. Active public involvement in the policy process is essential to ensure that opinions of the entire citizenry are aggregated and articulated. To accomplish this, a variety of informal and formal mechanisms is designed to link the public with governmental policy.

As biomedical issues increasingly are considered within the realm of public concern,[10] it is not surprising that an often-expressed theme is the need for greater public participation in the decision-making process. Comroe (1978: 937) concludes that in the long run a well-educated and well-informed public will more often than not make the correct decision. Kaplan (1975) argues that in solving questions of human values raised by biomedical technologies we must rely upon the experience of the ordinary citizen, not the experts. Likewise, Veatch (1975) asserts that the "reasonable man" must be depended on to make the complex moral decisions common in genetic issues. Finally, Schoenberg (1979: 92) concludes that a public debate is needed to "quickly bring to the surface the moral issues and ethical issues that confront science."

One question emerging from these calls for increased public involvement in technological decision making is to what extent public opinion should determine such decisions. It is popular to express a desire for aggrandizing the role of the public, but there is a risk in putting too much faith in the public's desire or ability to accept this responsibility. Also, public opinion on issues tends to fluctuate as the social and economic context changes, which results in a problem of inconsistency. The social trends described in Chapter 1, for instance, might lead to acceptance by the general public of eugenic programs that reduce the economic costs to society by eliminating those considered "abnormal." Certainly, the record of the public on racial matters and other moral questions is less than reassuring to those who would trust implicitly the "will of the people." In spite of this assumption that following the desires of the public can be risky, it seems reasonable to suggest that public policy reflect, to the maximum extent possible, the interests of a broad public rather than some elite. This can be accomplished by opening up the decision-making process to public scrutiny and by assuring public awareness of the issues and of the policy options. Although the decision should not be bound by any one segment of society, whether a minority or the majority, the process must accommodate the views of all citizens.

From what is known about public involvement in other issue areas, effective public input is limited. Public knowledge is minimal and motivation to participate other than by voting is retarded (Verba and Nie, 1972). Only a small proportion of the public actually participates in the policymaking process. The public wields strong influence only on unique decisions of utmost importance and even then influence is concentrated in the attentive public — those most informed and interested in that particular issue (Devine, 1970). According to Best (1973: 217), few decisions can be categorized as unique. Instead, the bulk of policy decisions are routine, with clearly defined alternatives and unambiguous decisional criteria. He contends that the bureaucratic structure routinizes decisions and thus lowers the levels of political awareness and political conflict.

However, the most controversial issues tend to be those with the greatest uncertainty as to which decision to make. The less clear the alternatives available and the criteria for making the decision are, the larger the role public opinion can play in the policy process. Under such circumstances, the public functions to define the situational context, delineate the alternatives, and clarify the criteria for making the decision (Best, 1973: 222). The most potential influence of the public, then, occurs when the issues are unique and the criteria for making the decision are ambiguous. It seems that the issues surrounding human genetic technology readily fit this description and, therefore, might accentuate the influence of the public.

Despite the limited impact of the public on most policy decisions, there is a variety of mechanisms available in the United States for translating public opinion into policy. Although none is an ideal "linkage," together they would appear to be an adequate means of ensuring public input. That they are not is a function as much of lack of public demand as of inherent limitations in the mechanisms themselves. It is crucial to analyze each of these institutions within the context of genetic issues. Although public involvement on such issues might involve "many of the same processes and mechanisms that determine lay participation in other aspects of American society" (DHEW, 1978: 54), the issues raised here appear qualitatively different from most political concerns. Certainly, the sensitive and dynamic nature of these problems would place them among the most difficult and controversial issues and warrant substantial levels of public interest and participation toward their resolution.

Political Parties and Elections

The formal mechanisms for public input include elections, political parties and interest groups. The first two of these have been dismissed by some political observers as inadequate linkages between the public and the decision makers on matters of public policies (see Blank, 1980: 273–278). Elections in the United States tend not to be issue dominated, due to structural as well as situational factors. The power of incumbency in Congress, the lack of a single-issue dimension in most elections, and the fragile link between election results and policy minimize the role of issues in U.S. elections. This, combined with the low importance of most issues to most of the public, results in little genuine debate or even discussion of specific policy alternatives. The complex and emotion-laden nature of biomedical issues, especially those concerned with genetic questions, ensures their obscurity in the election process. Few candidates have found it in their political interest to take strong and consistent stands on these ethical issues. The lack of political commitment on the abortion issue and the continual attempts by most candidates to make it a nonissue imply similar treatment of other life-death related issues.

When discussing political parties as a linkage between the public and policy in the United States one must focus on the two major parties, as third parties are generally of little importance. Neither the Republican nor the Democratic party can be expected, without a complete restructuring and reorientation, to deal adequately with the issues raised by biomedical research. It has been argued that the parties were unable to deal with the social issues of the 1970s (Scammon and Wattenberg, 1970), and it is questionable at this point whether either party can deal with the traditional "bread-and-butter" issues around which New Deal politics was built. Certainly, there is no indication that either party is willing to take stands on the politically elusive issues raised by biomedical technology or that either party would be able to handle these issues even if it were so disposed.

Although both parties have in recent national platforms acknowledged the abortion issue, neither has dared tie its political fortune to it, knowing well that a majority supports abortion on demand, but an active and therefore very influential minority opposes it. Therefore, it is most feasible politically to shroud a very complicated issue in vague rhetoric and attempt to placate the antiabortion minority without arousing the ire of the less intense majority.[11] It is clear that the political parties are neither willing nor able to deal with the issues raised by biomedical technology. The lack of widespread knowledge and visibility of these issues in the general public, the orientation of our electoral process away from specific issues, and the hesitancy of the parties and most party candidates to become involved or identified with such issues assures the continued absence of biomedical technology from electoral politics.

Interest Groups

Many political scientists (Dahl, 1967; Truman, 1971) have placed much faith in interest groups as the primary means of aggregating and articulating public opinion in a "pluralist" democracy. They assume (1) that anyone who feels strongly enough about an issue can join or form an interest group to pursue his/her objective, (2) that all groups will have access to the decision makers, and (3) that the public interest will evolve from competition among interest groups. However, these assumptions have been challenged (Lowi, 1969; Edelman, 1964) and appear not to reflect reality. Despite the emphasis on interest groups in American society, effective participation in them is limited to that small proportion of the population with sufficient motivation, skill, and time. Even among those with strong feelings on an issue, few are able to influence a group directly. Furthermore, access to the decision makers is not as open as the proponents of interest-group politics assume. Groups that are able to expend resources consistently over a period of years gain inordinate influence over specific issue areas, while other groups are excluded from exerting influence. Finally, it is doubtful that the public interest is served through the competition of specialized groups, each of which attempts to maximize its own interest (Lowi, 1969).

In order to refine the description of interest groups, Best (1973: 176ff) makes a distinction between stable, multi-interest groups that seek to influence policy over a long period of time and single-issue groups created and dissolved with great rapidity in their quest to influence a specific decision. According to Best, ad hoc, single-issue groups are the most effective vehicles for expression of public opinion as they arise out of concern for one issue and focus on a narrowly defined political objective upon which the membership agrees. Recent efforts to block recombinant DNA research (Grobstein, 1979) and obtain legislation for Huntington's disease (DHEW, 1977) are examples of successful group activity of this type.

Despite their ability to mobilize and reflect public opinion, however, these groups generally have difficulty gaining access to decision makers, establishing legitimacy, and building resources. In order to gain access, the single-issue group must expand its appeal and increase its membership. Ironically, however, through this process the group loses its ability to serve as a vehicle for public opinion. As it becomes involved in a broader range of issues and expands its base, the division of labor within the group becomes institutionalized (Michels, 1949). Leaders become most interested in perpetuating themselves in power to achieve their own political goals. At the same time, they attempt to satisfy the membership by providing it with primarily nonpolitical benefits (Olson, 1965; Salisbury, 1970). The leaders also control the internal lines of communication. As a result of this process, lobbying activities of the large, influential organizations seldom represent an attempt to articulate the interests of the group membership, much less so the public interest. Instead they reflect the interests of the leadership, which might or might not be those of the members. Despite the appearance and the claims that interest groups protect "the public interest" or even "a public's interest," often the most politically successful groups fall far short of that ideal.

Still, there is no doubt that interest groups do play a central role in the decision-making process. We have seen earlier that the federal bureaucracy as well as Congress are most receptive to and dependent on interest-group activity and that little is accomplished without the approval of key groups in each substantive area working to protect their own interests. According to Nelkin (1977: 399), "Perceptions of urgency are influenced by special interests. . . . more often it is the needs of large, formal organizations that dominate policy decisions. Public needs often become equated with organizational imperatives that follow from existing investments." Grobstein (1979: 103) argues that public-interest groups in the recombinant DNA debate represent their own view of the public good, and he decries their dependence on "worst-case scenarios" to gain public attention. On the other hand, Fanning (1978) contends that genetic screening and counseling have been dominated by an elite composed of scientists, physicians, family-planning professionals, and medical directors of life insurance companies. He concludes that these interests have assumed the role of "biosocial engineers" with the hope of reshaping social policies.

The Mass Media

In order for the printed and electronic media to become effective linkages between the public and governmental policy, they would have to undergo a radical transformation. At present they are designed to transmit messages from the officials to the public. Best (1973: 205) asserts that the "beat system" of reporting makes it difficult for persons not regularly covered to gain the attention of the media and gives the advantage to persons already considered newsworthy. As a result of this and other characteristics, the public seldom has access to the mass media for communicating its view to the government.

Advocacy groups are aware of the "power of the press" and have utilized the mass media effectively to publicize their concerns and provide the public with information about technological developments. As the media find genetic issues extremely newsworthy, dramatic and widespread coverage is common. Front page headlines of the first "test tube" baby, the wide coverage given Rorvik's (1978) claim to the first human clone, and media attention to the debate over recombinant DNA research indicate the type and scope of coverage these issues attract.

In his critique of the recombinant DNA debate, Grobstein (1979: 104) contends that the press itself is an interest group of consequence that "finds grist for its own mill in emphasizing the more spectacular alternative scenarios and the clash of the more charismatic personalities." He asserts that in their own version of the public interest, the media exaggerate confrontation while ignoring the duller details of the resolution of such conflicts. Grobstein (1979: 104) concludes that due to the distorted impression it conveys to the public "the press cannot foster an optimum climate for formulating sound policy in a novel and technically complex area."

In spite of these limitations and inherent biases of the media toward sensationalism and simplification of the issues, they (especially the electronic media) remain for most citizens the single source of information concerning these issues. There recently have been some excellent programs on genetic technology on both public and commercial television networks, but the audience for these shows tends to be small and the broader social issues are generally obscured by the technical emphasis of the productions.

As cable television becomes more widespread, the potential for in-depth programming on the issues arising out of genetic technologies will increase. The audience is bound to remain small and to include the segment of the public most interested and concerned. Although widespread two-way communication via television appears to be far off, it does offer fascinating possibilities for educating the public as well as for eliciting public opinion. Until more in-depth and specialized programming is feasible, however, media presentation of these issues will continue to be periodic, dramatic, and generally simplistic. With a few exceptions, the public will not be exposed to comprehensive and systematic coverage of issues surrounding human genetic technology.

In the final analysis, despite problems of unequal representation, limited access, and oligarchical tendencies within the group, interest groups offer the most feasible means of assuring public input into the policy process. Elections, political parties, and the mass media fail to provide adequate mechanisms for public influence at the present time. There is a danger in equating the public interest with the interest of a single group, however. This danger is expanded when the media and/or the political leaders identify the public with the most vocal of the interest groups, thereby risking distortion of the broader will of the people. Interest groups often are the only visible manifestations of public input. Issues of a highly emotional nature, such as those raised by genetic technology, are particularly vulnerable to domination by well-organized groups as long as the majority of citizens remain uninformed and unaware of the issues and options.

Public Opinion and Genetic Issues

Given the limited degree to which public opinion directly influences public policy on most issues, one might conclude that what the public actually feels is unimportant. However, if we are to encourage wider public involvement and better ascertain public reaction to genetic technologies, it is crucial to make every effort to describe public opinion. This section summarizes limited data on public attitudes toward genetic technology and examines the group activity and alignments surrounding genetic issues.

In Chapter 1 the pattern of public opinion in the United States concerning abortion was presented. It indicated a massive shift toward acceptance of abortion for a variety of situations during the 1970s. The data demonstrated that public opinion, rather than being a static contextual factor, is dynamic and itself a reflection of broader changes in society. As a basic assumption of a democracy is that the desires of the public be, to some extent, translated into public policy it is crucial to discover the basic levels of public support of and interest in genetic technology. Similarly, it is important to determine levels of public knowledge of the technologies and their implications in order to estimate how best to approach these issues. It is also illuminating to see how the public perceives biomedical technology in general.

Although public opinion data can be extracted in a variety of ways, the most common and reliable means is through the random survey, in which a sample is selected through procedures providing a relative cross section of the public. In addition to the normal problems of surveys (Babbie, 1973), data relating to genetic technologies at present have other limitations. First, data on all issues but abortion are sparse and often based on the inclusion of one question on a national survey at infrequent intervals or on small, one-time samples that are substantially less reliable. Second, the kinds of complex issues raised by genetic technology are not adequately covered by the use of structured multiple-choice type questions. The survey instrument with its emphasis on simple responses, therefore, tends to distort the issues and obscure their multidimensional character. Despite these limitations, public opinion, as reflected in sample surveys, is a crucial factor to be considered in discussions of genetic and reproductive technologies.

Public Perception of Medical Science and Technology

Although public support for medicine and science has dropped over the last decade, it has declined less than support for other U.S. institutions and remains, therefore, relatively high. Fifty-four percent of the public have a great deal of confidence in medicine and 37 percent in science as a whole, compared to 29, 23, and 19 percent having confidence in the federal executive branch, Congress, and television, respectively (DHEW, 1978: 58). Despite the increasing public concern about the impact of technology and increased skepticism of all institutions during this decade, the institutions related to health care enjoy relatively high levels of public confidence.

This support is reflected in other data as well. In 1974, 75 percent of the public felt that science and technology had changed life for the better, while only 5 percent perceived an overall change for the worse. In assessing the benefits of science and technology, the public saw benefits in medical care as the most significant (DHEW, 1978: 57). The DHEW report also concludes that although the public is more worried today about the impact of technology and science than in the past, there still appears to be only marginal support for imposing stronger controls on them. In the 1974 study, 28 percent felt that the degree of control that society has over science and technology should be increased, and 46 percent felt that less control would be desirable (DHEW, 1978: 59).

Support for biomedical technology remains relatively high but is not uniform across all socioeconomic groups in the country. This uneven distribution of support accentuates divisions within society and escalates the conflict over these issues. Etzioni and Nunn (1974) report that the highest levels of disaffection with science are found among the politically weaker, less-informed, and less-educated segments of the population. Additionally, the 1974 National Science Board study found that those over 60 years of age also exhibit higher levels of opposition to science. These data reflect not only the lessened sense of efficacy of these groups and their higher degree of alienation from all societal institutions, but also an accurate perception that they will not be major beneficiaries of the research. Etzioni and Nunn (1974) also conclude that the public is in need of much more information concerning scientific and technological developments. Complicating this data on group differences is the LaPorte and Metlay (1975) finding that the greatest degree of support for political control of technology is concentrated among younger people and those who define themselves as politically "liberal." Perhaps some of this inconsistency will emerge more clearly in the analysis of public opinion on specific issues.

Prenatal Diagnosis and Screening. As noted in Chapter 1, approximately 90 percent of the U.S. population approves of abortion when there is a serious genetic defect in the fetus. This is almost identical to the approval rate in West Germany (Tünte, 1975: 192). Furthermore, 72 percent of a 1976 national sample (DHEW, 1978: 200) agreed that a woman should be able to have prenatal diagnosis "even if she can't pay for it herself and the government has to pay for it." An additional 12 percent contend that a woman should have prenatal diagnosis only if she can pay for it, while only 9 percent feel a woman should not be able to have prenatal diagnosis at all. Interestingly, McIntosh and Alston (1977) found that the large gap between Catholics and Protestants on acceptance of abortion when health of the child is involved has narrowed substantially over the last decade. In the 1975 survey, 86 percent of the Protestants and 77 percent of the Catholics supported abortion under such circumstances.[12]

When prenatal diagnosis is placed in the context of conflict between individual prerogative versus government control, 50 percent of the population agreed that a woman should not be forced to have an abortion in the case of a diagnosed affected fetus unless she desires it, even if society has to pay for the long-term care of the child. Seventeen percent said that a woman should abort the fetus "because it is wrong to bring children with serious defects into the world," while only 6 percent agreed that the fetus should be aborted because taxpayers would have to support the child (DHEW, 1978: 200). Twenty-one percent of this sample rejected abortion as an alternative in such cases because it is "wrong to destroy any life." Similar results were recorded in a survey of college students conducted in the late 1970s. Margolin (1979) found that a majority favored the use of techniques of genetic control to prevent the births of defective persons but also felt that specific decisions should be made by the parents, not government officials. Together, these data indicate that the public supports wide availability of prenatal diagnosis and abortions as options for all women, and the majority also feels that the final choice whether to use them or not is the woman's. One-fifth of the 1976 sample went so far as to contend that it would be better not to develop advances at all if they cannot be distributed equitably (DHEW, 1978: 173).

On related questions the data offer similar conclusions. For instance, 67 percent of the respondents in the DHEW (1978: 200) survey agree that individuals should be required to undergo carrier screening tests before being given a marriage license, while 27 percent disagree. As early as 1971, Gallup (1972) found that 69 percent of the public felt that young couples should obtain "professional information and guidance" before having children. Finally, a 1969 Harris survey (Margolin, 1979: 33) demonstrated the disagreement over the rationale for genetic intervention. Although a 58 percent majority favored the use of genetic engineering to correct defects in particular fetuses, only 21 percent agreed that it should be used for eugenic goals. This in part reflects attitudes common in the United States that medical advances are inevitably good but the present distribution is inequitable.

Artificial Insemination and In Vitro Fertilization. In a preliminary study of public attitudes toward in vitro fertilization (IVF) one month after the announcement of the birth of the first IVF baby in England, Gallup (1978) found that by a two-to-one margin the American public approved of IVF and that a majority would be willing to follow this procedure if they were childless and wished to have children. Nationwide, 53 percent would undergo this procedure, while 36 percent would not. The corresponding figures for college-educated respondents and those with a grade school education are 69 to 25 and 26 to 58 percent, respectively, indicating that education is strongly related to attitudes on this question. Similarly, those under 30 years of age are more prone to accept IVF (64 to 28), while those 50 and over are evenly divided (42 to 43). Despite some suggestions to the contrary, there are not significant differences by sex or religion. The corresponding data are: men, 54 to 33 percent; women, 52 to 38 percent; Protestants, 53 to 37 percent; and Catholics, 50 to 39 percent. The widespread coverage by the press of the birth of Louise Brown was illustrated by the amazing 93 percent of the respondents who said they had heard or read about it.[13] Furthermore, two out of five of those who heard about the procedure were able to explain "exactly what happened," and support of IVF was highest among those who were most knowledgeable.

Although a 1978 national survey of 1,501 women by Harris (Ethics Advisory Board, 1979: 88) found widespread approval for IVF, especially among women who actually planned to have children (66 percent), it also demonstrates the complexity of the issue. Most women saw IVF as a legitimate option, but when they were asked if they would prefer adoption or IVF, more than twice as many chose adoption (57 percent) as IVF (21 percent). Furthermore, 63 percent wanted IVF to be banned as standard medical practice until further research had determined whether this procedure increased the likelihood of birth defects. Only 24 percent wanted IVF available immediately, and 50 percent opposed federal funding of such research.

Another concern of the public appears to be the possible extension of the basic IVF procedure for other uses, such as surrogate motherhood. In a small random sample of women aged 18 to 23 near Stanford University,

Miller (1974) found that the circumstances under which reproductive technologies are used are crucial to levels of support. Most critical was whether the egg or sperm was contributed by the couple or by a donor. Approximately 90 percent indicated they would use AIH (artificial insemination with the husband's sperm) if it were the only way they could conceive, and 66 percent said they would use IVF with their husband's sperm and their own egg. However, when they were asked to consider AID (artificial insemination with a donor's sperm) or IVF with a donor egg, support dropped to 14 and 11 percent, respectively. Together these studies confirm high levels of support for reproductive technologies, but only when the genetic materials are contributed by the couple involved.

Sex Preselection. Another potential use of reproductive technology is the preselection for sex through various techniques, including amniocentesis followed by abortion of those not of the preferred sex. In discussing this possibility in Chapter 2, it was noted that problems will emerge if widespread acceptance of sex preselection is forthcoming. Miller (1974: 149) concludes that preliminary evidence suggests that further development of such techniques might "lead to their widespread use." He bases this on his finding that 36 percent of his sample would select the sex of their children if given the opportunity, while an additional 31 percent said they might. It might be expected, however, that specific reference to amniocentesis and abortion in the question would lower this support, which is so far expressed in vague and hypothetical terms.

Data from the 1976 DHEW survey (1978: 201) do seem to conflict with Miller's findings and at least imply that wording of the question is a crucial variable. This study posed a hypothetical situation in which a company has developed a safe medical product used before a woman becomes pregnant to preselect a boy or a girl baby. Only 19 percent of the respondents reported they would use this technique should it become available, while 67 percent stated they would not. Furthermore, only 12 percent perceived this development as having a good effect on society, while 52 percent saw it as having a bad effect, mostly through alteration of the sex ratio favoring males. Seventy-three percent felt that people would select a boy for the first child and only 3 percent envisioned people selecting a girl. Interestingly, social controls over the distribution of these devices were strongly supported. Only 14 percent said they should be readily available; 41 percent felt they should be available only by prescription from a physician;[14] and 38 percent would ban their use.

In sum, the sparseness of the data suggests more than anything the need for a systematic, comprehensive, and continuing survey of public opinion on genetic issues. Still, even the presence of such data is encouraging and reflects the growing interest in these issues. Although the findings generally imply a public awareness of the development of many techniques, the understanding of the technologies as well as the policy issues they raise is superficial and mirrors the current coverage by the press. Etzioni and Nunn (1974) point out the need of the public for more scientific information and note that this poses a significant challenge as those least informed also tend to exhibit the lowest levels of confidence. Medical technology would appear to have the edge in support because "the public has much interest in, and gives great support to, health related or medical science and technology: there may be concern about the costs of health care, but the public still strongly supports research aimed at solving problems that threaten life or health" (DHEW, 1978: 65). Even so, the public does not seem to have a clear sense of desired priorities for medical research (p. 173) and lacks an adequate understanding of the choices available.

Interest-Group Involvement

Due to the crucial role interest groups play in the policy process through their lobbying efforts and their function as the major linkage between the public and the policies, any attempt to describe the political context of genetic technology must include a discussion of interest-group activity. Most groups concerned with genetic issues are recent in origin, but the technical specialization emerging from genetic technology has quickly multiplied their number and scope.[15] As genetic intervention enhances or challenges the strongly held values of many individuals, interest-group activity surrounding these issues is bound to continue. In a period of economic constraint and increased competition for scarce resources, groups must press their demands even harder if they are to achieve their goals. The advocacy climate of the 1970s has encouraged the creation of groups while the mass media have provided a forum and given them prominence.

One area where substantial interest-group activity has been documented is in the creation of PKU screening programs. The National Academy of Sciences (NAS) Committee for the Study of Inborn Errors (NAS, 1975: 47) rejects Swazey's (1971: 883) contention that the DHEW Children's Bureau engineered the national lobbying effort that resulted in PKU legislation in most states; it asserts instead that the major forces behind such laws were the state chapters of the Association for Retarded Children. Reilly (1977: 45), however, cautions that the NAS report makes it clear that these associations lobbied heavily in many states, but "it does not offer convincing proof that the legislation owes its existence to these efforts." At the least, the advocacy for mandatory PKU screening by the National Association for Retarded Children provided credible support to the proponents of such legislation. Given the lack of early opposition, the minimal costs of such programs, and the political attractiveness of reducing genetic disease, it is not surprising that even this limited influence was enough to carry the legislation through.

It will be apparent later, when reviewing federal action for a series of genetic disorders, that legislation for each was influenced by lobbying efforts of a number of groups in favor of governmental action. Although some inclusive and established organizations such as the National Genetics Foundation and the National Foundation–March of Dimes have encouraged federal legislation for a variety of programs, most success appears to be centered in groups organized around a specific disorder. To a large extent the National Sickle Cell Anemia Control Act (1972), the National Cooley's Anemia Control Act (1972), and the Huntington's Chorea and Hemophilia Act (1975) reflect the lobbying efforts of individuals and groups concerned with each particular disease.

Furthermore, in order to protect and extend their influence over legislation, nonprofit organizations have been established for virtually every genetic disease. Cerami and Washington (1974: 103ff) list over twenty major groups organized around sickle-cell anemia. Under the impetus and guidance of Marjorie Guthrie, the Committee to Combat Huntington's Disease[16] successfully lobbied the government to assume a larger proportion of the cost for care of affected persons. Similarly, strong associations exist for hemophilia, cystic fibrosis, muscular dystrophy, tuberous sclerosis, familial dysautonomia, retinitis pigmentosa, and others (Chulew, 1980). These organizations most often have a medical advisory board composed of clinicians and researchers and a professional staff that conducts the organization business. In addition to raising public consciousness and community support for the specific disease and providing services to those affected by genetic disease, these groups lobby for increased funding for research, screening (if appropriate), and counseling, and attempt to influence public policy favorable to their objectives.

Often these voluntary groups have been joined in their support of legislation by individual researchers involved in the development of screening techniques and by clinicians responsible for primary care of patients with genetic disease. Obviously, industries that develop and market medical products used in genetic screening and people in the public-health community whose jobs depend on continued public support are most conscientious in their advocacy of programs that benefit them. Together, then, the interests favoring genetic screening represent a rather imposing coalition of people directly affected by particular diseases, clinicians and researchers, and interests with a monetary stake in the legislation.

Most opposition to screening programs or government funding for specific genetic disorders has been directed either at poorly designed and implemented programs (Murray, 1978) or toward technical problems in the tests (Bessman and Swazey, 1971). Broader genetic intervention, however, has drawn attacks from a variety of directions. In fact, one of the most fascinating developments in the debate over genetic and reproductive issues is the new alliance evolving in opposition to these technologies, an alliance traversing traditional liberal-conservative political lines. This results in cleavages among traditional allies and, more importantly, thrusts unlikely groups together in opposition to genetic and reproductive technologies. On the right are groups who tend to oppose genetic intervention on moral grounds. They are most clearly represented by the right-to-life movement, which in itself is a unique coalition of Catholic Democrats and fundamentalist Protestant Republicans. Similarly, conservatives who label themselves "libertarians" oppose government intervention of almost any type, including that in reproductive matters.

Until now, perhaps because of the attention paid to the abortion issue, these "conservative" groups have been the most salient opponents to genetic technology. Recently, however, they have been joined by traditionally liberal or even radical elements that fear repression, stigmatization, or invasion of privacy. Minority-group leaders, especially black and Hispanic, as well as some Orthodox Jewish spokespersons, have criticized publicly various genetic and reproductive technologies as counter to the interests of their communities. Also, the presence of a "concerned scientists" lobby, reflected by such organizations as Science for the People, has added the dimension of largely liberal scientists concerned with the effects of technology on society.

More recently, feminists representing the National Organization for Women, the National Women's Health Network, and the Federation of Organizations of Professional Women called for a moratorium on the use of in vitro fertilization, sex preselection techniques including those utilizing amniocentesis, and birth-control methods designed only for women (Kotulak, 1980). They note that women bear increased health risks for these technologies, which also threaten women's role in society. Hubbard (1980: 12) adds that in vitro fertilization, for instance, is expensive and will "distort our health priorities and funnel scarce resources into a questionable effort." According to Hubbard, "we must find better and less risky solutions for women who want to parent but cannot bear children of their own."

One obvious dilemma emerging from this opposition from women's groups is that much of the demand for genetic screening and reproductive technologies comes from women who desire to bear their own healthy children. Furthermore, the arguments that women ought to be able to make their own reproductive choices and control their own bodies has been central to the women's movement's support for abortion on demand. To set limits on the alternatives available to women in procreative matters, especially sex preselection and in vitro fertilization, would appear to produce a paradox for those who otherwise support the choice of women. Opposing research and application of technologies that expand these choices does result in inconsistencies that must be resolved.

Interest-group activity in genetic issues will continue to cut across traditional social and political lines in American society. Due to the complexity of the problems raised by these technologies and the value conflicts they produce, future alignments of groups will differ substantially from those on other political issues. This makes it highly unlikely that either major political party will be able to adopt a strong policy stand on genetic technologies without risking the loss of substantial elements in their bases of support. At the same time, the high stakes involved in policy decisions concerning genetic intervention will accentuate group activity and magnify conflict among the interests.

Current Governmental Activity in Biomedical Issues

The 1970s witnessed a resurgence of governmental interest in the impact of science and technology on society and a limited beginning of activity directed specifically at biomedical research. This concern emerged in part at least as a reaction to a growing recognition that advances in biomedical technology threatened to alter social values drastically and had broad policy implications to which little attention had been paid. In 1971, Senator Mondale recommended establishment of a Commission on Health Science and Society, which would incorporate studies of these advances and their implications into the policy process so that the public would have a say in its own future. "The public's stake is too great. And the need for consensus as to how society should deal with these profound problems is too clear. . . . I think we need something far more official and far more public if we are to reach agreement on the ways in which society is to organize itself to handle these unprecedented problems" (DHEW, 1978: 9). Although Mondale's congressional advisory commission was not directly instituted, this proposal seems to have provided impetus for related developments in a variety of governmental units.

As noted earlier, the Office of Technology Assessment (OTA) was established in 1972 by Congress and has conducted a series of inquiries into the impact of innovations in biomedical technology and services, including in vitro fertilization and genetic screening (OTA, 1978). In 1976, a National Science Policy Act that defined for the first time congressional and executive responsibilities in this area was passed (Schmandt, 1977: 11). In addition, the Senate Committee on Human Resources (Subcommittee on Health and Scientific Research) and the House Committee on Science and

Technology (Subcommittee on Science, Research, and Technology) have conducted hearings and prepared reports on biomedical research. Unfortunately, these hearings have suffered from the traditional shortcomings of the congressional hearing format[17] and have failed to provide comprehensive and adequate analysis of genetic issues. Their very presence, however, indicates the growing importance of such issues.

Within the Department of Health, Education, and Welfare, an Office of Health Technology has recently been established to coordinate analysis and testing by agencies to determine safety, efficacy, and cost effectiveness of new and existing biomedical technologies, and to assist in determining which mechanisms should be used to promote, inhibit, or control the use of these technologies. In response to the growing ethical implications of these technologies, the Ethics Advisory Board was created in 1978 by then Secretary of DHEW Califano, to make recommendations concerning the ethical appropriateness of research in these areas. During 1978 the board[18] held eleven public hearings throughout the United States and took testimony from scholars in many fields in considering whether to lift the moratorium on federal funding of research involving in vitro fertilization of humans. The original purpose for this action was a grant application submitted to the National Institutes of Health (NIH) by Pierre Soupart to study human embryos created through in vitro fertilization and to observe them for up to six days in culture before destroying them. The announcement of the first "test-tube" baby in July 1978 broadened the scope and implications of the study considerably.[19]

Also within DHEW, NIH has created an Office for the Medical Applications of Technology and has attempted to broaden the roles of its various national advisory councils to enlarge the contribution of public representatives to the development of research policies and priorities. NIH has continued to come under criticism, however, for its medical-elite–dominated decision-making process.[20] Those concerned with the impact of biomedical technology also welcomed the reintroduction of science policy advisors into the executive office of the president with the creation of the Office of Science and Technology Policy (OSTP) in 1976. It is doubtful, however, that the broad scope of the OSTP will offer much consideration of biomedical technologies. To date, most attention has been directed toward energy-related technologies.

Advisory Boards

Although the creation of permanent bodies for technology review and assessment both in Congress and the executive agencies demonstrate a growing realization of the importance of technological problems, the primary mechanism for public involvement in biomedical and genetic issues continues to be the establishment of temporary, advisory commissions. From the general concern of the President's Biomedical Research Panel (1976) to the specialized focus of the Commission for the Control of Huntington's Disease and its Consequences (1977), national commissions provide a forum for discussion of these issues.

Most active of these recent bodies was the National Commission for the Protection of Human Subjects of Biomedical and Behavioral Research, established by the National Research Act of 1974. Before ending its statutory existence in October 1978, the commission held numerous hearings, solicited input from a range of scholars, and issued a series of final reports. Among these was the report, "Research on the Fetus," which detailed the technical status of fetal research and offered a variety of views concerning the ethical and social implications of such research.

More central to the concerns of this study is the commission's special study (DHEW, 1978) on the "Implications of Advances in Biomedical and Behavioral Research," which presented the results of three distinct projects involving: (1) a national panel of 121 consultants, (2) a random national sample of 1,679 adults, and (3) a four-day colloquium of 25 scientists and scholars. The commission (DHEW, 1978: 6) asserted the need to "create new institutions to monitor the development and introduction of new technologies in the biomedical and behavioral fields, and to draw the attention of legislatures and the public to social problems arising from the use of these new technologies." The report reiterated the need for an independent national agency that would: (1) formulate national policy and facilitate coordination of agencies that implement policy, (2) monitor and evaluate agencies charged with implementing policy, (3) review and evaluate the implications of research and technology, and (4) inform the public and scientific community and facilitate public participation in policymaking (DHEW, 1978: 35).

In 1978, Congress passed a bill etablishing the President's Commission for the Study of Ethical Problems in Medicine and Biomedical and Behavioral Research, which presumably might serve a function similar to the agency recommended in the special study. Unlike past advisory bodies, it was given jurisdiction over all federal agencies. Although its specific recommendations to an agency are not binding, they are published in the Federal Register and must be responded to by the agency within six months. Congress authorized a budget of $5 million per year for four years, at which time the panel will have completed its work. Among its numerous duties, the commission is to conduct a study on the legal and ethical implications of "voluntary testing, counseling and information and education programs with respect to genetic diseases and conditions taking into account the essential equality of all human beings, born and unborn"

(Public Law 95-622). It will be interesting to see how active a role this commission takes in leading the debate over genetic issues. Given the normal operation of the political institutions, it is unlikely that the Commission will be able to exert substantial influence over permanent agency decisions or the policy process.

Legislation

Although Congress has not expressed a desire to make genetic intervention policy, several pieces of legislation in the 1970s demonstrate pressures for national action. Although Congress has long appropriated monies for research into specific genetic diseases and has contributed to care of those affected through general health and social security acts, a new awareness of genetic problems and developments in genetic technology has emerged only in the last decade.

Prior to 1970, NIH had never allocated more than $250,000 at any one time for research of sickle-cell anemia (Cerami and Washington, 1974: 84). By 1972, however, Congress had passed the Sickle Cell Disease Control Act, which authorized federal expenditures of $115 million over a three-year period: $85 million for establishment and operation of voluntary sickle-cell anemia screening and counseling programs and $30 million for research on sickle-cell anemia and development of educational programs. Furthermore, between 1971 and 1972, 12 states and the District of Columbia rushed to enact laws designed to identify persons with the sickle-cell trait (Reilly, 1977: 65). Why this swift and dramatic increase in government involvement? Cerami and Washington (1974: 90) argue that this sudden interest was politically motivated. By 1970, the blacks had emerged as a crucial political entity. Once it was made clear that sickle-cell disease was largely concentrated in the black community, blacks as well as socially or politically conscious whites came out strongly for legislation designed to ameliorate this condition. Despite an obvious political motivation behind Nixon's request in his 1971 health message for $5 million for research of this "long-neglected" disease, politicians jumped at the chance to gain political advantage and expressed escalatory demands for federal expenditures for sickle-cell anemia. Demands were especially strong among liberal and black legislators, many of whom later were to speak out against the means through which the programs were implemented. DHEW officials actively opposed a large-scale screening program until basic research provided adequate methods for implementing it (Reilly, 1977: 79), but there was little vocal opposition from any other quarter (Culliton, 1972a and 1972b).

Due to the relatively small cost and seemingly rare opportunity to benefit an identifiable constituency, sickle-cell legislation was approved rapidly. It also created the incentive for other groups to press for similar legislation for diseases that most affected their communities. First to respond were members of Congress of Mediterranean heritage who sponsored legislation to screen for Cooley's anemia (beta thalassemia), which is disproportionally high among that population. They, too, were successful in gaining support. The National Cooley's Anemia Control Act of 1972 authorized spending of approximately $11 million for research, education, screening, and counseling. Again, some concern was expressed that a disease-specific approach for genetic programs was irrational from a planning perspective despite its political attractiveness (see Culliton, 1972: 590).

Following the passage of these statutes, a move began to secure passage of a National Tay-Sachs Control Act. Ultimately, however, Congress approved an omnibus bill that included a variety of genetic diseases in addition to sickle-cell and Cooley's anemia. According to Reilly (1977: 103), "Most of the better-organized associations concerned with specific genetic disorders managed to be included." The National Genetic Disease Act of 1976 authorized $90 million to "establish a national program to provide for basic and applied research, research training, testing, counseling, and information and education programs with respect to genetic disease." Despite its guidelines calling for voluntary programs, confidentiality of data, community representation, and a guarantee of genetic counseling for affected persons, limited appropriations and failure to fully develop the guidelines have minimized the policy impact of this statute.[21]

Maryland Commission on Hereditary Disorders

Although most of the states developed screening programs during the 1960s, Maryland was the first state to create a policy mechanism to provide coordination and centralize responsibility for state genetic programs. According to the enabling legislation,[22] the eleven-member Commission on Hereditary Disorders has the power to:

1) establish and promulgate rules, regulations, and standards for the detection and management of hereditary disorders in the state of Maryland;
2) gather and disseminate information to further the public's understanding of hereditary disorders;
3) establish systems for recording information obtained in programs regulated by the commission;
4) reevaluate on a continuous basis the need for and efficacy of state programs on hereditary disorders; and
5) investigate unjustified discrimination resulting from identifica-

tion as a carrier of a hereditary disorder, and make recommendations as it deems necessary to end such unjustified discrimination.

Unlike the fragmented and disease-specific screening programs found in most states, the presence of this commission with its attendant powers and funding provides a rational and accountable alternative to genetic programming.

In spite of the approval of the Maryland law as a model statute by the Committee on Suggested Legislation of the Council of State Governments, few states have adopted similar legislation.[23] There is no doubt that the Maryland approach is more expensive and that it places substantial authority in the hands of an independent commission — power that is otherwise retained by existing executive agencies or the legislature itself. Also, it might be that the most powerful lobby groups already have what they desire under existing legislation or at least that they prefer the status quo to the uncertainty of change. Whether the reason for this is monetary or political, however, most states continue to depend on piecemeal screening legislation.

Alternative Mechanisms for Policy Input

One of the themes of Chapter 1 that reemerges in discussions of governmental activity in biomedical issues is the interdependency between technology and society. In a democratic society a recurring question is: What constitutes a democratic decision-making process? The discussion of the political context thus far suggests that the present process is lacking in the extent to which a broad public interest is articulated through "public" policy. The critical implications of biomedical issues for society and its members now and in the future call for more urgency in delineating and establishing mechanisms for making effective, democratic decisions. The problem centers on the degree to which decisions must reflect both the desires of the mass public and the choices of scientific experts in each particular field.

Public Input

Despite recent attempts by policymakers to expand public involvement in developing priorities and making technological decisions through public hearings and membership on various commissions and review boards, Funke (1979: 19) concludes that "we have not yet found wholly appropriate mechanisms for allowing, much less facilitating, public input in the policy process." Given the framework of interest-group politics in the United

States, it is not surprising that proposals designed to increase the role of the public in technical policy decisions have become controversial, as particular groups will either gain or lose influence through this process. Several examples are presented here to illustrate the problems and principles involved in increasing citizen involvement.

There are two aspects to public involvement: one involving the need for more effective means of educating the public to make informed decisions and the other focusing on the need for increased public input into the policymaking process. It would seem obvious that public education must precede involvement in the policy process, but this has not always been the case in the rush to include lay participation. Baram (1971: 536) suggests that a major contribution of citizen groups has been to provide the public with more information about technological developments. Despite this, the public remains largely unaware of the alternatives available.

It is crucial to distinguish between making technical decisions requiring substantial expertise and establishing broad priorities based on social values. In light of the interface between social values and technology, it seems that most emphasis should be placed on the latter. Lay participation on technical review committees might under some circumstances provide useful input, but concern has shifted toward creation of mechanisms for effective representation on the broader concerns regarding the direction and application of scientific research. This demand for direct citizen participation in science decisions is apparent both inside and outside the government. Often these demands are articulated by single-issue groups or more general citizen advocacy groups such as Common Cause and the Nader citizen involvement program, which purport to address a broader public concern. Within the government, many attempts have been made to increase citizen action in policy decisions—usually with minimal success because of inherent "procedural biases that mitigate against effective implementation" (Nelkin, 1977a: 76).

One example of a recent attempt to encourage effective public involvement is the Science for Citizens Program proposed for the National Science Foundation budget in 1976 (Culliton, 1976). This program was supposed to improve public understanding of the issues, encourage scientists to participate in activities aimed at resolving policy issues, and enable nonprofit citizen groups to acquire technical expertise to assist them in dealing with the technical aspects of the issues. In addition to continuing traditional methods of educating or involving the public, such as conferences and hearings, this proposal would create regional science centers across the nation to achieve the above program objectives. Predictably, the proposal generated strong opposition from those who saw Science for Citizens as primarily a means of subsidizing groups that intervene to block programs already authorized by government officials. Some feared that citizen groups might subvert the program by using funds to pay scientists who assist them in other activities (Boffey, 1976a: 349). Although over $1 million was authorized by Congress for this program in 1977, the focus of the program has narrowed in its shift toward funding research proposals involving science education of citizens and away from the more innovative and therefore controversial provisions.[24]

Critics of attempts to increase public participation see it primarily as a means of delaying or blocking the use of technology rather than as an objective evaluative mechanism, and they fear domination by groups opposed to specific technologies. Stine (1977: 431) notes that it is difficult to think of a single instance in which the participatory process has advanced a technological project. Although Baram (1971: 536) agrees that citizen groups have proved to be "somewhat effective technology-curbers," he contends that they have not provided coherent, a priori control and that ultimately they must depend upon legal action. Tribe (1973a: 26) acknowledges that although antitechnology forces are "often much too weak, they are sometimes far too strong."

It seems that public involvement in genetic issues can be increased meaningfully through the dissemination of information concerning the state of genetic technology, the policy alternatives available, and the implications of each technological innovation. Expanded use of open meetings and conferences, organized debates among conflicting viewpoints through the electronic media, and broad public education programs would seem to be reasonable mechanisms at this stage. It is doubtful that meaningful citizen involvement, if defined more broadly than representation of citizen advocacy groups, is possible until public consciousness concerning genetic issues is raised. According to DHEW's special study (1978: 38), a prerequisite of informed public input is the availability of valid information.

Expert Input

Methods of securing input from researchers and clinicians, although numerous, are seldom satisfactory and often are criticized as biased or inadequate (Casper, 1976: 32). At present, much of the input from scientists occurs in committee hearings where "experts" are paraded past in rapid procession to give their testimony, generally to a handful of members present. In addition to hearings, other mechanisms for scientific input include ad hoc commissions, task forces, consulting services, conferences, and informal solicitation of advice by government officials. As we shall see, much governmental activity in genetic technology has occurred in such mechanisms. Both Congress and the bureaucracy depend on internal technical advice. Congress has established the Office of Technology Assessment (OTA) to serve this function, and various mechanisms, including a science advisor, a science advisory council, and an office of science and technology, have been used in the executive branch. As usual, their impact has been inconsistent and sporadic and their ability to present a well-balanced perspective on scientific fact has been questioned.

Lately, there has been a growing concern that the complex technological developments require a renewed effort to establish new mechanisms to ensure continuous yet balanced scientific input. These bodies would be responsible for analyzing technical aspects of major policy problems, developing alternative responses to these problems, making recommendations for policymakers, and providing continuing review and analysis of programs. In spite of the debate over how much input experts ought to have in policymaking, there seems to be a consensus that the current mechanisms for such input must be improved substantially.

Science Courts. One outgrowth of the controversies surrounding the ozone layer depletion, nuclear power, and recombinant DNA research, among others, is the presence of glaring differences of opinion within the scientific community itself. In each area there are cases in which lack of agreement on scientific facts that are relevant to public and official understanding of the issue fuels the debate over use of the technology. As the present institutions are dependent on expert testimony of some form, the disagreement among experts results in confusion. Those who testify often represent groups that have a stake in the policy decision, so it is not surprising that they will give scientific fact an interpretation favorable to their position. For instance, when one expert testifies that PKU screening is safe and accurate and another emphasizes the risk of false negatives and positives, the broader social-moral issues regarding PKU screening become clouded. The escalating claims of expert opponents often appear to generate "enormous confusion in the minds of the public." In response to this situation the Task Force of the Presidential Advisory Group on Anticipated Advances in Science and Technology proposed a "series of experiments" to resolve factual disputes and provide a sounder basis for public decisions (Task Force, 1976: 653).

The most prominent of these proposals is the "science court," which concentrates solely on clarifying questions of fact while leaving social value questions to the normal decision-making process. The purpose of the science court (Task Force, 1976: 653) is to "create a situation in which adversaries direct their best arguments at each other and at a panel of sophisticated scientific judges rather than at the general public." The basic mechanism is an adversary hearing open to the public and chaired by a "distinguished referee." The "distinterested judges" before whom the arguments are made are experts in scientific areas adjacent to the dispute.

After the adversary proceedings, the judges prepare a report "noting points on which the advocates agree and reaching judgements on disputed statements of fact." According to the Task Force, the result is to describe the current state of the technology and "obtain statements founded on that knowledge, which will provide defensible, credible, technical bases for urgent policy decisions."[25]

The science-court concept has gained much attention, including criticism (Nelkin, 1977b). One concern is that facts and values are inseparable when considering public-policy issues, and the more controversial the issue is, the greater the uncertainty over the facts is. Stine (1977: 428) raises questions concerning the selection of judges, case managers, and referees. He argues that it will be difficult to get competent, objective scientists who are willing to devote the time and risk their careers. In addition to these procedural questions, Casper (1976: 29) asserts that interested parties may try to use the science-court proceedings to promote their own ends. In a process that already overemphasizes the technical aspects of the problems, there is fear that this mechanism will further obscure the political and social dimensions. There is also the possibility that the science court will bring out the extremes when the facts might be somewhere in between. Casper (1976: 31) also questions the need for "scientific judges," noting that this assumes that politicians and other citizens are unable to weigh the claims of experts and judge for themselves. He argues that one does not need detailed technical knowledge to make decisions on policy implications and priorities.

Adversary Hearings. As an alternative to the science court, some have proposed restructuring congressional hearings into a formal adversary hearing in which a genuine debate format is used. Casper (1976: 34) argues that such a format, if made public, would improve the quality of information available to both the decision makers and the public so that they could arrive at independent judgments. He also favors public forums in which expert insights into social and political as well as technical implications would be offered. The biases of the experts would be stated and the broader issues argued through the medium of television. Casper (1976: 32) sees a need for "a tradition of public dialogue" concerning the implications of new technologies.

Other Input Mechanisms for Experts. Bevan (1977: 541) proposes an "institute for Congress" that would "put interdisciplinary teams of research scholars to work on broadly defined legislative problems." The institute would work under the guidance of a board made up of "distinguished scientists, lawyers, former members of Congress, and others who have served in the public sector." Pancheri (1978), taking a different approach, asserts that policy decisions in genetic technology should be made by "value specialists" who are trained in "one or several aspects of value theory and its application," not by the scientific community or the public. She would restrict the exercise of democratic methods to the election of adversary groups of value theorists who "would assist the decision-makers in learning public values." The final authority to make decisions would reside in "those who by their training are most skilled at discerning the values and value conflicts implicit in some situation and at tracing out the implications of some proposal" (Pancheri, 1978: 70).

Spilhaus (1972: 715) asserts that we should set up a permanent United States Planning Board now to formulate long-range goals for our society. "Otherwise the future serious realities will be lost in the noise of immediacies and solutions by crises." He contends this will require continuity comparable to the Supreme Court as well as the capability of addressing hard truths. Similarly, Rosenfeld (1977) calls for establishment of a permanent Early Alert Task Force, whose mission would be to warn all interested groups of the benefits and hazards implied in biomedical research.

The Need for Alternative Mechanisms

The complex issues raised by human genetic technology require mechanisms designed to provide more adequate public as well as expert input. Reconstituted forms of national commissions, with expanded public hearings supplemented with more extensive survey data and widespread dissemination of the conclusions, would seem to be a beginning in achieving both goals. Although there are inherent limitations both in the commission approach and in public hearings, they appear to provide an adequate foundation upon which to improve. The most recent President's Commission for the Study of Ethical Problems shows promise for incorporating some of these ideas. Ultimately, however, if such a mechanism is to have an impact on policy, it must be established as a permanent, autonomous commission with the authority to make policy decisions. The Commission on Hereditary Disorders of Maryland might serve as an excellent starting point. Membership on such a body should be on a rotating basis and the selection process should be less political than is now common on presidential commissions. Etzioni's (1973: 55) suggested two-tiered approach would establish a permanent national commission "charged with formulating alternative guidelines for public policy," supplemented by a "myriad of local review boards" that would review individual decisions and attack specific problems.

Finally, there is a great need for the creation of similar organizations at the world level. Etzioni (1973), Galey (1977), and Sinsheimer (1973) have argued that international bodies must be established, especially in the field of genetic technology. Etzioni (1973: 184) proposes an international commission composed of scientists and humanists to "mobilize greater social responsibility and responsiveness" to biomedical questions.

Many institutions contribute to the policy process, but none appears capable, at least as presently structured, of dealing with the complex and sensitive issues raised by the technologies discussed here. The fragmented decision-making process is hampered by its slowness to react, its passive nature, its tendency to concentrate on immediate problems and offer only short-term solutions, and the dominance of special interest groups in the American political process. The major political institutions of Congress, the courts, and the federal bureaucracy manifest these limitations. Mechanisms designed to link the public with these government officials largely fail to aggregate and articulate the broader "public interest." Despite some positive trends toward action displayed in recent genetic legislation, national commission reports, and attempts to design more effective mechanisms for public as well as expert input, the conclusions here reaffirm the findings of the Panel on Technology Assessment of the National Academy of Sciences over a decade ago: "Our study has revealed that existing mechanisms, whether they involve government agencies, private industries, or professional groups possess intrinsic limitations, some structural and others psychological, that leave serious gaps in the spectrum of processes that assess and direct the development of technology in our society" (Tribe 1973: 617).

Although broad public involvement in the policy process appears warranted, given the critical social and political implications of human genetic technology reviewed in Chapter 3, the process itself should not create needless obstacles to genetic research and application that might be beneficial for society. The goal of ensuring that all legitimate public interests are fully and fairly represented in setting priorities is not to hamper process, but to assure that it is directed and conducted in "fruitful, responsible, and discriminating ways" (DHEW, 1978: 90). Also, although it is of some urgency that effective mechanisms for accomplishing these goals be established, some effort must first be directed at adaptation of current mechanisms to meet particular goals, such as: (1) increasing public participation and accountability, (2) setting social priorities, (3) assessing and monitoring technologies, and (4) defining and evaluating risks and benefits associated with each technology.

Assessing Human Genetic Programs

Up to this point this book has argued that difficult political decisions must be made soon concerning human genetic research and application. In Chapter 3 attention was directed toward the political implications emanating from tension between individual rights and societal good. Chapter 4 concluded that political institutions as now constituted appear unable to deal with the complex emotional issues raised by genetic technology. Until now, problems and issues raised by genetic technology have been examined in isolation from other health and nonhealth concerns, which has been necessary in order to delineate the political implications but is not realistic.

Obviously, decisions as to whether or not to allocate public funds for genetic research and technology must be made within a broader political context. The expanded role of government in these areas results in part from the rapid increase in governmental funding of such endeavors. As medical costs have risen dramatically because of inflation, expensive midlevel technologies, and duplication and waste due to poor planning and improper administration, the government has assumed a larger proportion of these costs. Federal funding of research, Medicare and Medicaid coverage, and genetic screening and diagnostic programs is crucial. Federal expenditures for biomedical research have increased from $110 million in 1950 to $2.75 billion in 1975, an average rate of increase of about 100 percent per year.

Unfortunately, this increased dependence on public funding comes at a time when public resources are increasingly constrained. Not surprisingly, policymakers are looking for places to make cuts, not for new ways to spend money. With the realization that all resources are limited and that it costs money to develop as well as use any technology, it follows that monies for new programs must be taken from some other, perhaps well-established, program. The result is an increased emphasis on assessment of technology, cost-effectiveness of programs, and the creation of cost-benefit formulas for distributing limited public resources. Accompanying these trends is the demand by officials for more government control over how public funds are spent, resulting in further centralization of these programs. Any moves toward national health insurance or a similar program will accentuate rather than diminish the use of cost-benefit analysis and other assessment procedures on specific genetic proposals (Pliskin and Taylor, 1977: 6).

Given these patterns, emphasis in policymaking has shifted to establishing criteria for judging the effectiveness of specific programs. This means that interest-group activity has taken on another dimension, that of attempting to define the criteria and maximize the perceived advantages of their proposals. It also means that interests with entrenched programs will fight hard to maintain or increase funding. Although all ongoing and potential programs are in competition for a share of the funds even in an expanding economy, this competition intensifies when public funds are scarce. Under such circumstances, funds are allocated to a specific program not on the basis of its merits or even the strength of interest-group support, but on how well it meets the economic criteria upon which the decision ultimately rests, whether or not those criteria are reasonable. At present the criteria focus on cost-benefit formulas designed to maximize the return to society per unit of cost. This chapter describes the techniques used to evaluate programs from this pragmatic, utilitarian perspective of social cost and benefit and examines some of the problems they raise for genetic intervention programs.

It will be evident that this mode of policy analysis relies heavily on formulation of goals and setting of priorities among competing spending proposals. "Resource allocation" for genetic programs depends on at least three levels of priorities:

1. What proportion of public monies ought to go into health programs?
2. What proportion of public-health spending ought to go into genetic programs?
3. Within funds for genetic programs, what are the priorities for spending?

The first priority appears to be relatively well-defined in the United States: It is possible that spending for health programs could be increased in the future, but it is unlikely that they will be successful in drawing substantial funds away from other major areas of government spending, especially defense. The second question is far from answered and much disagreement remains over what proportion of health spending should go to preventive health programs, which at present receive relatively low priority. Given the continuing debate over the second question and the newness and controversial nature of genetic programs, it is not surprising that little attention has been directed toward establishing priorities for spending within genetic programs themselves. This chapter examines the scattered attempts to set these priorities, however limited they might be at present.

This chapter, then, focuses on the methods of technology assessment and cost-benefit analysis to see to what extent and through what means they might be adapted to genetic technology. It is argued that some type of technology assessment is necessary, and any such attempt must adapt the assessment process to these new issues and broaden it considerably. The author disagrees with Green's (1973: 385) statement that "the issues involved in the genetic area may be different, but the mechanisms for public policy decision-making are, or at least should be, exactly the same as they are with respect to any kind of public issue." The issues raised by biomedical technology, especially genetic technology, are qualitatively different from traditional public issues revolving solely around expenditures of funds. Biomedical issues include that dimension and also comprise difficult ethical and moral aspects that political institutions have normally avoided. If we rely on current political procedures, based heavily on compromise, trade-off, and bargaining, it seems that we will fail to recognize the complexity of these new issues. Although Green is correct in observing that we must decide these issues within a democratic institutional framework, I have less confidence in the present institutions than Green displays. As Coates (1978: 33) asserts, "cut and fit accommodation and incremental change, the traditional strategies of government, are increasingly ineffective, if not sterile modes of operation." Spilhaus (1972: 714) agrees that the elective system does not lend itself to long-range planning but rather "encourages focusing on immediate crises." This chapter examines the need for long-range planning and more inclusive assessment of technologies prior to their widespread use.

Cost-Benefit Analysis in Public Policymaking

Although cost-benefit analysis (CBA) was developed originally as an aid in the allocation of public monies among alternative river irrigation projects, this method is now applied in some form to most areas of public-policy evaluation. Despite its expanded use, it is most applicable to programs in which the costs and benefits are tangible, unambiguous, and easily translated into standardized units. Considerable caution is warranted, however, in attempts to apply this type of analysis to biomedical programs, where costs and benefits cannot be measured adequately in monetary terms and where intangibles often outweigh values that can be operationalized effectively.

Although the specifics of each CBA model vary somewhat and assumptions might differ substantially from one application to the next, the basic intent of CBA is to fully enumerate the relevant costs and benefits of each project and to compute a benefit/cost ratio for each. If expected benefits exceed the costs, the project is feasible on economic grounds; conversely, if costs are greater than benefits, the project should not be funded. A natural extension of this methodology is to compare alternative programs on the basis of their benefit/cost ratios and to establish priorities from most to least justified. Although CBA is straightforward in theory, in practice it is extremely difficult and arbitrary to calculate, especially across a set of disparate programs. Questions remain as to which costs and benefits should be included in a model, how they can be reduced to common units, and, ultimately, who should make the value judgments inherent in the final policy decision.

There is much disagreement surrounding the role of CBA in policymaking. Although the National Research Council (1975) concludes that there is no objective way of making decisions, "the use of techniques developed by decision theory and benefit-cost analysis can provide the decision-maker with a useful framework . . . help to clarify the alternatives . . . [and] facilitate communication." Similarly, Conley (1973: 241) argues, "Benefit-cost considerations are crucial to decisionmaking. No decision on the use of resources should ever be made without some estimate, even if crude and subjective, of benefits and costs over time. Ultimately, benefit-cost considerations are the basis for determining whether a particular project should be adopted, how large it should be, and the composition of the resources that are utilized."

On the other hand, Twiss (1976: 37) sees CBA of limited value in setting priorities in biomedical policy and contends that the norm of equity is of greater importance. According to Twiss, CBA cannot solve issues of health policy, determine the social validity of health programs, or provide proof of the social value of any health program. Murray (1976: 164) contends that CBA is an "oversimplification of a large number of interlocking and interdependent factors." Twiss (1976: 167) adds, "It is my view that cost/benefit analysis should not be the sole means for determining the allocation of resources for the development of biomedical technology and . . . could easily result in an undesirable consequence: systematic discrimination against treating certain types of illness in the population." Gustafson (1974) stresses the importance of including consideration of human values in any attempt to assess benefits and costs, while Kass (1976: 321) decries the reduction of the social standard "to its lowest common denominator: money." Not surprisingly, the obvious utilitarian assumptions of CBA produce opposition from proponents of other philosophical frameworks (discussed in Chapter 3), who emphasize rights, justice, or other principles as the basis for distributing resources in society.

Neuhauser (1977) argues that the application of CBA to medical decision making is callous and notes that the assumptions of CBA are clearly at odds with those of a traditional doctor-patient approach, in which no expense is spared for the patient. Until now, according to Altman and Blendon (1979: 1) new biomedical technologies have been introduced when clinicians believed they would benefit the patient, irrespective of cost. The emphasis on cost effectiveness is altering substantially this traditional mode of operation. Blumstein (1976: 233) points out the great inconsistency in the way we deal with costs as they relate to the value of life: Most people are willing to spend unlimited funds to maintain the life of a particular individual, yet we consciously make decisions on a cost-benefit basis that result in the probability of death to x number of individuals.[1] He suggests that although CBA might work when the immediate human consequences are not apparent, it breaks down and appears cruel when hypothetical cases become concrete.

Taking a more moderate position, Swint et al. (1979: 464) argue that CBA should not be taken to imply that economic consequences are the only decision criterion for program approval. "CBA provides decision-makers with information designed to improve their ability to make rational decisions, i.e., it functions as one source of information that they must combine with ethical, sociopolitical, and other (intangible) information for net evaluation." Pliskin and Taylor (1977: 6) agree that CBA cannot make value judgments for society, but it can frequently "clarify the issues by identifying advantages and disadvantages, quantifying effects, and measuring the resources involved." Grosse (1972: 89) also describes the usefulness of CBA in "framing the right questions," while noting some limitations in its application to health programs.

Given the reality of widespread dependence on cost-benefit studies in the United States, it seems that this last approach of explaining the limitations as well as the uses of CBA is most productive. As it is unlikely that such analyses will be terminated, it is crucial to establish the boundaries of influence of CBA in policymaking and place more emphasis on including less tangible costs and benefits in the formulas used. There is no doubt that some method of efficiently and fairly allocating scarce public resources among competing projects is desperately needed; it is also clear that CBA must be modified substantially before it can serve that objective for health-related programs.

General Procedures

As noted earlier, CBA attempts to enumerate and measure the costs and benefits of a particular program and compute a benefit/cost ratio. Due to the need for expressing both costs and benefits in the same unit, generally the dollar, the tendency is to include only factors that can be readily operationalized and for which adequate data is available. Once this data is collected, it is placed into the formula and several values are computed. The first of these is *net present value,* or the mathematical difference between the present sums of benefits and costs. The second is the *benefit/cost ratio,* which is simply the division of present benefits by present costs.

In CBA it is crucial that all future benefits and costs be translated to present value, as many benefits will be spread over future years.[2] The *discount rate* is the adjustment factor used to express future benefits in terms of their present value. This is based on the economic assumption that individuals prefer consumption today to the same amount of consumption in the future. The present value, then, is the price that people would be willing to pay today for a benefit in the future. Theoretically, it denotes how many dollars today must be set aside for expenditures of x dollars of future costs. Although selection of the discount rate is arbitrary, a common figure is 6 or 7 percent. A 6 percent rate means that in order to meet costs of $1.06 next year a person must set aside $1.00 today. The higher the discount rate is, the greater the weight on the present. By using a lower discount rate, costs and benefits in the future become more crucial to the analysis. Obviously, a high discount rate will affect the benefit/cost ratio unfavorably in genetic programs in which many benefits occur in the future while costs are largely in the present.

Conley (1973: 243) notes three methods of comparing costs and benefits: (1) comparison of program with alternative of no program, (2) comparison of the differential costs and benefits of various options, and (3) comparison of programs with CBA of each program carried out against alternative of no program and then compared with each other. The first technique has limited aplication for policymaking as it makes no determination as to what alternative is most efficient. Instead, it simply indicates whether a single program is worthwhile in cost-benefit terms. Until now, most cost-benefit studies for genetic programs have been of this type. The second method, termed "cost effectiveness," compares the costs of providing the same benefit in different ways; for example, given the goal of reducing genetic disease, which program gives the most return per dollar spent? This method does not make an overall determination of whether either program is worthwhile. The third method determines not only which programs are

TABLE 5.1
Cost-Benefit Data for Three Hypothetical Screening Programs

Program	Benefits	Costs	B/C Ratio
PKU	$400,000	$100,000	4
Down's	480,000	80,000	6
Tay-Sachs	400,000	80,000	5

economically desirable but also which of the alternative programs gives the greatest return. For instance, all three of the hypothetical screening programs in Table 5.1 are justified on economic grounds, but if resources are too limited to fund more than one, screening for Down's syndrome would be selected. Although this third method is most useful for policymaking, it maximizes problems of assumptions and measurement, as the fate of each program depends on its comparison with others, even though the costs and benefits of each differ qualitatively.

Problems

Measurement is a major problem of CBA, especially when comparing disparate programs. Many benefits, especially intangible psychological ones, cannot be expressed in terms that are directly comparable, much less in dollar terms. Also, there are many second-order costs and benefits that tend to be ignored because data is either sparse or unavailable. Furthermore, instruments for measuring benefits and nonmonetary social costs are primitive at best. On the positive side, however, measurement is one area where improvement is likely as more attention is placed on the importance of now-obscured variables.

According to Conley (1973: 264), the "choice of the discount rate is one of the most critical tasks confronting the benefit-cost analyst." The discount factor greatly affects the present value of costs and benefits and therefore favors particular distributions across time. One means of reducing bias derived from the discount rate is to compute benefit/cost ratios based on several different discount rates and examine whether priorities are influenced by changes in the rate. This does not resolve the problem, but at least it brings it to the forefront and allows policymakers to make a final decision with more meaningful comparative data available.

Although CBA is widespread and becoming ingrained in the American policy process, these problems suggest that this approach must be used with caution, especially in comparing programs with divergent goals and dimensions. CBA appears to be a useful technique for providing information on the costs and benfits of competing programs, but only if it makes clear the limits of its conclusions. In order for CBA to contribute meaningfully to policymaking, measuring instruments must be refined, renewed emphasis must be placed on quantifying major social and psychological costs and benefits, assumptions and their implications must be explicated, and new efforts must be made to anticipate second-order costs and benefits. Even then, the final decision in each case ought to reflect the actual needs, values, and preferences of the people affected by a program and include consideration of other decision-making principles such as equity and justice.

Cost-Benefit Applications to Genetic Intervention Programs

There is no doubt that future genetic policy decisions will be even more dependent on CBA, despite the inherent limitations and special problems raised in applying CBA to human genetic technologies. As noted by Nelson, Swint, and Caskey (1978: 160), as the "continuation and the possible extension of such programs can only be accomplished with further commitments of scarce medical resources, it is inevitable that the issue of returns of this investment relative to alternative uses of the necessary resources must be addressed." Thomas (1971) notes that it will be increasingly necessary to justify all elaborate investments in technology and he places the burden of proof on those who desire these investments. Leach (1970: 292) strongly argues in favor of establishing benefit/cost ratios for screening programs and concludes that "mass prevention campaigns against disease" are generally not efficient investments.

This section is an attempt to synthesize the fragmented cost-benefit data available on screening and diagnostic programs. Although it is clear from the data that most current programs can be justified on this basis, ultimately the choice of goals and selection of priorities involve consideration of a wide variety of social costs and benefits that cannot adequately be included in the commonly used cost-benefit models. Some suggestions are offered as to how inclusion of the complex and critical intangible factors might be accomplished, and a general warning is issued that cost-benefit analysis in itself ought to have limited application in making genetic policy decisions. (Most analysts who have published cost-benefit studies relating to genetic programs have expressed similar caution regarding dependence on this technique.)

Measuring Costs and Benefits

Although the criteria for computing the monetary costs of screening will vary somewhat by type of screening program, possibility for therapy, and so forth, generally these tangible costs depend upon four factors:

1. The number of cases that must be screened to identify one prenatally defective fetus;
2. The per-unit cost of the screening procedure;
3. The cost of treatment and followup procedures, when appropriate; and
4. The cost of the subsequent abortion, when appropriate.

The first two elements are common to all screening and diagnostic efforts, the third element is crucial to screening for metabolic disorders such as PKU, and the fourth applies to programs designed to prevent the birth of a diagnosed defective fetus.[3]

The monetary costs of any screening program are also dependent on the size and organization of the testing laboratory as well as the tests performed. For instance, a regional facility might reduce per-unit costs significantly under certain conditions.[4] The tangible costs of any screening program, therefore, must be measured as carefully and accurately as possible, given the current state of testing procedures. These expenses should include direct costs such as salaries and laboratory tests as well as indirect costs for resources that are prevented from being used elsewhere by existence of the program (such as overhead costs not used exclusively for the program itself, or the value of travel time).

Much more difficult to operationalize and therefore not usually included in cost-benefit analyses are intangible costs not easily translated into monetary terms. The social costs of genetic intervention might include deprivations of certain fundamental individual rights such as reproductive freedom, privacy, and self-determination. Certainly, these value costs must be included in any evaluation of a potential program. Discrimination, stigmatization, and anger have resulted from screening for sickle-cell anemia and from efforts to determine the prevalence of the XYY complement in several communities.

Additionally, cost-benefit analyses must establish a better data base on the potential impact of a program on such social aspects as self-image, emotional stability, social status, employability, security, and so forth. Although genetic programs are likely to influence values relating to these dimensions and to have an impact on the family structure (for example, in increasing divorce rates among identified carriers) none of these factors is included in traditional cost-benefit studies. In fact, until now little effort has been directed at obtaining such data. More inclusive methods of technology assessment will require a much better understanding of the social and ethical aspects of human genetic intervention if they are to measure effectively all of the relevant costs of each potential program, especially if these costs result in irreversible alterations.

The costs of a particular screening procedure are difficult enough to estimate; benefits of screening programs are even more difficult to measure. Few persons are callous enough to ignore the human benefits of preventing the birth of a grossly abnormal being, but reduction of the pain and suffering of the affected child and the family is a benefit that is not easily introduced into a cost-benefit equation. Although screening and prenatal diagnosis might create tensions, they might also relieve anxiety in parents whose fetus is identified as free from genetic disorder, and in some cases they might allow parents who are carriers of a particular trait to have healthy children by providing them with information upon which to make a choice. It is tempting to assume that these intangible costs and benefits will balance out within a particular program or that they will be identical in all health-related programs, but such assumptions ignore the realities of meaningful analysis.

Unfortunately, these humanitarian concerns alone will seldom ensure legislative support. Instead, in this era of budgetary constraints, genetic programs must stand or fall on the monetary benefits they provide. It is difficult to dismiss the human benefits of screening for the few that benefit directly, but politically emphasis is placed on the monetary benefits to society as measured by: (1) increased productivity of the treated person or in some cases a replacement person; (2) decreases in medical costs, institutionalization, and so forth; and (3) increases in individual well-being over original circumstances (i.e., in the case of a treatable disorder such as PKU). Usually it is necessary to compute benefits for several classes of persons and then weigh them in some way. Nelson, Swint, and Caskey (1978), for instance, compute overall benefits of a Tay-Sachs screening program by totaling medical costs averted for unmarried carriers discovered by screening, marriages with one carrier, and couples identified as being at risk (both are carriers). Although such studies of genetic screening programs are fragmentary at present, cost-benefit studies will proliferate as the need for policymaking data increases. Available data are summarized here for inborn errors of metabolism, neural tube defects, and Tay-Sachs disease.

Screening for Phenylketonuria (PKU). Due to widespread and relatively long-standing neonatal programs, the most complete data on screening costs and benefits are available for programs for detection of inborn metabolic disorders. Chief among these is PKU, although multiple testing generally includes several other similarly tested disorders.[5] Although PKU screening

TABLE 5.2
Cost-Benefit Data for Massachusetts Newborn Metabolic
Disorders Screening Program

ITEM	COST($)	
Cost of specimen collection	155,730	
Cost of laboratory testing	200,971	
Cost of PKU care	68,187	
Cost of other disorders care	35,750	
Total		460,638
Averted Costs:		
Institutionalization		
PKU	648,240	
Other disorders	162,060	
Evaluation & Hospitalization:		
PKU	6,000	
Other disorders	9,000	
Total		825,300
Estimated Savings (1972-73)		364,662

Source: Massachusetts Department of Health (1974: 1415).

costs vary from state to state, the data for Massachusetts (see Table 5.2) are representative. Certainly these figures are supportive of the continuance of PKU screening even from a narrow cost-benefit perspective. "In fact . . . PKU screening has proved itself not merely a medical but also an economic success, figured in the most hard-nosed budgetary terms" (Guthrie, 1973: 229). When the relief of human suffering is included (as PKU is treatable) the modest expenditure in Massachusetts is an exceedingly good investment.

For the United States as a whole the cost for screening well over 3 million newborns each year is about $10 million. Pressures from some state legislatures to discontinue PKU screening programs might be expected, but "discontinuance of PKU screening would represent not merely medical but also fiscal irresponsibility of the grossest sort" (Guthrie, 1973: 232). Although it costs at a maximum approximately $40,000–$50,000 to identify one case of PKU, failure to do so means that a child must be institutionalized at a lifetime cost of at least $250,000. This figure does not include the future earnings and productivity of the treated patient and the suffering experienced by the parents, especially with the knowledge that their child could have been treated through testing and proper diet. It is also possible that states that discontinue such programs could be the target of suits from parents with affected children.

There is evidence that the maximum cost stated above could be reduced somewhat through the use of automated test equipment if regional screening programs could be established. Part of the cost now is the result of duplication of testing equipment, some of which is used rarely. Consolidation would also result in further use of multiple tests to identify other inborn errors at little additional cost. "By 'regional' program I mean . . . one in which a sufficient number of newborn specimens are screened daily to permit application of those methods of automation already routine in a number of laboratories for the purpose of carrying out at least 8 of the 13 tests available" (Guthrie, 1973: 235). Even though Hsia and Holtzman (1973) criticize PKU screening programs as less impressive than first promised, they do not suggest that such programs should be discontinued. Instead, they opt for increased quality control, redoubled efforts at multiple testing procedures, and flexible application of the laws in light of new knowledge. Most observers agree that more emphasis should be placed on family counseling, the establishment of a proper diet, and long-term follow-up procedures.[6]

Neural Tube Defects. The findings of cost-benefit analyses for screening of neural tube defects are less conclusive than the PKU data. The major British study (Hagard, Carter, and Milne, 1976) concludes that screening for spina bifida is worthwhile only in populations in which the incidence of that condition is high. Since that time, however, tests for alpha-fetoprotein levels have improved substantially, lowering the per-unit cost. In a more recent study, Layde et al. (1979) find a favorable benefit/cost ratio for a multitiered screening program of a theoretical cohort of 100,000 pregnant women at risk for having an affected fetus. It is assumed that each woman would elect to terminate her pregnancy if an affected fetus were diagnosed. As usual for this type of analysis, the authors calculate ratios for both a replacement and nonreplacement situation. A replacement situation occurs when an affected fetus is aborted and later "replaced" with a subsequent child assumed to be normal. The benefit here will include the productivity of the replacement. In a nonreplacement situation, the aborted fetus is not replaced by a normal child and the resulting increase in production. Table 5.3 presents a summary of the figures.

Layde et al. (1979) conclude that the overall benefit/cost ratio would be somewhere between 1.95 and 2.35, depending on the proportion of families replacing the aborted fetus. They also note the problem of false

TABLE 5.3
Cost-Benefit Data for Alpha-Fetoprotein Screening

Cost of screening 100,000 women	$2,047,780
Benefits (non-replacement)	4,046,012
Benefits (replacement)	4,861,718
Benefit/cost ratio (non-replacement)	1.95
Benefit/cost ratio (replacement)	2.35

Source: Layde et al. (1979: 570).

positives—i.e., normal fetuses aborted because they were diagnosed wrongly as having a neural tube defect—and suggest that the favorable benefit/cost ratio shifts the onus of justification to the outcome of the ethical debate, as on cost-benefit grounds abortion of an affected fetus is justified.

Tay-Sachs Disease. Cost-benefit studies of three different Tay-Sachs programs have concluded that such programs are justified on grounds of reducing monetary costs.[7] In each case, the authors compute benefit/cost ratios for both the low- and high-cost estimates of care for a Tay-Sachs child.[8] Both the Nelson and Swint studies assume an average length in hospital of two and one-half years and use a discount rate of 7 per cent. Further, they assume that couples at risk will consent to amniocentesis and abortion when appropriate and that children diagnosed as carriers by the screening program will later at their own volition undergo screening and counseling by a private physician. Table 5.4 presents a summary of the cost-benefit data from these three programs.

In each program the net present value is positive, suggesting that the program costs are less than the program benefits as measured in solely monetary terms. The benefit/cost ratios reinforce the cost effectiveness of the programs. Even with the lower hospital cost estimate in Houston, for instance, for every $1.00 spent today, there are $3.20 in benefits discounted to today. Interestingly, Swint et al. (1979) do not even note the significant difference between the screening program conducted on a weekly basis and the program conducted three to four times annually in the Baltimore community. The benefit/cost ratio of the community program (5.0) is over three times that of the in-house program (1.6). Certainly this type of data is useful in determining how limited screening resources can be used most advantageously.[9]

Although they admit that humanitarian benefits have not been included

TABLE 5.4
Cost-Benefit Data for Three Tay-Sachs Programs

Program	Benefits	Costs	B/C	Net Present Value
Houston[a]				
$20,000 est.	$ 75,102	$23,413	3.2	$ 51,689
$40,000 est.	$150,204	$23,413	6.4	$126,791
Johns Hopkins Hospital[b]				
$20,000 est.	$ 27,930	$17,626	1.6	$ 10,304
$40,000 est.	$ 55,860	$17,626	3.2	$ 38,234
Johns Hopkins community[b]				
$20,000 est.	$101,442	$20,307	5.0	$ 81,135
$40,000 est.	$202,884	$20,307	10.0	$182,577

a) Nelson, Swint, and Caskey (1978)

b) Swint et al. (1979)

in their study, Nelson, Swint, and Caskey (1978: 161) argue that "if a program can be justified on economic grounds alone, then measurement of intangible benefits is unnecessary, as they would merely reinforce the excess of measured benefits over costs." But, as Inman (1978: 221) notes, neglecting these benefits will obscure the true social value of a program. As the ultimate use of cost-benefit data is to compare the benefit/cost ratios of many competing programs and to give higher priority to those that are most cost effective, dependence solely on tangible costs and benefits may lead to unfortunate decisions. According to Inman (1978: 222), "Benefit-cost analysis demands a full enumeration of gains and losses to be a useful guide to decision-making. In applications to health care decision-making, this means that the humanitarian benefits must be counted. It is a delicate and demanding job, but either you confront this task, or you should leave benefit-cost analysis alone. There is no useful middle road." We must be cautious in accepting findings based on limited data that is utilized only because it is available; at the same time we must realize that the reality of politics demands such figures.

Conley and Milunsky (1975) have computed the value of benefits for four genetic disorders, including Tay-Sachs disease. As illustrated in Table 5.5, the monetary benefit of eliminating fetuses with chromosomal abnormalities is higher than that for Tay-Sachs, implying that prenatal diagnosis programs for these conditions also might be cost effective. In fact, Thomp-

TABLE 5.5
Comparison of Benefits for Four Disorders

Type of Condition Prevented	Replacement	Non-Replacement
Tay-Sachs	$ 95,000	$ 30,000
Hunter's Syndrome	$113,000	$ 65,000
Down's Syndrome	$100,000	$ 65,000
Trisomy 18	$100,000	$ 65,000

Source: Conley and Milunsky (1975).

son and Milunsky (1979: 35) conclude that "chromosomal and neural tube defects constitute by far the most cost-effective targets for general testing."

As the benefit/cost ratio is heavily dependent on the expense of averting each affected birth, selection of the population to be screened is an important aspect of any proposed program. For instance, although Conley and Milunsky (1975) arrive at a benefit/cost ratio of 75 under the most favorable assumptions regarding the population to be screened, this drops substantially to a ratio of 1.9 under the least favorable assumptions. For their test population they found the cost of averting an affected fetus to be $34,000 (p. 457). If screening is targeted to those at risk, the cost can be reduced significantly, perhaps to as low as $2,000.[10]

Limitations of Cost-Benefit Applications

In addition to the technical problems of cost-benefit analysis discussed earlier, such as selection of the discount rate and computation of costs and benefits in dollar units, applications to genetic programs are limited by their inability to never satisfactorily account for intangible benefits or more subtle social costs. Although this data might be interesting and especially useful in maximizing cost effectiveness for similar programs (in hospital or community settings, for example), it is dangerous to base policy decisions solely on the results of such analyses, given their questionable assumptions and selective inclusion of factors that are most easily operationalized.

One critical assumption of the Tay-Sachs studies cited here is that parents would always choose to abort a fetus diagnosed as defective. Although there is evidence that among those who request genetic screening significant proportions submit to abortion of defective fetuses, Neel (1973: 356) questions whether the reproductive patterns of those screened without requesting the service will be changed: "In assigning priorities to genetic programs, we must keep in mind that a screening program for carriers that does not alter the reproductive pattern of the population concerned, has failed its ostensible purpose, no matter how interesting the data collected." Before cost-benefit analysis can represent a meaningful contribution to decision making in genetic matters, more adequate data must be collected as to comparable compliance rates relating to specific disorders (e.g., Tay-Sachs versus Down's syndrome) and between various populations. Built into any program, then, should be procedures designed to maximize the effectiveness of the screening effort. This can be accomplished only through strengthening the data base of the attitudes and prospective behavior of the target population.

Difficult decisions must also be made as to where to concentrate screening efforts in order to not only maximize efficacy but also protect fundamental rights of individuals. It was demonstrated in Chapter 1 that for many genetic diseases such as Tay-Sachs, sickle-cell anemia, and thalassemia, the incidence among particular ethnic groups is significantly higher than the population as a whole. Economically and logistically, screening of such high-risk groups is practical, but screening the entire population is not feasible because of the low overall incidence of carriers. "Several estimates of cost effectiveness have been made which indicate that it would cost only one fifth to one third as much to screen the entire Ashkenazi Jewish population in the United States as to care for the affected children that would be born without a preventive program" (Kaback and O'Brien, 1973: 262). However, it is specifically these diseases that result in stigmatizing certain groups. When groups already are the target of social discrimination, identifying them as carriers of a genetic disease can be devastating. This is especially the case in screening for the sickle-cell trait, as there is little medical value in detecting the carrier state unless it is used in conjunction with prenatal diagnosis.

In addition, more work is needed to develop an effective means of forecasting the need for genetic services and facilities. For instance, Selle, Holmes, and Ingbar (1979) project an increase of 61 percent in the number of women over thirty-five years of age who give birth by the year 2000, due to the crest of the baby boom and a delayed fertility pattern. At this rate, while fertility rates overall are declining, the annual births to women 35 to 44 are expected to increase from 158,000 to 254,000. Given current patterns, those born with chromosomal abnormalities will jump from 3,900 to 6,400, an increase of 64 percent. These projections are based on assumptions that might prove to be in error, but they at least offer some help in attempts to more realistically build knowledge of future trends into policy.

At a minimum, the time allowed for calculating costs and benefits must be expanded to account for benefits that might accrue in the future as well as second-order or irreversible costs that might arise. Although this is extremely difficult under the cost-benefit formulas currently in use, it is not impossible. More effort to include intangible variables, increased use of supporting data to refine assumptions, and delineation of the benefits accruing to a wide range of individuals should strengthen the applicability of cost-benefit analysis to genetic policies. Given the state of program evaluation and scrutiny at present, there appears to be no other choice but to work on modifying cost-benefit models to better reflect and anticipate the complex yet subtle benefits and costs of human genetic intervention.

Technology Assessment

Although the need for more comprehensive long-range planning and assessment of future alternatives has been recognized for many years, only recently has a genuine effort been made to include future considerations as a crucial dimension in policymaking. Still, the short-term, pragmatic emphasis of policymaking continues to constrain such long-range considerations, and as yet no political mechanism has been established to assess continuously the consequences of human genetic technology. Genetic policies, however, require inclusion of future dimensions, as the major effects of current research efforts will be apparent in the coming generations. Traditional cost-benefit analysis can be adjusted to account for estimated future costs and benefits, although it tends to focus on immediate consequences, normally for a narrow range of interests most directly involved in the development of the technology.

Technology assessment (TA) is a process normally viewed as more inclusive than cost-benefit analysis, as it expands the scope of consequences accompanying the introduction of a new technology. In practice, the term "technology assessment" has been applied to studies that vary considerably in purpose and methodology. Some useful distinctions relate to the prospective or retrospective nature of the study and the extent to which the assessment is evaluative or primarily descriptive. A basic distinction appears to be between what might be termed narrow technical assessment and a broader assessment that details the interplay of the technology, values, and society. Although the primary concern of this chapter is the second, more inclusive defintion, an example of the technical form is presented to illustrate the difference between the two and perhaps clarify the controversy over TA discussed later in this section.

In 1978 the Office of Technology Assessment (OTA) appraised the efficacy and safety issues raised by 17 medical procedures, including amniocentesis. That study represents a highly specialized form of TA, focusing on the technical dimensions while basically ignoring the social, legal, and ethical aspects. To some extent, this application is a cost-benefit study that considers the benefits, the medical problem, the population affected, and the conditions under which the technology is applied. Conversely, safety is measured in terms of risks and defined by OTA (1978: 17) as a "judgement of the acceptability of the risk associated with a medical technology." (OTA acknowledges that both safety and efficacy reflect value judgments concerning acceptability of risk and perception of benefit.) The purpose of this narrow technology assessment is to explicate the technical risks and benefits inherent in the specific technique. The OTA study (1978: 97–104) also outlines current assessment activities in the areas covered and notes policy alternatives available for making such decisions.

Although assessments of this type are necessary in order to evaluate the more limited technical components of each biomedical application, thorough technology assessment must include the social, ethical, and political dimensions as well. Therefore, without detracting from the importance of technical assessments, concentration here is on the need for inclusive assessment procedures and mechanisms designed to analyze the nontechnical as well as technical effects of a technology. Joseph Coates (1971: 225) defines this expanded concept of TA as "the systematic study of the effects on society that may occur when a technology is introduced, extended, or modified, with special emphasis on the impacts that are unintended, indirect, and delayed." This definition refers to two aspects that are viewed as crucial for effective assessment. Most obvious is the broad scope of concern for effects on "society," which would include all of the elements perceived as important in this study. The second, and more subtle, aspect is the special emphasis on second-order consequences: those that are "unintended, indirect, or delayed." According to Walters (1978: 1653), the most important contribution of TA has been "to broaden and lengthen the perspective from which technological developments are viewed." By requiring consideration of a broad range of effects on society both in the present and in the future, TA as defined by Coates promises a more comprehensive analysis of the complex interactions between technology and society.

There is no single accepted methodology for performing technology assessment as defined above. Walters (1978: 1650) suggests that a comprehensive assessment would include seven major steps presented by Jones (1971: 26):

1. defining the assessment task
2. describing relevant technologies
3. developing state-of-society assumptions

4. identifying impact areas
5. preparing a preliminary impact analysis
6. identifying possible action options
7. completing the impact analysis

Step one entails detailing the scope of the inquiry by setting the boundaries as to specific time period, type of impact, and inclusiveness. Step two describes the current state of the technology to be assessed, surveys related technologies, and attempts to estimate the future state of the art and the scope of its use. Step three attempts to identify major nontechnological factors that might influence the development and application of the technologies, and the fourth stage involves describing the social characteristics that will be most influenced by introduction and use of the technology. Basically, the first four steps involve establishing the framework for the analysis and describing the social context. (At a general level, this book is largely an attempt to provide this framework for assessing human genetic technologies.)

The last three steps of technology assessment as outlined by Jones involve analysis of the anticipated social consequences of the technology. In step five, the assessor posits which social groups and institutions will be affected by the technology and how they will be affected. Stage six involves identification of alternative courses of action. Attempts are made to develop options that will provide maximum public benefit while reducing to a minimum the negative consequences of the technology being assessed. Finally, in step seven, each option is analyzed for its social impact, given the potential modifications of this impact by changes outlined in the preceding step.

Although this process appears complex and is extremely difficult to carry out, it tends to proceed quite logically from the first to the last step. Basically, it results in an explication of the many technical and nontechnical considerations that ought to be, but seldom are, part of each policy decision regarding the development and/or application of a technology. Cost-benefit analysis is often necessary for comparing the alternative courses of action while emphasis in TA is expanded substantially toward broader social consequences and away from exclusively monetary considerations.

Assessing Human Genetic Technologies

According to the National Academy of Science (NAS) report (1975: 2), little thorough and systematic investigation of biomedical technologies has been conducted. To date most of the major technology assessments have been in nonbiological fields such as energy, transportation, communications, and natural resources (Coates, 1975: 6). Walters (1978a: 224) explains the lack of TA for biomedical technology: As two-thirds of funding for such research comes from the federal government, "advances in biomedical technology already reflect public-policy decisions to a much greater extent than do technical advances in the field of physics and physical engineering."

The last decade has seen more activity in assessing biomedical technologies, although the preponderance of TA activity is in the physical sciences. Among these recent efforts has been a general discussion of future biomedical developments and their potential social impact (Gordon and Ament, 1969), an assessment of four biomedical techniques (NAS, 1975a), and an overview of nine biomedical candidates for further assessment (OTA, 1976). Finally, several of the national commissions discussed in Chapter 4 have issued reports demonstrating the social, legal, and ethical implications of such research. The volatile action of government officials, public-interest groups, and some scientists in response to recombinant DNA research and in vitro fertilization in the latter half of the 1970s resulted in more attention to the need for continued and greatly expanded assessment efforts in genetic technology. Although he recognizes that physical technologies are different, Walters (1978: 225) hypothesizes that the "same methodology, with minor adjustments is applicable to the biomedical field." The National Academy of Sciences (1975a: 3) suggests that modification is necessary to consider better the "deeply ingrained feelings" about the nature of humans, their freedom, integrity, dignity, and beliefs, which are much more clearly operative in biomedical areas. Also, as these technologies are likely to be introduced through the health profession, it is crucial to examine the special features of the physician-patient relationship in analyzing their potential use.

Glass (1972: 253) appeals for broad interdisciplinary involvement in assessment of genetic technology, including representation from experts in the fields of philosophy, religion, and political science.[11] Hanft, in testimony reported in Powledge and Dach (1977: 23), agrees that too little attention has been paid to the consequences of the introduction of new biomedical technologies. She warns: "Once given the Good Housekeeping seal of the community, it is very difficult to withhold introduction of a new technology into the health services system, even when efficacy and costs have not been established." Rising expectations of the public, fueled by press reports of miraculous advances in genetic technology, might very easily create a route of no return if adequate assessment is not conducted early in the development process. Again, we cannot afford to wait until after technologies are fully developed and publicized in order to make the policy decisions, because that often makes the decision that much more difficult. Technology assessment as currently practiced might not be the ideal mechanism for evaluating genetic programs, but some means of assessment is vital now. For Walters (1978a: 232), "the technology-assessment methodology provides a coherent framework for analyzing the social impact of technological change."

Appraising Assessment Methodology

Walters expresses considerable confidence in technology assessment, despite the controversy that has surrounded the application of this methodology to policymaking on biomedical technologies. Some of this opposition comes from philosophers who are critical of the utilitarian assumptions in which technology assessment is firmly rooted. Others criticize attempts to force complex decisions into a predetermined analytical process. In their assessment of four of the more straightforward biomedical technologies, theorists at the National Academy of Sciences (1975a: 4) concluded that "the breadth and complexity of the subject matter posed serious obstacles to developing a uniform mode of analysis . . . different technologies presented different kinds of problems for analysis and assessment." They found assessment of biomedical technology helpful in illuminating important public-policy questions and identifying stages in the use of a given technology at which decisions and value choices can be made and by whom, yet overall they were cautious concerning the desirability and feasibility of technology assessment for making the final decision.

Although technology assessment often is viewed as largely descriptive, it contains a prescriptive component as well in the many value judgments made at each stage of the analysis. This evaluative dimension is certainly apparent in cost-benefit analysis as well as in broader assessment methodologies. Tribe (1973: 627) contends that by emphasizing impacts and outcomes, technology assessment minimizes the role of "soft" variables that cannot be measured easily. As a result, "entire problems tend to be reduced to terms that misstate their underlying structure and ignore the 'global' features that give them their total character." Like any other form of applied policy analysis, technology assessment can become a weapon for the "disguised advancement of narrow interests."

Unless complemented by other methods of evaluation, technology assessment is only another exercise in "instrumental rationality," in which policy decisions are viewed simply as a product of trade-offs among existing interests and values in the community. Simply broadening the range of factors under consideration by expanding the spectrum of affected interests, including social costs and benefits, and extending the time frame will not resolve the underlying problems of the instrumental mode of analysis. Tribe argues that given the rapid advances in biomedical technology, we can no longer depend solely on expanding the instrumental method.

The policy-analytic mode itself is flawed due to its focus on outcomes at the expense of questions of process. Tribe does not dismiss technology assessment entirely, but he does suggest that emphasis should be placed on what the ends and values *ought to be* rather than accepting them as givens. The goals of society must be explicated before the process can proceed. According to Tribe (p. 641), if technology assessment and environmental analysis cannot address the question of what one's ultimate ends and values ought to be, then they "will either have to be silent as to an increasing significant range of problems that both disciplines should be called upon to illuminate or will mistakenly treat the choice of ultimate ends as though that task were really one calling only for the selection of means to attainment of ends already given." At the least, Tribe (p. 659) requires increased attempts to enrich policy analysis by adding a constitutive dimension that will deal with these crucial value problems.

Huddle (1972: 155) reiterates the necessity to establish new societal goals and rules of behavior in light of the rapid technological advances. He suggests the need for a more comprehensive, integrative function, which includes the forecasting of technology, the development of social indicators, and the identification of national goals as well as the technology assessment itself. "Technology assessment is meaningless except when it is accompanied by technology forecasting and some form of social indicators. We cannot judge the merits of a technology except in the context of the alternative technological options, present and future" (p. 162). Although some progress has been made toward meeting these goals in the decade since Huddle's comments were made, these deficiencies in technology assessment remain.

According to Baram (1971: 537), technology assessment and control are essentially policymaking processes and as such will be embroiled in political controversy, another dimension to consider. Brooks (1973: 251) agrees that there are no objective or scientific bases upon which a final choice can be made. Instead, the "choices themselves are political, depending upon a complex interplay or bargaining process among conflicting economic, political and ideological interests and values." The National Academy of Sciences (1975a: 4–5) submits that insights provided by technology assessment might be ignored when policy decisions are made, as these decisions ultimately are political and emerge from a "welter of competing claims, motives, interests and pressures," including some "forces hostile to the public good." Ferkiss (1978: 7) similarly concludes, "Whatever the facts may be in a particular case, whatever methods of analysis may be used, one thing is clear. Appropriate technology and technology assessment have political and moral dimensions, and they rest on political and moral assumptions." The difficulties involved with technology assessment are compounded when technology is judged within the context of "political and social goals which are themselves subject to controversy" (p. 4).

Due to these ubiquitous political boundaries, some observers have been highly critical of technology assessment. Brooks (1973: 251) notes that technology assessment can lead people to rethink their own value preferences by revealing the relative costs of the options available; he also views it as a ready means of legitimizing political consensus through its supposedly value-free analysis. Elliot and Elliot (1977: 135) are highly critical of technology assessment, asserting that it is naive to separate it into discrete elements of (1) an objective apolitical process of technical investigation and (2) a political decision-making process following the technical findings. Not only do the techniques fail to be value-free, they say, but also, "vested interests and dominant values have a profound effect on the type of questions asked and the kinds of alternatives considered during the technical investigation process." Elliot and Elliot see technology assessment as one more "tool for legitimizing the inequalities of the status quo." As long as the persons conducting the assessment receive funds and are therefore beholden to certain interests, it is difficult to visualize a truly independent assessment mechanism with no prior commitment to the values and priorities of those interests.

On a more practical level, Freeman (1974) outlines constraints on technology assessment: (1) inadequate theory and data, (2) lack of reliability in foreseeing advances in technology, (3) limits in the ability to determine safe thresholds,[12] and (4) the inability to predict new societal values. Each of these constraints limits the applicability of a particular assessment methodology and each must be faced in assessment efforts. In addition to the political aspects discussed above, current technology assessment mechanisms are also inhibited by the combined effects of what Freeman terms "organizational constraints": the competitive pressures to externalize as many costs as possible, the domination of goal setting by narrow interests instead of some broader public, and the constraints imposed by territorial and functional jurisdictional divisions. As a result, these mechanisms are too slow to respond to rapid technological advances and too unbalanced in approach (Freeman 1974: 164).

Technology Assessment: A Summary

In spite of the flurry of activity and highly optimistic reports concerning technology assessment, it continues to be controversial. Continuing problems relate to: (1) its ultimate grounding in traditional values; (2) the difficulty of determining the impact of each of a multitude of subtly interrelated variables on society, especially through a chain of probabilistic future events; and (3) the inability to create a socially neutral mechanism for conducting the assessment free from political and social constraints.

Despite these meaningful and accurate criticisms, it is here argued that TA has contributed positively toward evaluation of biomedical technologies and that, given major modifications, it will play an even more crucial role in the future. Walters (1978a) is correct in his contention that we must work to improve the tools we have at our disposal, while altering them to better serve our goals. Technology assessment is highly flexible and should be adapted to disparate types of technology. The more inclusive form of technology assessment emphasized here has broadened substantially the perspective of analysis by allowing intangible factors that have been largely ignored in past analyses to be considered. Furthermore, it has helped expand the concept of moral responsibility (Walters, 1978a: 231) by holding policymakers responsible for the remote as well as the immediate consequences of their decisions. More than any other recent development in the policy process, technology assessment serves to bring control over technology one step closer to reality. Still, technology assessment alone does little to solve two crucial questions: What criteria are used to establish societal priorities? And who makes the final decision?

Genetic Policymaking

Although the moves toward more inclusive forms of technology assessment described in the last section are welcome and at least raise questions regarding the long-term, second-order consequences of biomedical innovations, until now little attention has been given to human genetic technology. In light of the intensity and scope of the controversy genetic intervention elicits, it is not surprising that policymakers have avoided the introduction of these complex issues into the policy process as long as possible. Genetic issues, which strike at the underlying assumptions concerning individualism and the role of social policy, prove most difficult to evaluate through political mechanisms founded on those very assumptions. The discussion here, however, implies that these issues are within the public-policy realm, that they will be more so in the future, and that an appropriate political response is both necessary and warranted.

Until now, genetic policies appear to be largely the result of ad hoc, fragmented, and inconsistent decisions made without adequate consideration of the unique dimensions and broad implications that accompany advances in human genetic technology. Given the paucity of efforts to assess genetic innovations and the apparent inability of existing political institutions to face the policy issues created as these technologies expand, it seems that efforts in the 1980s must be aimed at establishing procedures and mechanisms for integrating genetic issues into every stage of the policy process. The remainder of this section examines some of the ways in which this objective might be approached.

The Policymaking Process

The policymaking process itself has been defined in varied ways. There is some agreement, however, that analytically at least the process can be parcelled into a set of discrete steps or stages. For instance, Williams (1977: 30) asserts that policymaking activities can be divided into three parts: (1) the formulation and analysis of alternative courses of action, (2) the decision-making process, and (3) the means used to translate decisions into action. He envisions that process as a closed cycle with constant feedback, which affords an interconnectedness among the stages. This study uses a more detailed scheme of the policy cycle (May and Wildavsky, 1979), moving chronologically through six steps:

1. Setting the policy agenda
2. Formulation of policy alternatives
3. Making the decision
4. Policy implementation
5. Policy evaluation
6. Policy termination

It is obvious that adequate genetic policies can emerge only through accomplishment of all six stages, including the continuous evaluation of ongoing genetic programs and the termination of those deemed unsatisfactory, but immediate attention must be directed toward the first two stages. If genetic-related issues are to receive the necessary public consideration, they first must be viewed as a legitimate element of the public agenda. Once that occurs, it is crucial that feasible and comprehensive policy options be formulated and, concurrently, that mechanisms designed to make and implement genetic policy decisions be developed. In light of the actual and potential political controversies surrounding these technologies, success at each of these stages will not be easily achieved.

Agenda Setting. According to Cobb and Elder (1972: 85), the "governmental agenda" includes "all issues that are commonly perceived by members of the political community as meriting public attention . . . and involving matters within the legitimate jurisdiction of existing governmental authority." The process through which concerns and conflicts receive governmental attention and become "public" issues recently has been referred to as "agenda setting." Nelson (1978: 19) claims that too little attention has been directed at the means through which programs reach the public agenda. Others have noted that the haphazard and uncoordinated agenda-setting attempts in the United States are due to the numerous points of access across a multitude of government agencies (Gergen, 1968) and the relatively high degree of autonomy among the various governmental units (Aldrich, 1973).

Nelkin (1977: 413) contends that the policy importance of a technological innovation — i.e., whether or not it appears on the public agenda — depends on the degree to which it provokes a public response and on its relationship to organized political and economic interests. Political demands focus on issues that are highly visible or dramatic, especially if their potential impact on public health or safety is clear. The resulting interest in these issues is followed by a proliferation of interest groups, protests confronting the technological development, and governmental committees, conferences, and so forth (Nelkin, 1977: 408). It seems that genetic issues now reflect the criteria outlined by Nelkin. Ostheimer (1979: 19) suggests that as these issues are too volatile or emotional for most politicians to touch willingly, the politicians must "study their experiences with the various theories of agenda formation in mind."

Two tasks appear vital if genetic issues are to be given a place on the public agenda. First, national health goals must be defined more clearly and consistently, especially in the context of constrained public resources. To date, little success is apparent in setting national objectives regarding preventive health care, including most potential genetic technologies. Furthermore, much health policy continues to be fragmented among the fifty states and the various health-related agencies in the national government. According to Spilhaus (1972: 714), "Now is the time to revive ideas of how to plan for large national objectives that transcend local and state interests and that look far beyond present immediacies." The second task is to determine where genetic programs fit into these national health objectives in a manner that accounts for the complex ethical framework surrounding genetic technology. Only by delineating broader social goals can the direction of genetic research and development and the social priority attached to each potential application be ascertained. One such option would include various methods of genetic intervention as parts of a broader effort to prevent mental retardation and genetic disease. Figure 5.1 demonstrates how genetic screening and prenatal diagnostic programs might contribute to these goals.

Application of genetic technology under such an approach would be multifaceted and goal directed, rather than fragmented into programs with narrow or ambiguous objectives. The primary goal of such genetic policies would be to reduce genetic disease and produce healthy children. They might also serve to reduce the suffering of those affected, the anxiety of parents, and the costs to society — an unlikely scenario due to the political,

FIGURE 5.1
Strategies for the Prevention of Mental Retardation and Genetic Disease

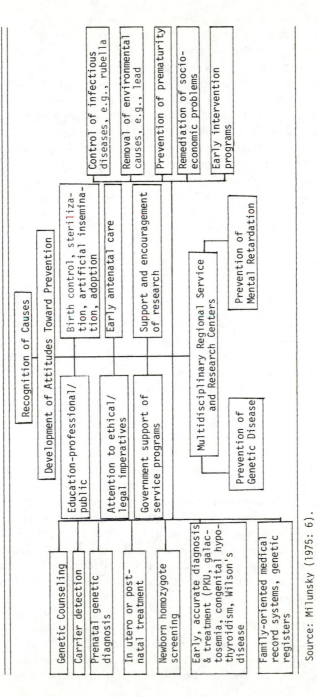

Source: Milunsky (1975: 6).

economic, and social constraints outlined in this study. Still, it is critical at this juncture to define how genetic-related issues can be included most effectively in the public agenda. The question no longer is whether they are matters of public concern; genetic issues are already among the most controversial and potentially explosive issues. Given the ethical and political complexity of genetic issues discussed in earlier chapters, it is essential that intensive efforts be made to include genetic technologies on the public agenda in a way that is both reasonable and sensitive to these broader concerns. Highest priority must be given to setting national goals and a truly future-oriented agenda for achieving those goals.

Formulation of Policy Alternatives. Robbins (1979: 174) notes that we must "improve our capacity to assess technologies during the developmental stage and to encourage those projects which have the greatest promise for yielding effective outcomes." According to R. Williams (1977: 30), the formulation and analysis of alternative courses of action depends on the ability to accurately predict technological development as well as to evaluate the impact of each development. Joseph Coates (1978: 36) points out the principal needs for forecasting, feedback, and flexibility in designing public policies.

Nowhere is the need for intense evaluation of alternatives more crucial than in human genetic technology. As noted above, technology assessment and forecasting are vital elements in the formulation of meaningful, inclusive policy options. Without successful completion of this stage, decision making and implementation will continue to be flawed. In order to frame policy alternatives for genetic technology, a two-tiered approach seems necessary. First, each genetic innovation must be examined separately through the broadly defined technology-assessment process defined earlier. Included in this analysis would be evaluation of the technical considerations such as efficacy, safety, scope of use, and so forth. Also included would be an inventory of the social impact of each application of the technique on a wide range of values such as privacy and individualism[13] as well as on social institutions and patterns of behavior. Although the social consequences of many genetic technologies overlap, many nuances remain and should be explicated. This level of assessment of alternatives will necessarily contain cost-benefit analyses, but these alternatives must be broadened substantially to comprise intangible social benefits and costs as well as the narrow monetary ones.

The second level of assessment needed is more comprehensive and therefore more difficult. At this level, all biomedical technologies must be evaluated as to their contribution to achieving the national goals delineated during agenda setting. Due to the interconnectedness among biomedical technologies, priorities must be set to deal with complex second-order consequences, both adverse and beneficial. For instance, the technique of in vitro fertilization, although distinct from its potential use in surrogate motherhood and possibly cloning, is a necessary means through which these extensions might be conducted. In other words, the achievement of one technology might serve as the means through which other, perhaps less desirable and unanticipated, developments occur. Priority setting must take into consideration these connections between technologies and be based on attempts to anticipate second- and third-order consequences of each application. Each of these decisions will require hard choices by policymakers, but they can be aided significantly by adequate formulation of the alternatives.

Implementation: Federalism and Genetic Policy. So far this discussion of genetic policy has assumed that the kind of decision needed to deal with the broad social implications of human genetic technology requires concentrated effort at the national level. Only by setting national goals and priorities can the alternatives be defined uniformly and the rights of all U.S. citizens be assured. Although it is argued here that such a national effort is essential in order to deal with the moral-legal-social dimensions of these technologies as well as to make the technical assessments of the safety and efficacy of particular applications, implementation of genetic policies might best be accomplished through the states. In fact, there are some dangers in centralizing even the agenda-setting and assessment function at the national level. This illustrates still another dilemma: Although comprehensive genetic planning and evaluation is critical, thereby necessitating a coordinated assessment mechanism, guarantees must be included to ensure protection of all interests and representation of all viewpoints. This frequently is difficult in a highly centralized policymaking context. Also, there is fear among some observers that creation of such a public agency would produce an attendant bureaucracy that would be irresponsible, restrictive, and dependent on its own survival (Department of Health, Education, and Welfare, 1978: 23).

One must also take into consideration the federal system. Although this study is critical of the present uncoordinated health policy that is the result of our fragmented political system, constitutionally the fifty states retain the basic responsibility for making such policy. In recent decades the funding lever of the national government has exerted some influence over state policy, though Daniels (1980) notes that the impact of such incentives in some health areas has been minimal. For example, the national funding for sickle-cell screening introduced in 1972 encouraged some states to switch from a mandatory to voluntary screening policy, but it had little impact on the majority of states, which still have no such screening legislation.

Until now Congress has demonstrated little propensity to preempt state responsibility for health policy, especially in the area of genetics. For a variety of political and legal reasons, it is likely that policymaking and implementation of genetic applications will remain largely at the state level, although funding of genetic research and development will be mainly national. As a result, programs, where they exist, will continue to vary substantially from state to state, in terms of both quality and format. Obviously, this will continue to produce great unevenness of genetic services, as in other health services (Verner and Zins, 1980), from state to state. On the other hand, this decentralized process does allow for needed experimentation with alternative concepts and might better reflect the values of the communities they serve than programs designed at the national level would.

In the absence of significant deliberation and assessment of genetic intervention by Congress, some states have made substantial efforts to include the genetic dimension in their overall health programs. For example, the Prenatal and Clinical Genetic Services Project in Wisconsin, supported by state Maternal and Child Care funds, is a multifaceted attempt to "prevent genetic disorders and birth defects and to improve the condition of affected persons by providing statewide comprehensive genetic services." This program provides a range of prenatal and clinical genetic services, including genetic evaluation, genetic counseling, prenatal diagnosis, carrier detection, teratologic evaluation, and resource information.

Current activity in Wisconsin and several other states[14] is directed toward establishment of state networks of regional centers to serve their residents more equitably. For instance, the Statewide Genetics Services Network Project is designed to coordinate services throughout Wisconsin and on its borders; to plan and develop training and outreach programs; and to facilitate data collection, documentation, and exchange (see Figure 5.2). In addition to providing these services, the program eventually is expected to allow the clinicians actually performing the services to be freed somewhat from time-consuming administrative duties. In Wisconsin, four levels of key groups are involved in planning and developing the genetic services network: (1) genetic professionals,[15] who meet regularly to determine program goals and ways to approach common clinical problems; (2) an advisory committee composed of representatives from state agencies, charitable organizations,[16] and consumers; (3) appropriate state agencies;[17] and (4) genetic contacts throughout the state.[18]

For each of the states with integrated approaches toward genetic health services, there are many others with fragmented or otherwise inadequate programs. Furthermore, most ongoing programs tend to focus on counseling and diagnosis and often do not deal with the broader social questions raised by human genetic and reproductive intervention that are explored in

FIGURE 5.2
Activities of Wisconsin Statewide Genetics Services Network Project

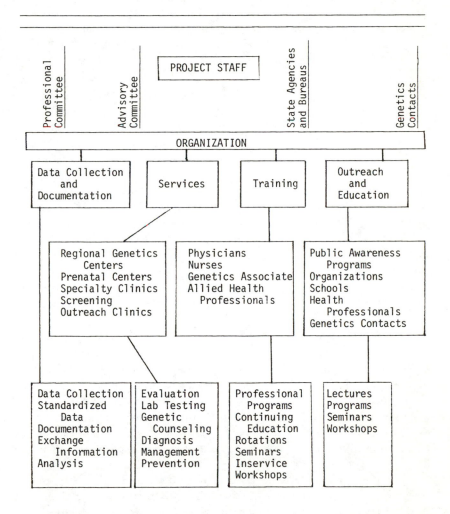

Source: Renata Laxova and Raymond Kessel, "Project to Develop Statewide Genetics Services Network in Wisconsin." Presentation at 1979 Great Plains Clinical Genetics Society meeting.

this study. Although implementation of genetic services appears well served by many state efforts, a long-range national genetic policy appears necessary if all Americans are to share in these services. To a large extent, the scope of genetic education and services available is still dependent on the state in which people reside and whether or not they live in an urban center. The few resources currently directed toward genetic services, therefore, continue to be distributed unequally in the United States.

Allocation of Resources for Genetic Technology

Public policies relating to the acceptance or rejection of any technology are made within a complex political-social-cultural context that must take into account intense competition among varied interests, public expectations, and the personal biases of a range of decision makers. Certainly, policy regarding genetic technology is no exception. According to Nelkin (1977: 397), three factors are crucial to the allocation of public resources to specific research areas: (1) national objectives, (2) the perceived urgency of specific problems, and (3) the convergence of the political will with technological opportunity. The problem must not only be viewed as urgent, but also be seen as a matter of public concern with resulting pressure for immediate resolution through governmental action. These perceptions of urgency may be influenced by interest groups, but perhaps the "overriding factor shaping priorities for science and technology is the convergence of technological opportunity; that is the availability of an appropriate technology, with political readiness to accept technological change" (Nelkin, 1977: 399).

Although human genetic technology is an area in which appropriate techniques are available, there is as yet no consensus as to the necessity of placing a high priority on their widespread application. Major differences of opinion exist even within the scientific community concerning the public-health threat of genetic disease. Disagreement concerning the implications of a deteriorating gene pool or even its presence is further evidence of the ambiguity of the problem. Debate over whether this should be a matter of utmost public concern and therefore of high priority in the allocation of resources is still in the preliminary stages.

Until now, human genetic research has not fared well compared to research on cancer or even the less-emphasized cardiovascular diseases.[19] Another factor working against genetic disease research is the high priority placed on diseases of the aged versus those of children.[20] Despite the scope of genetic disease in the United States and the availability of technologies to reduce it, human genetic technology has not received a reasonable level of funding relative to other areas of health technology. It is not at present seen as a crucial national objective, as is cancer, nor is it perceived as either a politically attractive or an immediate problem.

Rogers (1962) offers five characteristics of genetic innovation that affect its chances of adoption: (1) its relative advantage over competing ideas; (2) its compatibility with existing values and practices; (3) its complexity; (4) its divisibility, which allows for use on a limited basis; and (5) its communicability. Most genetic and reproductive technologies have difficulties with the last four factors. In addition to their perceived threat to existing values by small but intense minorities, the complexity of these technologies results in attempts at simplification that distort the issues. Furthermore, genetic technologies are to some extent separable, allowing for their use on a limited basis, yet often criticism focuses on the indivisible nature of genetic technology and the linkages to a variety of potential uses. This in part reflects a strategy of those opposed to genetic intervention and also illustrates the susceptibility of genetic technology to such attacks. The "slippery slope" argument is used frequently by those who wish to emphasize the lack of discrete divisions between potential extentions of use and the more extreme applications that follow acceptance of a particular technique.[21]

Although genetic technology promises many benefits, the extent to which it is applied in the future depends on how it is perceived by public authorities, the general public, and interest groups. If it is viewed as a crisis and interests can be mobilized to support it, the obstacles reviewed above might be minimized. Conversely, if these technologies continue to be seen as a threat to the basic values of even a small proportion of the population, utilization will remain difficult and the allocation of resources in these areas will be constrained. The cost-benefit and technology-assessment techniques described in this chapter are probably necessary in order to set public priorities and allocate limited public resources, but they must be applied with caution in this sensitive and volatile policy area.

6
Conclusions

Each of the first five chapters has drawn heavily from literature in bioethics, human genetics, and the social sciences in order to synthesize that vast array of information into a meaningful examination of the political aspects of human genetic technology. This chapter serves primarily to summarize the implications of the materials introduced in earlier chapters. Additionally, it presents the views of the author concerning what options are available to us and what priorities ought to be established regarding the role of the government in genetic research and application.

Emerging Genetic Issues in the United States

The continually expanding arsenal of genetic and reproductive technologies described in Chapter 2 is certain to produce fertile ground for political controversy. One premise of this study is that biomedical applications, especially those relating to human genetic intervention, will emerge as major political issues in the coming decades as we attempt to grapple with their widespread social ramifications. One need not search long to demonstrate the increasing visibility and political salience of these technologies. Fetal research, in vitro fertilization, prenatal diagnosis, genetic screening, and various negative and positive eugenic applications already are the object of close government scrutiny and involvement. New genetic innovations, especially those relating to genetic engineering and therapy, are bound to accentuate the role of the government. The reasons for politicization of genetic technology are complex; this study has summarized the more critical ones.

One factor drawing genetic issues into the public arena is the severe value conflict produced when accelerating advances in genetic technology challenge traditional values. Not only are these values among the most basic, relating to individual rights and human existence itself, but in addition they are being changed over a very short time span. Normally, the alteration of values and beliefs is more gradual and is eased in through a socialization process. This incremental process recently appears to have been bypassed in favor of more dramatic and sporadic shifts in response to new technological innovations in genetics. This has altered expectations and caused uncertainty over further changes.

The nature of genetic technologies causes concern among many observers because they raise the specter of the implementation of eugenic programs and of social control through manipulation of human genes. Although this study has demonstrated that it is unlikely that genetic technologies would be used in the near future for mass eugenic programs, these technologies inherently raise problems relating to reproductive rights, due process, and other political-legal concepts. Furthermore, due to the selective nature of genetic disease, attempts to intervene are seen as threats by many minorities and are therefore met with suspicion, fear, or hostility. For example, bad experiences with poorly planned and implemented sickle-cell screening programs in the early 1970s were heightened because of their concentration on blacks. Stigmatization and invasion of privacy in any case should be a matter of grave concern; when they are directed at minorities, whether by design or not, they become highly volatile political issues.

If all by-products of genetic applications were negative, leading to value conflict and social disruption, the issue would disappear. However, genetic technologies promise broad opportunities and potentially vast benefits to many people. They are viewed by some as the means to reduce or eliminate particular genetic disorders and by others as the means through which humans will be able to control their destiny. It is this promise of vast benefits combined with the potential threats to various conceptions of rights and human life that raises the issue to the level of political conflict.

The second factor contributing to the politicization of genetic technology is also a product of the value conflict. Technology and the specialization it encourages has multiplied the number of interests, each with its own particular goals and demands for action. Ultimately, these conflicting demands must be resolved in the political process. As each technical application benefits some interests and deprives others, especially in times of scarce public resources, some groups have much at stake in the acceptance or rejection of particular technologies. The demand for access to policymakers and for representation in decision-making mechanisms has increased as these groups compete for the constrained public support.

The establishment of these interest groups has been reinforced by the advocacy climate that came largely out of the environmentalist movement and the Vietnam protests of the 1960s and 1970s. Group advocacy on issues has become a common political activity, to some extent replacing traditional institutions such as political parties. Freedom of information, open access to government, and group action have become political code words. This climate has accelerated the demand for a public role in a wide range of areas, including biomedical research, and has led to increased concern for public input through hearings, impact statements, and public-opinion surveys.

This new or at least revitalized form of political activity has been supplemented by an acceptance of the mass media in a more active advocacy role. The mass media, especially television, provide a forum for these groups and increase their ability to carry their messages to the broader public. As noted earlier, genetic technologies, because they are considered newsworthy, are certain to receive widespread coverage in the press. Reports on the Nobel sperm bank, the "test-tube" baby, and biohazards of recombinant DNA research apparently make attractive headlines. Although media coverage is often oversimplified and at times misleading or sympathetic toward one position, it does help to define the issues and mobilize public concern for the issues.

A final factor leading to the inclusion of genetic issues in the political arena results from the expanded role of government in general, and especially in genetic research and application. This follows the rapid increase of government funding of biomedicine. As costs in these areas have risen dramatically, the government has assumed an increasing proportion of them, both directly through funding of research and applied programs and indirectly through Medicare and Medicaid. As this comes at a time when federal and state resources are tightened substantially, it is not surprising that expenditures of all public funds, including those for genetic programs, are scrutinized very closely. The demand for more public control over governmental expenditures and for more representation in the policymaking process reinforces the assumptions of cost-benefit analysis, cost effectiveness, and broad technology assessment.

Despite the inherent fears of most politicians of becoming involved with volatile and emotional moral issues, their responsiveness to perceived pressures from interest groups and the media has produced an awareness of and concern for the issues raised by genetic and reproductive technologies. The rapid passage of PKU and sickle-cell screening programs was largely a response to pressures for action from one side. Now that opposition has developed, it is more likely that future attempts at human genetic intervention of any type will generate considerably more political controversy and become important matters of public concern.

Defining the Public Role in
Human Genetic Intervention

Given the emerging political implications of human genetic technologies and the increased awareness of the public issues encompassing genetic intervention, one would expect to see more effective governmental activity than here described. However, another thesis central to this study is that the political process as now structured creates almost insurmountable obstacles to the resolution and even the definition of the dilemmas raised by these technologies. The U.S. political system is highly fragmented, with authority for policymaking dispersed among a myriad of public agencies at the national, state, and local levels. Each of these decision-making bodies is protective of its own jurisdiction and wary of other agencies that might infringe upon it. Decisions are based primarily on immediate or short-range objectives that maximize not the interests of the general public but rather the more narrow interests of the most powerful groups in each area of influence. Under these circumstances, policy most often is the product of a bargaining process and represents some sort of compromise among the interests able to compete for public resources. This process is not well suited for determining public policy regarding use or nonuse of human genetic technologies.

The record of U.S. political institutions in making decisions on issues with substantial moral content is less than encouraging. The intensity, complexity, and sensitivity of the concerns raised by the genetic and reproductive innovations described in this book demonstrate clearly the added difficulties encountered in making policy on such matters. Any government involvement in genetic research or application requires substantially more foresight and rigorous, comprehensive assessment than is now available. Also, political ambitions and narrow group interests must give way to a balanced and future-oriented policy process. From agenda setting to program termination, the process must be made responsive to a more broadly defined "public interest," one that accounts for the interests of the affected persons, the parents and family, society, and future generations. This task is not easy but will only become more difficult as decisions are delayed. Some of the trends reviewed in Chapters 4 and 5 reflect at least a recognition of the scope and intensity of the issues raised by technological advances in genetics.

Before significant progress in defining the proper role of government in genetic intervention can be made, several conceptual distinctions must be clarified. First, much of the controversy surrounding public involvement in genetic decisions stems from the ambiguity and confusion as to what actions constitute "public involvement." This results in part from the conscious effort of opponents of genetic intervention to focus on actions involving possible mandated eugenic programs that violate individual rights, while proponents place emphasis on the possibility of government prohibition of specific genetic research and/or applications. As noted in Chapter 4, government involvement more accurately comprises a continuum of actions ranging from prohibition to compulsory use of a technology. If a meaningful dialogue is to exist, more attention must be directed toward the less severe forms of involvement — regulation and encouragement of the utilization of particular techniques. The examples frequently proposed by observers fearful of public involvement have a tendency to obscure rational consideration of less intrusive government action. Although the prohibition or mandated use of certain genetic techniques might prove appropriate, the more immediate role of the government should be to assess the technologies, refine the issues, and propose policy alternatives upon which informed and representative decisions can be made. It would seem that the common result of this procedure will be a combination of funding and regulation of genetic programs deemed to be of high priority for the good of all interests. With few exceptions, such programs would be conducted on a voluntary basis, although a wide range of incentives is available for use where appropriate and vital.

Another factor contributing to the emergent debate over human genetic intervention is the inability or unwillingness of many people to distinguish between the technological developments themselves and their potential uses. It is apparent that each genetic technique has a variety of possible applications or extensions, depending on the desires of those who would use it. In addition, the means through which a specific genetic policy is implemented can alter the political ramifications drastically. Although the technologies themselves do not infringe upon individual rights as we normally define them, and in some cases might extend these rights, certain uses of any of these technologies represent tangible intrusions into procreative freedoms. For instance, the technique of in vitro fertilization can be used alternately as a method of overcoming blocked oviducts, a means leading to a variety of surrogate motherhood forms, a technique for basic research in fertility and contraceptive studies, or one element in a mass eugenic program. Similarly, artificial insemination, sterilization, prenatal diagnosis, carrier screening, and other techniques described in this book are all open to a broad range of applications. Therefore, each genetic technology can be interpreted in completely different ways depending not only on a person's value framework but also on which uses appear probable for that person. Not surprisingly, those opposed to genetic technology focus primarily on the potential eugenic applications of each technique, while those favoring genetic technology deal almost exclusively with clinical applications and minimize the eugenic aspect. The result again is to obscure the debate and generate controversy. Comprehensive technology assessment should provide a realistic appraisal of the potential uses and abuses of each innovation before it becomes commonplace.

According to Hetman (1977: 5) there are three main courses of action possible at this time: (1) continuation of uncontrolled scientific and technological development, (2) termination of scientific and technological advancement, or (3) socially responsible management of scientific and technological innovation. Given the tremendous benefits and risks inherent in human genetic technology, this study concurs with Hetman's contention that the third strategy is the only reasonable choice. Although the selection of this approach is a difficult one for policymakers, as it forces them to assess the broad implications of each technology and make decisions often unpopular with politically important interests, neither of the other strategies is appropriate in light of the developments described in this study.

Genetic Priorities in the United States

This book has argued that all technical applications are made within a complex cultural-social-political context. The issues raised by human genetic technologies are among the most sensitive and volatile the government has faced. In addition, the technologies are advancing so quickly that the public sector has little time to appraise the state of the art without becoming woefully out of touch with the technical possibilities. Although the issues created by genetic technology are being drawn into the political spectrum, the political agencies are ill prepared to deal with them.

In order to produce a meaningful framework within which political decisions can be made that account for the variety of interests affected by genetic technology, a multifaceted and intensive effort is necessary. First, there is an eminent need for creation of a continuing mechanism for reviewing the social and ethical dimensions of genetic technologies throughout their development. Although various national commissions and governmental agencies have dealt with specific social aspects or particular techniques, in general their time frame has been limited and their attention constrained by prior commitments or assumptions. Broad technology assessment, both of specific techniques and the cumulative impact of human genetic technology on society, must be forthcoming if we are to have a reasonable chance of directing their development and use.

Second, high priority must be directed toward improving genetic education if we are to utilize technologies effectively and minimize their abuses. McInerney (1979: 3), for example, cites the lack of public understanding about human genetics as a key impediment to effective genetic counseling and asserts that the average person is unaware of the relationship of one's genetic constitution to matters of health and disease. "For the lay person 'genetic diseases' are rare occurrences that always affect someone else." Scriver and Clow (1979: 9) talk of decreasing the "prevailing illiteracy" in human genetics, and Childs (1979: 7) notes that provision for teaching genetics to medical students is "at best irregular and at worst nonexistent."

The Center for Education in Human and Medical Genetics, which is spearheading efforts to improve genetic education, views this education as a multifaceted, multistage process beginning in elementary school and continuing throughout adult life (Biological Sciences Curriculum Study, 1978: 21). Formal education should not only include the transfer of technical genetic knowledge, but also produce an understanding of the social and ethical dilemmas raised by genetic technologies. Students ought to be aware of the implications of genetic intervention and have a much firmer grounding in the mechanics of human genetics. Due to the politically sensitive nature of genetics, this must be done with great care and attention to the social context of genetic variation. In addition, public education is crucial for expanding public understanding of the options available, increasing public awareness of the complexity and importance of the issues raised by genetic technology, and encouraging public involvement in genetic policymaking.

Prior to the implementation of any genetic program a full-scale education campaign must be conducted to inform the public of the services available and to assure a basic understanding of the objectives, rationale, and meaning of the program. Efforts to inform the clinical and research communities of the social and political implications of their work must be extended and strengthened. Finally, policymakers themselves, whether elected officials, public employees, or private officials, must be convinced of the importance of these issues and the need for decisive yet well-reasoned responses to these challenges. It is unlikely that the resources needed to conduct a comprehensive education program in human genetic technology can be mobilized without active government support.

Ultimately, it seems, the government does have a responsibility to ensure the best possible uses of genetic and reproductive technologies and to guarantee that social abuses do not occur. The public has a substantial stake in how genetic intervention programs are designed and, to the maximum extent possible, all such programs must be directed toward the needs and well-being of the participants. The provision of such services to those who desire them within a framework of broader national goals of reducing genetic disease appears to be a reasonable application of governmental authority. At the same time, any government involvement must be limited to the least intrusive alternative possible in each case. Programs must be designed to maximize the rights of individuals and reflect community goals and attitudes. Voluntary informed consent is a critical concept for any genetic intervention program.

Although some of the trends in social values discussed in Chapter 1 and the moves toward cost-benefit analysis described in Chapter 5 imply potential support for eugenic programs, values concerning human dignity and autonomy basic to our culture and our social institutions seem to preclude the enforcement of genetic intervention solely on eugenic grounds. Given the fine lines of distinction between the various applications of any single technique and the different degrees of government involvement in implementing genetic technologies, we must constantly be on the alert for misuses.

Government encouragement and regulation of human genetic intervention appears imminent and on balance positive, but there are significant dangers inherent in expanding government's role without more public awareness, debate, and input. Also required is a thorough reexamination of the political process and substantial modification where appropriate so that it might become more attuned to these issues of the coming decades. Although decisive political action concerning human genetic technologies is needed soon, we still have time for thorough investigation of the ramifications and serious consideration of what the societal priorities ought to be. The time for reflection is slipping away, however, as the technologies become more inclusive and more entrenched in the political process.

Notes

Chapter 1

1. Emphasis in this study is on science and technology directed toward technological implementation. The demarcation between "science" and "technology" is less clear than some observers assume and no attempt is made here to enter the debate.

2. We must be cautious not to assume that these models pit scientists against humanists. Many of the strongest proponents of genetic-oriented models are biologists and much of the opposition to that model comes from those in the "soft sciences" and from ethicists, although there is a wide variety of views within each community. The major distinction is most often one of degree: What is the mix of genetic and environmental factors?

3. Others (King and Wilson, 1975) have estimated that humans share approximately 99 percent of their genes with chimpanzees. This reduces even further the possible genetic variation among humans than suggested by Corning.

4. See Cavalli-Sforza (1974) for a history of hereditary mutation using the sickle-cell gene as an example.

5. Baer (1977: 86–91) provides an excellent bibliography on research on environmental hazards.

6. Although emphasis here is on humans, direct genetic intervention is new for both humans and nonhumans. Reproductive controls are the basis for plant and domestic-animal genetics.

7. The goal of eugenics is improvement of the human species by decreasing the propagation of the physically and mentally handicapped (negative eugenics) and by increasing that of the more desirable types (positive eugenics).

8. Living wills are legal documents granting terminally ill persons the right to authorize by prior directive the withdrawal of life-sustaining procedures when death is believed imminent. Although only a handful of states have passed enabling legislation as of March 1, 1977, at least 49 death-with-dignity bills were pending in 33 states (Ramsey, 1978: 318). The vast implications of such legislation and the fear by some that this action will lead ultimately to active euthanasia has raised considerable attention. For a detailed look at the California Natural Death Act see Ramsey (1978: 318–332).

9. See Griffin (1976) for the counterargument that animals, too, have an intellectual awareness.

10. More recent sickle-cell programs have included better counseling, education, and follow-up procedures and have shifted screening from the preschool-age cohort

to young adults where it might be more effective.

11. By classifying these individuals into three groups, there is no presumption that each category represents a unified ethical perspective. In fact, within each group are individuals with vastly different moral justifications for their stand for or against genetic intervention. Also, in disussing ethical frameworks here, it is crucial to distinguish the present emphasis from that of most ethical theories. Generally, discussions of ethical decisions focus on personal-level choices. For instance, is it moral for a woman to undergo in vitro fertilization or have an abortion? The ethical framework at that level provides justification for one's choice and enumerates circumstances and/or rules under which the choice is made. Ethics here is applied instead at the societal level; questions of right or wrong are defined in the public dimension. Is it moral for society to intervene in human evolution? If it is, what conditions and rules apply in coming to that decision? Although the private and public dimensions are not mutually exclusive, and the latter is based on the former, it is vital to recognize the distinction and note that emphasis here is directed to the latter.

12. The five models of genetic responsibility presented by Twiss (1974) are: (1) parental role, (2) parent–family member role, (3) parent-citizen role, (4) parent–species member role, and (5) parent–ethnic population role.

Chapter 2

1. Walters (1978a) also utilizes this broader definition of genetic technology.

2. For a review of the debate over recombinant DNA research including the philosophical, legal, and social issues see Jackson and Stich (1979). Also minimized here are the impressive advancements being made in gene therapy. For a summary of these recent developments see Stine (1977: 472–482). Also, Volume 265 of the *Annals of the New York Academy of Sciences* (1976) is devoted to the ethical and scientific issues posed by human uses of molecular genetics (see Twiss; Beckwith; Lappé; and Morison [all 1976]).

3. NIH (1979: 27) notes that the percent of infant deaths resulting from congenital malformations has risen from 6.4 in 1915 to 17.3 in 1976.

4. Heller (1973) notes that approximately 3.6 percent of the cases are of translocation type.

5. Conversely, available data, although still inconclusive, demonstrate little if any increase in frequency of Down's syndrome with advanced paternal age (Erickson, 1979).

6. Marjorie Guthrie, widow of folksinger Woody Guthrie (who died of Huntington's disease), provided much of the impetus for publicizing the disease and increasing congressional and public awareness.

7. Fetoscopy utilizes a fiber optic endoscope that, under ultrasound and a local anesthetic, is inserted through the abdomen of the pregnant woman. This procedure allows the physician to see the surface of the fetus in 2 to 4 cm segments. Fetal blood samples, if needed, are generally taken from the vessels on the inside surface of the placenta. See NIH (1979: 108–118) for more details.

8. For instance, in San Francisco this rate is approximately 40 percent. According to Milunsky and Atkins (1975: 231), prenatal genetic studies are routinely recommended for women over 35 in Boston.

9. Milunsky (1977: 172) notes three additional rare sex-linked disorders that can now be identified prenatally.

10. On the other hand, there are instances in which gaps in technology and knowledge lead to abortion of unaffected or minimally affected fetuses. Examples include X-linked disorders such as hemophilia, in which 50 percent of the male fetuses aborted would have been normal, and the lack of specificity of alpha fetoprotein determination, which might lead to decisions to abort a fetus whose defect might be minor and correctable. See Lebacqz (1973) for a strong condemnation of prenatal diagnosis and selective abortion. She concludes that selective abortion, even more than abortion on demand, threatens basic human rights, and she urges instead that more public funds be given to support families with children with genetic defects.

11. Although genetic counseling is a central aspect of genetic intervention, it has been consciously excluded from this study so that full attention can be directed toward the technologies themselves. For good summaries of the issues surrounding counseling see Stevenson et al. (1977), Lebel (1978), and Y. E. Hsia et al. (1979).

12. Even screening research designed to collect data concerning the frequency and phenotypic variation of the XYY complement in the population has been terminated due to public pressure.

13. Although the XYY condition has not been used successfully in the United States in order to gain a defendant's freedom, in Australia a defendant was acquitted of a murder charge on this basis. In the recent murder case of San Francisco's Mayor Moscone and City Supervisor Milk, the defense argued that the accused suffered from genetically caused melancholia and should not be held responsible for his actions (*Time,* May 28, 1979: 57). The defendant in this case received a very light sentence. If XYY or other genetic anomalies are accepted as a proper defense, is it possible that society will favor protecting itself by incarcerating all such individuals before they commit the crimes for which they are supposedly genetically predisposed.

14. Although some physicians still feel that amniocentesis and other scarce diagnostic techniques should be performed only if the mother expresses prior commitment to abort a diagnosed defective fetus, Milunsky (1977: 185) contends that the woman must be able to use information as she sees fit and he therefore rejects the prior-commitment rationale. He points out that when faced with the prospect of bearing a fetus so identified, most parents opt to abort despite their opinions stated before the diagnosis.

15. These include methylmalonic acidura, for which massive doses of vitamin B_{12} are injected into the mother during pregnancy; hypothyroidism; and adrenogenital syndrome (Milunsky, 1977: 176–177).

16. For more details on Tay-Sachs disease and screening, see Kaback and O'Brien (1973) and Goodman (1979).

17. Bowman (1978) gives examples of the infringement on rights of individuals identified as having the sickle-cell trait. These include airlines' grounding of black

employees with the trait, the need for signed waivers of responsibility in order to enter the U.S. Air Force Academy, higher premiums or cancellation of insurance policies, and classmates' taunts and rejection.

18. At present, PKU tests are offered in all 50 states, although there is no ena-bling legislation in 7 of them. Only Washington, D.C., lacks a PKU screening pro-gram. It was abandoned in the mid-1970s after several years without uncovering a single case of PKU in the predominantly black population. See Steiner and Smith (1975) and Reilly (1977) for in-depth surveys of these screening programs and laws.

19. "Multiphasic" refers to procedures that test one sample simultaneously for several abnormalities. Massachusetts' multiphasic metabolic screening program, for example, makes use of three separate tests to screen for approximately ten disorders: an umbilical cord blood sample at birth, a peripheral blood sample at two to four days (normal PKU) and urine samples when the newborn is three to four weeks old (Lappé and Roblin, 1974: 8–9). According to Nyhan and Edelson (1976: 229), future screening for metabolic disease will involve multiple testing from a single drop of blood from the newborn. Research is being conducted at Stanford University to identify and sort fetal blood cells that cross the placenta into the mother's bloodstream (Iverson, 1978). Although there are substantial technical problems to overcome before this cell sorting process can be used clinically, success could lead to prenatal diagnosis of many disorders through a maternal blood test in-stead of amniocentesis and early identification and possible treatment of metabolic disorders in the fetus.

20. Nitowsky (1973: 1299) suggests that although the primary role of screening is preventative, it also "permits early detection of poorly understood diseases and pro-vides an opportunity to study them and to elucidate their pathophysiology." Guthrie (1973) also believes that the data obtained through mass screening is an invaluable fringe benefit as long as it does not increase the cost.

21. According to McLaren (1973: 5), a priori one would expect AI babies to ex-hibit less mortality and fewer congenital defects than normal as "considerable efforts are made to synchronize insemination and ovulation, so the risk of fertilization of stale eggs is correspondingly diminished." Stale eggs, those which have been ovulated one or two days before insemination, have been linked with higher in-cidences of some chromosomal abnormalities.

22. In February 1980, front-page headlines announced that three women had been inseminated by semen from a "Nobel sperm bank" established by California business tycoon Robert K. Graham. The only Nobel Prize winner to admit having his sperm in the bank was William B. Shockley, an outspoken proponent of various eugenic programs designed to increase "people at the top of the population." See Broad (1980) for further discussion of this sperm bank.

23. Although the probability is low, current reliance on a small number of donors in medical centers could result in unconscious incest between second-generation siblings.

24. See, for example, *Doornbus* v. *Doornbus,* No. 54, S. 13, 875 Sup. Ct. Cook Co. (November 1954).

25. *People* v. *Sorenson,* 66 Cal. Rptr. 7 (1968).

26. Annas (1979: 14) contends that the term "donors" is misapplied, as virtually

all are paid for their service. He suggests that sperm "vendors" is a more appropriate term and that although the distinction might seem trivial, it may have legal consequences.

27. A pending class-action suit on behalf of approximately 50 clients of a bankrupt San Francisco sperm bank that allowed their frozen sperm to thaw is only one example of legal issues raised by this technology.

28. This concern for a unique genotype inevitably leads to a comparison of clones with identical twins. Although such twins share a genotype, however, they are the product of chance, not a purposive effort to design them after a particular cell donor. Also, both are different from their parents and have been accepted by society as biological as well as social individuals. The status of clones, on the other hand, is uncertain and must be faced prior to the first clone.

29. See Farrow and Juberg (1969) for a discussion of coefficients of relatedness. Obviously, the growing trend toward consensual mating or illegitimate births, often the result of incest, demonstrates the limited impact of marriage restrictions.

30. In Georgia, a male may marry his daughter or grandmother and an uncle may marry his niece. In Rhode Island, the uncle-niece marriage is permitted among Hebrews only.

31. For instance, despite advances in genetic knowledge concerning carriers, there are presently no legal or social constraints on marriage or mating between two carriers of the same trait.

32. For a description of the federal government's role in sterilization, see DHEW (1978a), especially pages 17-1 to 17-14.

Chapter 3

1. For more detailed coverage of bioethics see Beauchamp and Childress (1979). The *Bibliography of Society, Ethics and the Life Sciences* of the Hastings Center offers a good general summary of the literature by area, and the *Bibliography of Bioethics*, edited by LeRoy Walters, offers a more inclusive listing of bioethics topics and a bioethics thesaurus.

2. For a detailed examination of the policy problems and options raised by the concept of brain death, see Veatch (1976), especially pages 55 to 76.

3. See Tooley (1972) for a discussion of the terms "person" and "human being" relative to the right to life.

4. Actually this is less altruistic than it appears as Rawls contends that the social contract will be drawn up from behind a "veil of ignorance." In other words, no person in the original position (a hypothetical situation prior to the establishment of a society) will know what his or her lot in life will be. Under such conditions, to protect themselves, all persons will attempt to maximize the least advantaged position, lest they find themselves in it after the contract is cast.

5. Rawls has been attacked by egalitarians for what is seen as his lack of enthusiasm for economic redistribution. See Bloom (1975) and Wright (1977).

6. For examples of two perspectives at variance see Mills (1959) and Dahl (1967). Dahl sees a pluralistic system resulting from the U.S. political context while Mills

sees the system as a power elite.

7. Other categories of individuals whose values become an integral part of the human genetic intervention process include physicians, scientists, and counselors (Hirschhorn, 1976). Also, Hare (1976) talks about the rights of the next in queue: healthy individuals who would be born if unhealthy prior siblings had been or are aborted.

8. Obviously, this approach can be attacked as presenting unsolvable problems relating to purely hypothetical persons or potential persons. Future persons and the unborn do not fit our predisposition concerning personhood, but they must be dealt with somehow. For more eloquent discussions of these concerns see Parfit (1976) and Hare (1976).

9. This latter argument seems especially weak justification in light of the small proportion of the total health dollars currently directed toward the severely abnormal.

10. For instance, Tay-Sachs disease is always expressed through an early and painful death, but the expression of many anomolies such as Down's syndrome varies substantially among those affected.

11. Despite the current interest of the U.S. government in advancing the rights of the handicapped, society as a whole appears unwilling or unable to grant the mentally handicapped equal status.

12. Often this is stated as the rights of the family, though legally the rights refer primarily to the parents. Despite this, siblings and other more distant family members are affected, both materially and emotionally, by any genetic decision. Meyerowitz and Lipkin (1976), for instance, note that the impact on healthy children of knowing that a potential sibling was destroyed because it was not healthy raises serious problems. Conversely, the birth of a genetically affected child in a family might be a heavy financial and emotional strain. In no case is an easy solution forthcoming.

13. Traditional custody proceedings after divorce often manifest the concept of children as property to somehow be divided.

14. This uncertainty, according to Rawls, will force one to provide "just savings" for future generations. This raises the question of whether the veil-of-ignorance concept (see note 4) can be used to make decisions on genetic intervention and fetus rights. What alternative would rational people take if they had no idea as to their fate?

15. This might be tested in the courts through "torts for wrongful life," in which children sue their parents for damages due to their birth with particular genetic defects. Although such damage claims until now have been denied by the courts, new technologies in prenatal diagnosis and screening might produce more favorable grounds for action if the parents fail to take what is considered reasonable precautions to avoid the situation. If such torts are successful, they might serve as a form of eugenics (Grant and Blank, 1980).

16. For example, although Beecher (1974: 110) generally opposes state intervention, he admits that the "collection of individuals called society tend to invade the individual's privacy." The test he suggests is whether the threat or invasion is unreasonable or intolerable.

17. For a summary of principles of justice see Beauchamp and Childress (1979: 168–200). Other theories of distributive justice include egalitarian, libertarian, Marxist, utilitarian, and entitlement.

18. Of course it is a possibility, however remote, that a vigorous eugenic program could produce persons of great genius who, in turn, would discover cures for ailments and thereby benefit the least advantaged.

19. Justice Holmes's terminology is from *Buck* v. *Bell* (1927).

Chapter 4

1. Specific opinions tend to fluctuate, but basic political values have been found to be quite stable and more resistant to alteration (Jaros, 1973). Also, as socialization tends to be cumulative in nature, values learned earliest in life appear to be most persistent.

2. In addition to the four types of action described here, another governmental response could be nonaction. In fact, many political decisions are nondecisions in that no action is taken or action is postponed. Given the nature of the genetic issues of the coming decades, it is unlikely that the government can long continue this route of nonaction. Another distinction made is between self-regulation and government regulation. Bass (1974: 625) sees four alternatives for evaluating eugenics: (1) self-regulation, (2) advisory bodies, (3) government funding policies, and (4) direct government control through legislation.

3. Early in 1980 the Supreme Court ordered states to pay for all "medically necessary" abortions for Medicaid patients, pending the outcome of an appeal of the Hyde Amendment. Furthermore, the Court agreed to expedite consideration of two cases challenging that amendment and schedule arguments in April 1980.

4. Although the broad moral issues do not appear to be amenable to bargaining and negotiation, specific biomedical applications, for example, recombinant DNA procedures, are.

5. Ray, however, examined only three states (Connecticut, Wisconsin, and Michigan) from 1893 to 1969.

6. Many state constitutions have provisions for special sessions to be called by the governor or through other means. As usual, the procedures and constraints vary considerably from state to state.

7. See Powledge (1979: 16) for an example of the impact of such torts on medical practice and the pressures they exert on physicians.

8. Even the relatively rare injunctions on future actions are commonly based on evidence of harm by similar actions in the past.

9. For further information on criminal cases involving submission of evidence concerning the XYY complement of the defendant, see Chapter 2.

10. Although the focus of this book is on more narrowly genetic issues, this discussion of policy encompasses the more inclusive category of biomedical issues. Because of the interrelationships among biomedical technologies, it is difficult to draw clear lines of distinction and isolate genetic policies.

11. See Stencel (1977) for an examination of abortion as an issue during the 1976

electoral campaign.

12. This compares to 73 and 39 percent, respectively, in the 1962 survey.

13. For comparison, this figure is approximately the same as the proportion of the public that reported hearing or reading about the Watergate scandals at the height of the congressional hearings in 1974.

14. This again illustrates the incredible reliance some people have on physicians in matters relating to use of reproductive technologies. It also demonstrates the responsibility of physicians to be aware of the genetic and reproductive matters of their patients.

15. Chulew (1980), for instance, lists 75 national organizations that provide services for persons with various genetic disorders or for their families.

16. This committee was joined in lobbying efforts by the Huntington's Chorea Foundation, the Hereditary Disease Foundation, and the National Huntington's Disease Association.

17. Problems of congressional hearings include poor congressional attendance, unbalanced testimony, unequal access, limited distribution of the findings, and the lack of genuine, structured debate.

18. The Ethics Advisory Board membership includes seven physicians, two lawyers, one businessperson, one philosopher, one religious ethicist, and one representative from a charitable organization (United Way).

19. The Ethics Advisory Board was not included in the 1981 budget because the administration decided to request funding only for the new commission designed to study ethical problems in medicine. As a result, the Board must terminate its ongoing work by September, 1980. According to the Hastings Center (1980: 3), if the Ethics Advisory Board is dissolved and no alternate body is named to take over its functions, "in effect a moratorium will be declared on certain types of research, primarily fetal research."

20. For a discussion of NIH policymaking and criticisms of it see Marston (1978).

21. One provision of this act in which substantial progress has been made is in information collection and dissemination. The National Clearinghouse for Human Genetic Diseases, established under this act in October 1978, is active in the publication of educational and informational materials, bibliographies, and directories of informational and clinical resources. It also has catalogued federal and state legislation dealing with genetics. Currently, a 27-member advisory council is being established. Substantial initiative in genetic education, for elementary and high schools as well as allied health professions and the general public, has come from the Center for Education in Human and Medical Genetics. Established under grants from the March of Dimes and the National Institutes of Health in 1975, the center is now a continuing program of the Biological Sciences Curriculum Study (BSCS) based in Boulder, Colorado. In addition to producing educational materials and designing curricula, BSCS conducts seminars, conferences, and surveys dealing with many facets of biology including human genetics. For a summary of the background and objectives of this program, see McInerney (1979).

22. See Maryland (1978: 369ff) for provisions of the most recent code.

23. The New York Birth Defects Institute, however, has similar functions.

24. The National Science Foundation Public Service Science Residencies and Internships Program awards 15 to 25 residencies to those with doctoral degrees and 15 to 25 internships annually under the Science for Citizens legislation. The goal of this program is to improve public understanding of science, engineering, and technology and their impact on public policy. Each resident or intern associates with a host organization, which might be an educational organization, a state or local government agency, or a professional association.

25. See Task Force (1976) for details on funding, selection, procedures, and so forth.

Chapter 5

1. For instance, in establishing safety standards in industry and failing to enact strict automobile safety-belt or motorcycle-helmet laws.

2. This is most difficult for health-related programs in which diseases are multifactorial and estimates for future benefits and costs are dependent on a broad range of intervening factors.

3. Or, in the case of some x-linked diseases such as hemophilia, the male fetus.

4. See Riccardi (1976) for a discussion of regional genetic counseling programs.

5. See Chapter 2 for a discussion of these tests.

6. Follow-up procedures are most crucial for females, given the risk of complications should they become pregnant later in life.

7. See Nelson et al. (1978) for a discussion of the Houston Tay-Sachs program and Swint et al. (1979) for a discussion of two separate programs conducted through the auspices of Johns Hopkins University in Baltimore.

8. These estimates come from Kaback and Zeiger (1973) and are twenty thousand and forty thousand dollars, respectively. Powledge (1974: 34) notes that complete care in a Tay-Sachs child's last years can cost forty thousand dollars annually and that, ironically, the better the care is, the longer the child will live.

9. These data indicate that screening money is better spent through community programs conducted infrequently than on continuous in-hospital programs.

10. This minimal figure of two thousand dollars represents the cost of amniocentesis for all four fetuses and abortion for the one in four that is diagnosed as being affected.

11. Blank and Ostheimer (1979) assert the need for social scientists to take a more active role in evaluating the public-policy implications of biomedical technology, including a wide range of genetic applications.

12. This always represents a value judgment as no technological application is absolutely safe. "Acceptable risk" is subjective.

13. Lubs (1976) contends that we must reexamine and most likely modify our attitudes toward privacy because of the increased availability of genetic information. Steinfels (1974) introduces a method of charting the impact of biomedical developments on five components of individualism including human dignity, privacy, self-fulfillment, autonomy, and external freedom.

14. Although no attempt was made here to survey systematically the 50 states,

the several states that consistently emerge in the literature as most progressive in establishing genetic services programs are California, Maryland, New York, Oregon, and Wisconsin.

15. The genetic professionals include clinical geneticists, counselors, and genetic associates from a variety of genetic centers and major hospitals in the state as well as representatives from several specialty clinics.

16. These organizations presently include the March of Dimes and cystic fibrosis, muscular dystrophy, and hemophilia foundations. In addition to providing a broad advisory capacity, these representatives serve to strengthen the lobby for unified genetic services in the legislature.

17. These include agencies dealing with public instruction, developmental disabilities, prevention, community health, and community planning.

18. These genetic contacts are approximately 130 public health nurses, developmental disabilities coordinators, social workers, and other professionals throughout Wisconsin who are aware of families in their area that are in need of genetic services and refer them to the appropriate center.

19. See Strickland (1972) for a review of the origins of national cancer policy, the rise of the cancer research lobby, and an assessment of policy results. Again, one must be cautious not to draw absolute lines between basic research areas as many of the advances in genetic technology, especially those dealing with recombinant DNA, have come from basic cancer research. Also, in vitro fertilization and other reproductive technologies have major applications in a wide variety of research areas, including cancer.

20. For instance, in 1974, $765 million was spent for cancer research, but only $106 million was spent for research on childhood diseases.

21. Some of these linkages are technically easy to visualize, however: the use of in vitro fertilization for surrogate motherhood, amniocentesis for sex preselection, carrier screening for social control over procreation, for example. The "slippery slope" argument assumes that once a technique is available (on the slope), it is difficult if not impossible to limit its use or restrain the momentum; as we become accustomed to application of a technique at one level, moral objections to its use at the next level on the slope are weakened, and so forth down the slope.

References

Abt, C. C. (1977) "The Issue of Social Costs in Cost-Benefit Analysis of Surgery," in J. P. Bunker, B. A. Barnes, and F. Mosteller, eds., *Costs, Risks, and Benefits in Surgery*. New York: Oxford University Press.

Aldrich, H. (1973) "Organizational Boundaries and Interorganizational Conflict," in F. Baker, ed., *Organization Systems*. Homewood, Ill.: Dorsey Press.

Altman, S. H., and R. Blendon, eds. (1979) *Medical Technology: The Culprit Behind Health Care Costs?* Washington, D.C.: Department of Health, Education, and Welfare.

Amdur, R. (1977) "Rawls' Theory of Justice: Domestic and International Perspectives." *World Politics* 29, 3: 438–461.

Annas, G. I. (1979) "Artificial Insemination: Beyond the Best Interests of the Donor." *Hastings Center Report* 9, 4: 14–15, 43.

Babbie, E. R. (1973) *Survey Research Methods*. Belmont, Calif.: Wadsworth.

Bach-y-Rita, G. (1974) "The Prisoner as an Experimental Subject." *Journal of the American Medical Association* 229, 1.

Baer, A. S. (1977) *Heredity and Society: Readings in Social Genetics*. 2nd ed. New York: Macmillan Company.

Banta, H. D., and S. B. Thacker (1979) "Policies Toward Medical Technology: The Case of Electronic Fetal Monitoring." *American Journal of Public Health* 69, 9: 931–935.

Baram, M. S. (1971) "Social Control of Science and Technology." *Science* 172: 535–539.

—— (1973) "Technology Assessment and Social Control." *Science* 180: 465–473.

Barry, B. (1978) "Utilitarianism, Contract Theory and Future Generations." Unpublished manuscript

Bass, I. S. (1974) "Governmental Control of Research in Positive Eugenics." *Journal of Law Reform* 8: 615–630.

Bayles, M. (1976) "Harm to the Unconceived." *Philosophy and Public Affairs* 5, 3: 292–304.

Beauchamp, T. L. (1976) "On Justifications for Coercive Genetic Control," in J. M. Humber and R. F. Almeder, eds, *Biomedical Ethics and the Law*. New York: Plenum Press.

Beauchamp, T. L., and J. F. Childress (1979) *Principles of Biomedical Ethics*. New York: Oxford University Press.

Beckwith, J. (1976) "Social and Political Uses of Genetics in the United States:

Past and Present." *Annals of the New York Academy of Sciences* 265: 46–58.

Beckwith, J., and J. King (1974) "The XYY Syndrome: A Dangerous Myth." *New Scientist* 64: 474–476.

Beecher, H. K. (1968) "Medical Research and the Individual," in D. H. Labby, ed., *Life or Death: Ethics and Options*. Portland, Oregon: Reed College.

––––––– (1974) "Definition of Death: The Individual's Right to Be Let Alone," in *Protection of Human Rights in Light of Scientific and Technological Progress in Biology and Medicine*. Geneva: World Health Organization.

Bender, H. (1974) "The Right to Choose or Ignore," in M. Lipkin and P. Rowley, eds., *Genetic Responsibility: On Choosing Our Children's Genes*. New York: Plenum Press.

Berman, D. R. (1978) *State and Local Politics*. 2nd ed. Boston: Holbrook Press.

Bernstein, M. H. (1955) *Regulating Business by Independent Commission*. Princeton, N.J.: Princeton University Press.

Bessman, S. P., and J. P. Swazey (1971) "Phenylketonuria: A Study of Biomedical Legislation," in E. Mendesohn, J. P. Swazey, and I. Taviss, eds., *Human Aspects of Biomedical Innovation*. Cambridge, Mass.: Harvard University Press.

Best, J. M. (1973) *Public Opinion: Micro and Macro*. Homewood, Ill.: Dorsey Press.

Bevan, W. (1977) "Science in the Penultimate Age." *American Scientist* 65, September-October: 538–546.

Biological Sciences Curriculum Study (1978) "Guidelines for Educational Priorities and Curricular Innovations in the Areas of Human and Medical Genetics." *BSCS Journal* 1, 1: 20–29.

Birch, C., and P. Abrecht (1975) "Findings on Genetics and the Quality of Life," in C. Birch and P. Abrecht, eds., *Genetics and the Quality of Life*. Australia: Pergamon Press.

Black, M. M., and C. Riley (1973) "Moral Issues and Priorities in Biomedical Engineering." *Science, Medicine and Man* 1: 69.

Blank, R. H. (1980) *Political Parties: An Introduction*. Englewood Cliffs, N. J.: Prentice-Hall.

Blank, R. H., and J. M. Ostheimer (1979) "An Overview of Biomedical Policy: Life and Death Issues." *Policy Studies Journal* 8, Winter: 470–479.

Bloom, A. (1975) "Justice: John Rawls vs. The Tradition of Political Philosophy." *American Political Science Review* 69, 2: 648–662.

Blumberg, B. D.; M. S. Golbus; and K. H. Hanson (1975) "The Psychological Sequelae of Abortion Performed for a Genetic Indication." *American Journal of Obstetrics and Gynecology* 122: 799–808.

Blumstein, J. F. (1976) "Constitutional Perspectives on Governmental Decisions Affecting Human Life and Health." *Law and Contemporary Problems* 40, 4: 231–305.

Boffey, P. M. (1976) "Office of Technology Assessment: Bad Marks on Its First Report Card." *Science* 193: 213–215.

––––––– (1976a) "NSF: New Program Criticized as 'Appalling' Subsidy to Activists." *Science* 194: 306.

Boggs, E. M. (1976) "The Making of Public Policy: What Others Do with What We Say We Know," in D. Bergsma and A. E. Pulver, eds., *Developmental Disabilities:*

Psychological and Social Implications. New York: Alan R. Liss.

Boorstein, D. J. (1978) *The Republic of Technology.* New York: Harper & Row.

Bowie, N. E., and R. L. Simon (1977) *The Individual and the Political Order: An Introduction to Social and Political Philosophy.* Englewood Cliffs, N.J.: Prentice-Hall.

Bowman, J. E. (1978) "Social, Legal, and Economic Issues in Sickle Cell Programs," in J. J. Buckley, ed., *Genetics Now: Ethical Issues in Genetic Research.* Washington, D.C.: University Press of America.

Breyer, S., and R. Zeckhauser (1974) "The Regulation of Genetic Engineering," in M. Lipkin and P. Rowley, eds., *Genetic Responsibility: On Choosing Our Children's Genes.* New York: Plenum Press.

Broad, W. J. (1980) "A Bank for Nobel Sperm." *Science* 207, March: 1326-1327.

Brooks, H. (1973) "Technology Assessment as a Process." *International Social Science Journal* 25, 3: 247-256.

―――― (1976) "Technology Assessment in Retrospect." *Newsletter on Science, Technology and Human Values* 17, January: 17-29.

Brooks, H., and R. Bowers (1970) "The Assessment of Technology." *Scientific American* 222, 2: 13-21.

Cairns, J. (1978) *Cancer: Science and Society.* San Francisco: W. H. Freeman.

Calder, N. (1970) *Technopolis: Social Control of the Uses of Science.* New York: Simon and Schuster.

Callahan, D. (1971) "What Obligations Do We Have to Future Generations?" *American Ecclesiastical Review* 164: 265-280.

―――― (1973) *The Tyranny of Survival: And Other Pathologies of Civilized Life.* New York: Macmillan.

Cameron, J. M. (1978) "Ideology and Policy Termination: Restructuring California's Mental Health System," in J. V. May and A. B. Wildavsky, eds., *The Policy Cycle.* Beverly Hills, Calif.: Sage.

Capron, A. M. (1975) "Legal Issues in Foetal Diagnosis and Abortion," in C. Birch and P. Abrecht, eds., *Genetics and the Quality of Life.* Australia: Pergamon Press.

Carr, D. H. (1970) "Heredity and the Embryo." *Science Journal* 6: 75-79.

Carroll, C. (1974) "Ethical Issues Raised by Advances in Genetics," in I. H. Porter and R. E. Shalko, eds., *Heredity and Society.* New York: Academic Press.

Carter, C., et al. (1971) "Genetic Clinics: A Follow-up." *Lancet* 1: 281-285.

Casper, B. (1976) "Technology Policy and Democracy: Is the Proposed Science Court What We Need?" *Science* 194: 29-35.

Cavalli-Sforza, L. L. (1974) "The Genetics of Human Populations." *Scientific American* 231: 80-89.

Cavalli-Sforza, L. L., and W. Bodmer (1971) *The Genetics of Human Populations.* San Francisco: W. H. Freeman.

Cerami, A., and E. Washington (1974) *Sickle Cell Anemia.* New York: Third Press.

Chapman, J. W. (1975) "Rawls's Theory of Justice," *American Political Science Review* 69, 2: 588-593.

Childs, B. (1979) "Education in Genetics for the Medical Profession and the Public." *BSCS Journal* 2, 2: 7-8.

Childs, B.; S. Miller; and A. Bearn (1972) "Gene Mutation as a Cause of Human Disease," in H. Sutton and M. Harris, eds., *Mutagenic Effects of Environmental Con-*

tamination. New York: Academic Press.

Chulew, J. (1980) *Directory of Organizations Providing Services for Persons With Genetic or Genetically Implicated Disorders and For Their Families.* Madison: Wisconsin Clinical Genetics Center.

Chung, C. S., and N. C. Myrianthopoulus (1968) "Racial and Prenatal Factors in Major Congenital Malformations." *American Journal of Human Genetics* 20, 1: 44–60.

Coates, J. F. (1971) "Technology Assessment: The Benefits . . . The Costs . . . The Consequences." *Futurist* 5: 225–231.

—————— (1975) "Technology Assessment and Public Wisdom." *Journal of the Washington Academy of Sciences* 65: 3–12.

—————— (1978) "What is a Public Policy Issue?" in K. R. Hammond, ed., *Judgement and Decision in Public Policy Formation.* Boulder, Colo.: Westview Press.

Coates, V. T. (1972) *Technology and Public Policy: The Process of Technology Assessment in the Federal Government.* Vol. 1. Washington, D.C.: Program of Policy Studies in Science and Technology, George Washington University.

Cobb, R. W., and C. D. Elder (1972) *Participation in American Politics: The Dynamics of Agenda-Building.* Boston: Allyn and Bacon.

Coleman, J. S. (1977) "Policy Research in the Social Sciences," in *Policy Analysis on Major Issues,* prepared for the Commission on the Operation of the Senate. Washington, D.C.: Government Printing Office.

Comroe, J. H. (1978) "The Road from Research to New Diagnosis and Therapy." *Science* 200: 931–937.

Conley, R. W. (1973) *The Economics of Mental Retardation.* Baltimore: Johns Hopkins University Press.

Conley, R., and A. Milunsky (1975) "The Economics of Prenatal Genetic Diagnosis," in A. Milunsky, ed., *The Prevention of Genetic Disease and Mental Retardation.* Philadelphia: W. B. Saunders.

Cooke, R. E. (1974) "Societal Mechanisms to Cope With the Application of Advances in the New Biology," in M. Lipkin and P. Rowley, eds., *Genetic Responsibility: On Choosing Our Children's Genes.* New York: Plenum Press.

Coombs, L. C. (1977) "Preferences for Sex of Children Among U.S. Couples." *Family Planning Perspectives* 9: 259–265.

Corning, P. A. (1978) "Biopolitics: Toward a New Political Science." Paper presented to the annual meeting of the American Political Science Association, New York, August.

Crandall, B., and M. Brazier, eds. (1978) *Review of Neural Tube Defects, The Role of Alpha-fetoprotein.* New York: Academic Press.

Creasy, M. R., and J. Crolla (1974) "Prenatal Mortality of Trisomy 21." *Lancet* 1: 473–474.

Culliton, B. J. (1972) "Cooley's Anemia: Special Treatment for Another Ethnic Disease." *Science* 178: 590.

—————— (1972a) "Sickle Cell Anemia: The Route From Obscurity to Prominence." *Science* 178: 138.

—————— (1972b) "Sickle Cell Anemia: National Program Raises Problems as Well as Hopes." *Science* 178: 283–285.

_____ (1975) "Amniocentesis: HEW Backs Test for Prenatal Diagnosis of Disease." *Science* 190: 537–540.

_____ (1976) "N.S.F.: Trying to Cope with Congressional Pressure for Public Participation." *Science* 191: 274–318.

Curie-Cohen, M.; L. Luttrell; and S. Shapiro (1979) "Current Practice of Artificial Insemination by Donor in the United States." *New England Journal of Medicine* 300: 585–590.

Curran, C. E. (1973) *Politics, Medicine, and Christian Ethics: A Dialogue with Paul Ramsey.* Philadelphia: Fortress Press.

Dahl, R. A. (1967) *Pluralist Democracy in the United States.* Chicago: Rand McNally.

Daniels, M. R. (1980) "Physicians' Assistants Programs as Health Care Delivery Systems." Paper presented to annual meeting of Midwest Political Science Association, Chicago, April 23–26.

Darlington, C. D. (1969) *The Evolution of Man and Society.* London: Allen & Unwin.

Davis, B. D. (1970) "Prospects for Genetic Intervention in Man." *Science* 170: 1279–1283.

Department of Health, Education, and Welfare (1977) *Report of the Commission for the Control of Huntington's Disease and its Consequences.* Washington, D.C.: Government Printing Office.

_____ (1978) *Special Study: Implications of Advances in Biomedical and Behavioral Research.* Report to the National Commission for the Protection of Human Subjects of Biomedical and Behavioral Research. Washington, D.C.: Government Printing Office.

_____ (1978a) *Ethical Guidelines for the Delivery of Health Services by DHEW.* Washington, D.C.: Government Printing Office.

Dershowitz, A. M. (1976) "Karyotype, Predictability and Culpability," in A. Milunsky, ed., *Genetics and the Law.* New York: Plenum Press.

Devine, D.J. (1970) *The Attentive Public: Polyarchical Democracy.* Chicago: Rand McNally.

_____ (1972) *The Political Culture of the United States.* Boston: Little, Brown and Co.

Diamond, E. (1977) "Microsurgical Reconstruction of the Uterine Tube in Sterilized Patients." *Fertility and Sterility* 28, November: 1203–1211.

Dobzhansky, T. (1962) *Mankind Evolving.* New Haven, Conn.: Yale University Press.

_____ (1973) *Genetic Diversity and Human Equality.* New York: Basic Books.

Douglas, B. (1976) "The Common Good and the Public Interest." Paper presented at the American Political Science Association seminar, Northwestern University, Evanston, Ill., July.

Downs, A. (1967) *Inside Bureaucracy.* Boston: Little, Brown and Co.

Drotar, D., et al. (1975) "The Adaptation of Parents to the Birth of an Infant with a Congenital Malformation." *Pediatrics* 56: 710–717.

Duff, R. S., and A.G.M. Campbell (1973) "Moral and Ethical Dilemmas in the Special-Care Nursery." *New England Journal of Medicine* 289, October: 890–894.

Dukeminier, J. (1970) "Supplying Organs for Transplantation." *Michigan Law Review* 68, April: 811–866.

Duncan, A. S. (1974) "Scientific and Technological Development in Biology and Medicine Which May Lead to the Infringement of Human Rights," in *Protection of Human Rights in the Light of Scientific and Technological Progress in Biology and Medicine.* Geneva: World Health Organization.

Dunstan, G. R. (1973) "Moral and Social Issues Arising from A.I.D.," in CIBA Foundation Symposium No. 17, *Law and Ethics of A.I.D. and Embryo Transfer.* Amsterdam: Elsevier.

Dworkin, G. (1972) "Paternalism." *The Monist* 56, January: 64–84.

Dworkin, R. (1977) *Taking Rights Seriously.* Cambridge, Mass.: Harvard University Press.

_____ (1979) "Three Concepts of Liberalism." *New Republic,* April 14: 41–49.

Edelman, M. (1964) *The Symbolic Uses of Politics.* Urbana: University of Illinois Press.

Edwards, R. G., and P. C. Steptoe (1973) "Biological Aspects of Embryo Transfer," in CIBA Foundation Symposium No. 17, *Law and Ethics of A.I.D. and Embryo Transfer.* Amsterdam: Elsevier.

Elliot, D., and R. Elliot (1977) "Limitations of Technology Assessment," in G. Boyle, D. Elliot, and R. Roy, eds., *The Politics of Technology.* London: Open University.

Ellison, D. L. (1978) *The Bio-Medical Fix.* Westport, Conn.: Greenwood Press.

Ellul, J. (1964) *The Technological Society.* New York: Random House.

Englehardt, H. T. (1975) "Ethical Issues in Aiding the Death of Young Children," in M. Kohl, ed., *Beneficient Euthanasia.* Buffalo, N.Y.: Prometheus Books.

Erickson, J. D. (1979) "Paternal Age and Down Syndrome." *American Journal of Human Genetics* 31: 489–497.

Ethics Advisory Board (1979) *HEW Support of Research Involving Human In Vitro Fertilization and Embryo Transfer.* Washington, D.C.: Department of Health, Education, and Welfare.

Etzioni, A. (1968) "Sex Control, Science, and Society." *Science* 161: 1107–1112.

_____ (1973) *Genetic Fix: The Next Technological Revolution.* New York: Harper and Row.

_____ (1974) "Social Implications of the Use or Non-Use of New Genetic and Medical Techniques," in *Protection of Human Rights in Light of Scientific and Technological Progress in Biology and Medicine.* Geneva: World Health Organization.

Etzioni, A., and C. Nunn (1974) "Public Appreciation of Science in Contemporary America." *Daedalus* 103: 191–206.

Fanning, T. R. (1978) "Political Genetics: The Case of Genetic Screening and Counseling." Ph.D. diss., State University of New York, Binghamton.

Farrow, M. G., and R. C. Juberg (1969) "Genetics and Laws Prohibiting Marriage in the United States." *Journal of the American Medical Association* 209, 4: 534–538.

Feinberg, J. (1973) *Social Philosophy.* Englewood Cliffs, N.J.: Prentice-Hall.

_____ (1974) *Doing and Deserving: Essays on the Theory of Responsibility.* Princeton, N.J.: Princeton University Press.

Ferkiss, V. (1969) *Technological Man: The Myth and the Reality.* New York: Mentor Books.

_____ (1978) "Technology Assessment and Appropriate Technology: The Political and Moral Dimensions." *National Forum,* Fall: 3–7.

Fineberg, H. V. (1979) "Clinical Chemistries: The High Cost of Low-Cost Diagnostic Tests," in S. H. Altman and R. Blendon, eds., *Medical Technology: The Culprit Behind Health Care Costs?* Washington, D.C.: Department of Health, Education, and Welfare.

Finegold, W. J. (1976) *Artificial Insemination.* 2nd ed. Springfield, Ill.: Charles C. Thomas.

Flathman, R. E. (1966) *The Public Interest.* New York: John Wiley & Sons.

_____ (1972) *Political Obligation.* New York: Atheneum.

Fletcher, J. C. [John] (1972) "The Brink: The Parent-Child Bond in the Genetic Revolution." *Theological Studies* 33: 457–485.

_____ (1974) "Genetics, Choice and Society," in M. Lipkin and P. Rowley, eds., *Genetic Responsibility: On Choosing Our Children's Genes.* New York: Plenum Press.

_____ (1975) "Abortion, Euthanasia, and Care of Defective Newborns." *New England Journal of Medicine* 292, January: 75–78.

_____ (1978) "Prenatal Diagnosis: Ethical Issues," in *Encyclopedia of Bioethics.* New York: Macmillan.

_____ (1979) "Ethics and Amniocentesis for Fetal Sex Identification." *New England Journal of Medicine* 301, 10: 550–553.

Fletcher, J. F. [Joseph] (1954) *Morals and Medicine.* Princeton: Princeton University Press.

_____ (1966) *Situation Ethics: The New Morality.* Philadelphia: Westminster Press.

_____ (1971) "Ethical Aspects of Genetic Controls: Designed Genetic Changes in Man." *New England Journal of Medicine* 285: 776–783.

_____ (1972) "Indicators of Humanhood: A Tentative Profile of Man." *Hastings Center Report* 2, November: 1–4.

_____ (1973) "Ethics and Euthanasia." *American Journal of Nursing* 73: 78–82.

_____ (1974) *The Ethics of Genetic Control: Ending Reproductive Roulette.* New York: Doubleday & Co.

_____ (1979) *Humanhood.* Buffalo, N.Y.: Prometheus Books.

Frankel, C. (1976) "The Specter of Eugenics," in N. Ostheimer and J. Ostheimer, eds., *Life or Death — Who Controls?* New York: Springer.

Frankel, M. S. (1973) *Genetic Technology: Promises and Problems.* Washington, D.C.: Program of Policy Studies in Science and Technology, George Washington University.

_____ (1973a) *The Public Policy Dimensions of Artificial Insemination and Human Sperm Cyrobanking.* Washington, D.C.: Program of Policy Studies in Science and Technology, George Washington University.

_____ (1978) "Artificial Insemination" and "InVitro Fertilization." *Encyclopedia of Bioethics.* New York: Macmillan.

Freeman, D. M. (1974) *Technology and Society: Issues in Assessment, Conflict and Choice.* Chicago: Rand McNally.

Freund, P. A. (1977) "Mongoloids and 'Mercy Killing'," in S. J. Reiser, A. J. Dyck, and W. J. Curran, eds., *Ethics in Medicine.* Boston: M.I.T. Press.

Fried, C. (1973) "Ethical Issues in Existing and Emerging Techniques for Improving Human Fertility," in CIBA Foundation Symposium No. 17, *Law and Ethics of A.I.D. and Embryo Transfer.* Amsterdam: Elsevier.

Friedman, J. M. (1974) "Legal Implications of Amniocentesis." *University of Pennsylvania Law Review* 123: 92–156.

Funke, O. (1979) "Governing Basic Science Research: Public Policy and the Recombinant-DNA Controversy." Paper presented at the annual meeting of the American Political Science Association, Washington, D.C., August.

Furlow, T. W. (1974) "Tyranny of Technology: A Physician Looks at Euthanasia." *Humanist* 34, 4: 6–8.

Galbraith, J. K. (1967) *The New Industrial State.* Boston: Houghton Mifflin Company.

Galey, M. E. (1977) "Trends and Dimensions in International Science Policy and Organization," in J. Haberer, ed., *Science and Technology Policy.* Lexington, Mass.: Lexington Books.

Gallup, G. H. (1972) *The Gallup Poll, Vol. 3: 1959–1971.* New York: Random House.

———— (1978) *The Gallup Opinion Index,* No. 161 (December): 5.

Gaylin, W. (1975) "Scientific Research and Public Regulation." *Hastings Center Report* 5, 3: 5–7.

Gergen, K. J. (1968) "Assessing the Leverage Points in the Process of Policy Formation," in R. A. Bauer and K. J. Gergen, eds., *The Study of Policy Formation.* New York: Free Press.

Glass, B. (1972) "Eugenic Implications of the New Reproductive Technologies." *Social Biology* 19, 4: 326–336.

———— (1975) "Ethical Problems Raised by Genetics," in C. Birch and P. Albrecht, eds., *Genetics and the Quality of Life.* Australia: Pergamon Press.

Golbus, M. S. (1978) "Prenatal Diagnosis of Genetic Defects — Where it is and Where it is Going," in J. W. Littlefield and J. DeGrouchy, eds., *Birth Defects.* New York: Excerpta Medica.

Golbus, M. S., et al. (1979) "Prenatal Genetic Diagnosis in 3000 Amniocenteses." *New England Journal of Medicine* 300: 157–163.

Golding, M. P. (1968) "Ethical Issues in Biological Engineering." *UCLA Law Review* 15: 443–479.

———— (1972) "Obligations Toward Future Generations." *The Monist* 56: 85–99.

———— (1978) "Future Generations, Obligations To," in *Encyclopedia of Bioethics.* New York: Macmillan.

Gomel, V. (1977) "Tubal Reanastomosis by Microsurgery." *Fertility and Sterility* 28, January: 59–65.

Gonzales, B. (1976) "Estimate of the Number of Voluntary Sterilizations Performed 1970–75." News Release, May. Association for Voluntary Sterilization, New York.

Goodfield, J. (1977) *Playing God: Genetic Engineering and the Manipulation of Life.* New York: Random House.

Goodman, R. M. (1979) *Genetic Disorders Among the Jewish People.* Baltimore: Johns Hopkins University Press.

Gordon, T. J., and R. H. Ament (1969) *Forecasts of Some Technological Developments and Their Societal Consequences*. Middletown, Conn.: Institute for the Future.

Gottesman, I. I., and L. Erlenmeyer-Kimling (1971) "Prologue: A Foundation for Informed Eugenics." *Social Biology* 18, September: Supplement S1-S8.

Grant, M. A., and Blank, R. H. (1980) "The Medical-Legal Biopolitical Dilemma of Wrongful Life." Unpublished manuscript.

Gray, J. C. (1976) "Compulsory Sterilization in a Free Society: Choices and Dilemmas," in N. C. Ostheimer and J. M. Ostheimer, eds., *Life or Death — Who Controls?* New York: Springer.

Green, H. P. (1967) *The New Technological Era: A View From the Law*. Washington, D.C.: Program of Policy Studies in Science and Technology, George Washington University.

_____ (1973) "Mechanisms for Public Policy Decision-Making," in B. Hilton et al., eds., *Ethical Issues in Human Genetics*. New York: Plenum Press.

_____ (1976) "Law and Genetic Control: Public Policy Questions." *Annals of the New York Academy of Sciences* 265, January: 170–177.

Green, H. P., and A. M. Capron (1974) "Issues of Law and Public Policy in Genetic Screening," in D. Bergsma, ed., *Ethical, Social, and Legal Dimensions of Screening for Genetic Disease*. New York: Stratton.

Green, J. R. (1977) "Cost-Benefit Analysis of Surgery: Some Additional Caveats and Interpretations," in J. P. Bunker, B. A. Barnes, and A. F. Mosteller, eds., *Costs, Risks, and Benefits of Surgery*. New York: Oxford University Press.

Griffin, D. R. (1976) *The Question of Animal Awareness: Evolutionary Continuity of Mental Experience*. New York: Rockefeller University Press.

Grobstein, C. (1979) *A Double Image of the Double Helix: The Recombinant DNA Debate*. San Francisco: W. H. Freeman and Co.

Grosse, R. N. (1972) "Cost-Analysis of Health Service." *Annals of the American Academy of Sciences* 339: 89.

Gustafson, J. M. (1973) "Genetic Counseling and the Uses of Genetic Knowledge — An Ethical Overview," in B. Hilton et al., eds., *Ethical Issues in Human Genetics*. New York: Plenum Press.

_____ (1973a) "Genetic Engineering and the Normative View of the Human," in P. Williams, ed., *Ethical Issues in Biology and Medicine*. Cambridge, Mass.: Schenkman Publishing Company.

_____ (1973b) "Mongolism, Parental Desires and the Right to Life." *Perspectives in Biology and Medicine* 16, 4: 529–557.

_____ (1974) "Genetic Screening and Human Values," in D. Bergsma, ed., *Ethical, Social, and Legal Dimensions of Screening for Human Genetic Disease*. New York: Stratton.

Guthrie, R. (1973) "Mass Screening for Genetic Disease," in V. A. McKusick, ed., *Medical Genetics*. New York: H. P. Publishing Co.

Hadden, S. G. (1977) "Technical Advice in Policy Making: A Propositional Inventory," in J. Haberer, ed., *Science and Technology Policy*. Lexington, Mass.: Lexington Books.

Hagard, S.; F. Carter; and R. Milne (1974) "Screening for Spina Bifida Cystica: A Cost-Benefit Analysis." *British Journal of Preventive Social Medicine* 130: 40–53.

Hanft, R. (1977) Testimony before Senate Subcommittee on Health and Scientific

Research, in T. M. Powledge and L. Dachs, eds., *Biomedical Research and the Public*. Washington, D.C.: Government Printing Office.

Hansen, H.; A. Shahidi; and Z. A. Stein (1978) "Screening for Phenylketonuria in New York City: Threshold Values Reconsidered." *Public Health Reports* 93, 3: 246–251.

Hardin, G. (1972) *Exploring New Ethics for Survival: The Voyage of the Spaceship Beagle*. New York: Viking Press.

———— (1974) "The Moral Threat of Personal Medicine," in M. Lipkin and P. Rowley, eds., *Genetic Responsibility: On Choosing Our Children's Genes*. New York: Plenum Press.

Hare, R. M. (1976) "Survival of the Weakest," in S. Gorovitz et al., eds., *Moral Problems in Medicine*. Englewood Cliffs, N.J.: Prentice-Hall.

Häring, B. (1975) *Ethics of Manipulation: Issues in Medicine, Behavior Control and Genetics*. New York: Seabury Press.

Harris, H. (1975) *Prenatal Diagnosis and Selective Abortion*. Cambridge, Mass.: Harvard University Press.

Harsanyi, J. C. (1975) "Can the Maximin Principle Serve as a Basis for Morality." *American Political Science Review* 65, 2: 594–606.

Hastings Center (1980) "H.E.W. to Cut Off Funding for Ethics Advisory Board." *Hastings Center Report* 10, February: 2.

Heim, W. G. (1975) "Moral and Legal Decisions in Reproductive and Genetic Engineering," in T. R. Mertens, ed., *Human Genetics: Readings on the Implications of Genetic Engineering*. New York: John Wiley & Sons.

Hellberg, J. (1974) Discussant in *Protection of Human Rights in Light of Scientific and Technological Progress in Biology and Medicine*. Geneva: World Health Organization.

Hellegers, A. E., and R. A. McCormick (1978) "Unanswered Questions on Test Tube Life." *America* 139, 4: 75–78.

Heller, J. H. (1973) "Human Chromosome Abnormalities as Related to Physical and Mental Dysfunction," in J. B. Bresler, ed., *Genetics and Society*. Reading, Mass.: Addison-Wesley.

Hetman, F. (1977) "Technology on Trial," in G. Boyle, E. Elliot, and R. Roy, eds., *The Politics of Technology*. London: Open University.

Hirschhorn, K. (1976) "Practical and Ethical Problems in Human Genetics," in J. M. Humber and R. F. Almeder, eds., *Biomedical Ethics and the Law*. New York: Plenum Press.

Holtzman, N. A.; D. W. Welcher; and E. D. Mellitis (1975) "Termination of Restricted Diet in Children with Phenylketonuria: A Randomized Controlled Study." *New England Journal of Medicine* 293: 1121–1124.

Hook, E. B., and A. Lindsjö (1978) "Down Syndrome in Live Births by Single Year Maternal Age Interval in a Swedish Study: Comparison with Results from a New York State Study." *American Journal of Human Genetics* 30: 19.

Howard, T., and J. Rifkin (1977) *Who Should Play God?* New York: Dell Publishing Company.

Hsia, D. Y., and N. A. Holtzman (1973) "A Critical Evaluation of PKU Screening," in V. A. McKusick, ed., *Medical Genetics*. New York: H. P. Publishing Co.

Hsia, Y. E., et al. (1979) *Counseling in Genetics*. New York: Alan R. Liss.

Hubbard, R. (1980) "Test-Tube Babies: Solution or Problem?" *Technology Review,* March-April: 10–12.

Huddle, F. P. (1972) "The Social Function of Technology Assessment," in R. G. Kasper, ed., *Technology Assessment: Understanding the Social Consequences of Technological Applications.* New York: Praeger.

Huxley, A. (1932) *Brave New World.* New York: Harper and Row.

Iizuka, R., et al. (1968) "The Physical and Mental Development of Children Born Following Artificial Insemination." *International Journal of Fertility* 13: 24–32.

Ingle, D. J. (1970) "The Ethics of Biomedical Interventions." *Perspectives in Biology and Medicine* 13, Spring: 364–387.

———— (1973) *Who Should Have Children?* Indianapolis, Ind.: Bobbs-Merrill.

Inman, R. P. (1978) "On the Benefits and Costs of Genetic Screening." *American Journal of Human Genetics* 30: 219–223.

Iverson, M. (1978) Personal conversation. August 4, Palo Alto, California.

Jackson, D. A., and S. P. Stich, eds. (1979) *The Recombinant DNA Debate.* Englewood Cliffs, N.J.: Prentice-Hall.

Jacobs, P. A., et al. (1965) "Aggressive Behavior, Mental Sub-normality and the XYY Male." *Nature* 208: 1351–1352.

Jaros, D. (1973) *Socialization to Politics.* New York: Praeger.

Jasper, H. N. (1974) "Congressional Interest in the Ethical Problems of Biomedical Technology," in M. Lipkin and P. Rowley, eds., *Genetic Responsibility: On Choosing Our Children's Genes.* New York: Plenum Press.

Jones, M. V. (1971) *A Technology Assessment Methodology.* 7 vols. Vol. 1: *Some Basic Propositions.* Washington, D.C.: MITRE Corporation.

Kaback, M. M., and J. S. O'Brien (1973) "Tay-Sachs: Prototype for Prevention of Genetic Disease," in V. A. McKusick, ed., *Medical Genetics.* New York: H. P. Publishing Co.

Kaback, M. M., and R. S. Zeiger (1973) "The John F. Kennedy Institute Tay-Sachs Program: Practical and Ethical Issues in an Adult Genetic Screening Program," in B. Hilton et al., eds., *Ethical Issues in Human Genetics.* New York: Plenum Press.

Kaback, M. M.; M. H. Becker; and M. V. Ruth (1974) "Sociologic Studies in Human Genetics: I. Compliance Factors in a Voluntary Heterozygote Screening Program," in D. Bergsma, ed., *Ethical, Social, and Legal Dimensions of Screening for Human Genetic Disease.* New York: Stratton.

Kan, Y. W., and A. M. Dozy (1978) "Antenatal Diagnosis of Sickle-Cell Anemia by D.N.A. Analysis of Amniotic Fluid Cells." *Lancet* 1: 910–912.

Kaplan, M. B. (1975) "The Case of the Artificial Heart Panel." *Hastings Center Report* 5, 5: 41–48.

Karp, L. E. (1976) *Genetic Engineering: Threat or Promise?* Chicago: Nelson Hall.

Kass, L. R. (1971) "The New Biology: What Price Relieving Man's Estate?" *Science* 174: 779–788.

———— (1972) "Making Babies—the New Biology and the 'Old' Morality." *Public Interest* 26, Winter: 18–56.

———— (1972a) "New Beginnings in Life," in M. Hamilton, ed., *The New Genetics and the Future of Man.* Grand Rapids, Mich.: William Eerdmans.

———— (1976) "Implications of Prenatal Diagnosis For the Human Right to Life," in J. M. Humber and R. F. Almeder, eds., *Biomedical Ethics and the Law*. New York: Plenum Press.

Kennedy, I. M. (1976) "The Karen Quinlan Case: Problems and Proposals." *Journal of Medical Ethics* 2, March: 3–7.

Kershaw, J. D. (1973) *Handicapped Children*. London: William Heinemann Medical Books.

Kieffer, G. H. (1975) *Ethical Issues in the Life Sciences*. New York: American Association for the Advancement of Science.

———— (1979) *Bioethics: A Textbook of Issues*. Reading, Mass.: Addison-Wesley.

Kindig, D. A., and V. Sidel (1973) "Social and Scientific Priorities: Process and Content," in B. Hilton and D. Callahan, eds., *Ethical Issues in Human Genetics*. New York: Plenum Press.

King, M. C., and A. C. Wilson (1975) "Evolution at Two Levels: Molecular Similarities and Biological Differences Between Humans and Chimpanzees." *Science* 188: 107–116.

Kotulak, R. (1980) "Scientific Gains Being Used Against Women, Panel Says." *Chicago Tribune*, January 7, Section 1: 3.

LaPorte, T., and D. Metlay (1975) "Technology Observed: Attitudes of a Wary Public." *Science* 188, April 11: 121–127.

Lappé, M. (1972) "Moral Obligations and the Fallacies of 'Genetic Control'." *Theological Studies* 33, September: 411–427.

———— (1973) "Human Genetics." *Annals of the New York Academy of Sciences* 216, May: 152–159.

———— (1976) "Reflections on the Cost of Doing Science." *Annals of the New York Academy of Sciences* 265, January: 102–109.

———— (1979) *Genetic Politics: The Limits of Biological Control*. New York: Simon and Schuster.

Lappé, M., and R. O. Roblin (1974) "Newborn Genetic Screening as a Concept in Health Care Delivery: A Critique," in D. Bergsma, ed., *Ethical, Social, and Legal Dimensions of Screening for Human Genetic Disease*. New York: Stratton.

Lappé, M., et al. (1972) "Ethical and Social Issues in Screening for Genetic Disease." *New England Journal of Medicine* 286: 1129–1132.

Largey, G. (1972) "Sex Control, Sex Preferences, and the Future of the Family." *Social Biology* 19, 4: 379–392.

———— (1979) "Reversible Sterilization: Socio-ethical Considerations." *Social Biology* 25, 2: 135–144.

Layde, P. M., et al. (1979) "Maternal Serum Alpha-Fetoprotein Screening: A Cost-Benefit Analysis." *American Journal of Public Health* 69, 6: 566–572.

Leach, G. (1970) *The Biocrats*. New York: McGraw-Hill.

Lebacqz, K. A. (1973) "Prenatal Diagnosis and Selective Abortion." *Linacre Quarterly* 40: 109–127.

Lebel, R. R. (1978) "Ethical Issues Arising in the Genetic Counseling Relationship," in *Birth Defects: Original Article Series* 14, 9. New York: The National Foundation, March of Dimes.

Lederberg, J. (1966) "Experimental Genetics and Human Evolution." *American Naturalist* 100: 519–526.

———— (1972) "Biological Innovation and Genetic Intervention," in J. A. Behnke, ed., *Challenging Biological Problems*. New York: Oxford University Press.

Lejeune, J. (1970) "On the Nature of Men." *American Journal of Human Genetics* 22, March: 121–128.

Lerner, I. M., and W. J. Libby (1968) *Heredity, Evolution and Society*. San Francisco: W. H. Freeman and Company.

Levin, L. S. (1976) "Developmental Disabilities: Educating the Public," in D. Bergsma and A. E. Pulver, eds., *Developmental Disabilities: Psychologic and Social Implications*. New York: Alan R. Liss.

Levitan, M. (1977) *Textbook of Human Genetics*. 2nd ed. New York: Oxford University Press.

Lewis, C. S. (1965) *The Abolition of Man*. New York: Collier-Macmillan.

Lipkin, M., and P. Rowley (1974) "Choosing Our Children's Genes: On the Need to Learn How People Choose," in M. Lipkin and P. Rowley, eds., *Genetic Responsibility: On Choosing Our Children's Genes*. New York: Plenum Press.

Lorber, J. (1974) "Selective Treatment of Myelomeningocele: To Treat or Not to Treat." *Pediatrics* 53, March: 307–308.

Lowi, T. J. (1969) *The End of Liberalism*. New York: W. W. Norton.

Lubs, H. A. (1976) "Privacy and Genetic Information," in J. M. Humber and R. F. Almeder, eds., *Biomedical Ethics and the Law*. New York: Plenum Press.

Ludmerer, K. M. (1972) *Genetics and American Society*. Baltimore: Johns Hopkins University Press.

McCormick, R. A. (1974) "To Save or Let Die: The Dilemma of Modern Medicine." *Journal of the American Medical Association* 229, July: 172–176.

MacCready, R. A. (1974) "Admissions of Phenylketonuria Patients to Residential Institutions Before and After Screening Programs of the Newborn Infant." *Journal of Pediatrics* 85: 383–385.

McDonald, L. C. (1978) "Three Forms of Political Ethics." *Western Political Quarterly* 31, 1: 7–18.

McInerney, J. D. (1979) "Human Genetics Education: Background and Rationale," *BSCS Journal* 2, 2: 2–6.

McIntosh, W., and H. Alston (1977) "Review of the Polls: Acceptance of Abortion Among White Catholics and Protestants, 1962 and 1975." *Journal of the Scientific Study of Religion* 16: 295.

McKusick, V. (1978) *Mendelian Inheritance in Man*. Baltimore: Johns Hopkins University Press.

McLaren, A. (1973) "Biological Aspects of A.I.D.," in CIBA Foundation Symposium No. 17, *Law and Ethics of A.I.D. and Embryo Transfer*. Amsterdam: Elsevier.

Marcuse, H. (1964) *One Dimensional Man*. Boston: Beacon Press.

Margolin, C. R. (1979) "Attitudes Toward Control and Elimination of Genetic Defects." *Social Biology* 25, 1: 33–37.

Marston, R. Q. (1978) "Influence of NIH Policy Past and Present on the University Health Education Complex," in H. H. Fudenberg and V. L. Melnik, eds.,

Biomedical Scientists and Public Policy. New York: Plenum Press.

Martin, M. B. (1978) "Test Tube Morality." *National Review,* October 13: 1285.

Maryland (1978) Annotated Code of Maryland, 1978 Cumulative Supplement. Art. 43, Sec. 814-821.

Massachusetts Department of Health (1974) "Cost-Benefit Analysis of Newborn Screening for Metabolic Disorders." *New England Journal of Medicine* 291: 1414-1416.

Matthews, D. R., and J. A. Stimson (1975) *Yeas and Nays: Normal Decision-Making in the U.S. House of Representatives.* New York: John Wiley & Sons.

May, J. V., and A. B. Wildavsky (1979) *The Policy Cycle.* Beverly Hills, Calif.: Sage.

Mayr, E. (1967) "Biological Man and the Year 2000." *Daedalus* 96, Summer: 832–837.

Medawar, P. B. (1969) "The Genetic Improvement of Man." *Australasian Annals of Medicine* 4: 317–320.

Meyerowitz, S., and M. Lipkin (1976) "Psychological Aspects," in *Prevention of Embryonic, Fetal and Perinatal Disease.* Washington, D.C.: Government Printing Office.

Michels, R. (1949) *Political Parties.* Glencoe, Ill.: Free Press.

Mill, J. S. (1863) *Utilitarianism.* London: Longman.

Miller, W. G. (1974) "Reproduction Technology and the Behavioral Sciences." *Science* 183: 149.

Mills, C. W. (1959) *The Power Elite.* New York: Galaxy.

Milunsky, A. (1973) *The Prenatal Diagnosis of Hereditary Disorders.* Springfield, Ill.: Charles C. Thomas.

_____ (1975) *The Prevention of Genetic Disease and Mental Retardation.* Philadelphia: W. B. Saunders.

_____ (1976) "Medico-Legal Issues in Prenatal Genetic Diagnosis," in A. Milunsky and G. Annas, eds., *Genetics and the Law.* New York: Plenum Press.

_____ (1977) *Know Your Genes.* Boston: Houghton-Mifflin.

Milunsky, A., and L. Atkins (1975) "Prenatal Diagnosis of Genetic Disorders," in A. Milunsky, ed., *The Prevention of Genetic Disease and Mental Retardation.* Philadelphia: W. B. Saunders.

Morison, R. (1976) "Closing Remarks." *Annals of the New York Academy of Sciences* 265, January: 206–208.

Muller, H. J. (1959) "The Guidance of Human Evolution." *Perspectives in Biology and Medicine* 3, 1: 1–43.

_____ (1961) "Human Evolution by Voluntary Choice of Germ Plasm." *Science* 134: 643–649.

_____ (1973) "The Radiation Danger," in E. A. Carlson, ed., *Man's Future Birthright.* Albany: State University of New York Press.

Murphy, E. A.; G. Chase; and A. Rodriguez (1978) "Genetic Intervention: Some Social, Psychological, and Philosophical Aspects," in B. H. Cohen et al., eds., *Genetic Issues in Public Health and Medicine.* Springfield, Ill.: Charles C. Thomas.

Murray, R. F. (1976) Panel discussion in *Annals of the New York Academy of Sciences* 265, January: 163–166.

_____ (1978) "Public Health Perspectives on Screening and Problems in Counseling in Sickle Cell Anemia," in B. H. Cohen et al., eds., *Genetic Issues in Public Health and Medicine.* Springfield, Ill.: Charles C. Thomas.

_____ (1979) Lecture to the American Association for the Advancement of Science Seminar on "Genetics and Society."

Nagel, T. (1975) "Libertarianism Without Foundation." *Yale Law Journal* 85: 136–149.

National Academy of Sciences (1975) *Genetic Screening: Programs, Principles, and Research.* Washington, D.C.: National Academy of Sciences.

_____ (1975a) *Assessing Biomedical Technologies: An Inquiry into the Nature of the Process.* Washington, D.C.: National Science Foundation.

National Center for Health Statistics (1978) *Facts of Life and Death.* Washington, D.C.: Department of Health, Education, and Welfare.

National Institutes of Health (1977) *Report of the Commission for the Control of Huntington's Disease and Its Consequences.* Washington, D.C.: Department of Health, Education, and Welfare.

_____ (1979) *Antenatal Diagnosis: Predictors of Hereditary Disease or Congenital Defects.* Washington, D.C.: Department of Health, Education, and Welfare.

National Research Council (1975) *Decision Making for Regulating Chemicals in the Environment,* Report of the Committee on Principles of Decision Making for Regulating Chemicals in the Environment. Washington, D.C.: National Academy of Sciences.

Neel, J. V. (1970) "Lessons from a Primitive People." *Science* 170: 815–822.

_____ (1973) "Social and Scientific Priorities in the Use of Genetic Knowledge," in B. Hilton and D. Callahan, eds., *Ethical Issues in Human Genetics.* New York: Plenum Press.

Neel, J. V., and A. D. Bloom (1977) "The Detection of Environmental Mutagens," in A. S. Baer, ed., *Heredity and Society.* New York: Macmillan.

Nelkin, D. (1977) "Technology and Public Policy," in I. Spiegel-Rösing and D. deSolla Price, eds., *Science, Technology, and Society.* Beverly Hills, Calif.: Sage.

_____ (1977a) "Trends in Science Policy: The Search for Controls," in J. Haberer, ed., *Science and Technology Policy.* Lexington, Mass.: Lexington Books.

_____ (1977b) "Thoughts on the Proposed Science Court." *Newsletter on Science, Technology and Human Values* 19, January: 20–31.

Nelson, B. J. (1978) "Setting the Public Agenda: The Case of Child Abuse," in J. V. May and A. B. Wildavsky, eds., *The Policy Cycle.* Beverly Hills, Calif.: Sage.

Nelson, W. B.; J. M. Swint; and C. T. Caskey (1978) "An Economic Evaluation of a Genetic Screening Program for Tay-Sachs Disease." *American Journal of Human Genetics* 30: 160–166.

Neuhauser, D. (1977) "Cost-Effective Clinical Decision Making: Implications for Delivery of Health Services," in J. P. Bunker, B. A. Barnes, and F. Mosteller, eds., *Costs, Risks, and Benefits of Surgery.* New York: Oxford University Press.

NICHD National Registry for Amniocentesis Study Group (1976) "Midtrimester Amniocentesis for Prenatal Diagnosis: Safety and Accuracy." *Journal of the American Medical Association* 236: 1471–1476.

Nitowsky, H. M. (1973) "Prescriptive Screening for Metabolic Disorders." *New*

England Journal of Medicine 28: 1299–1300.

Nozick, R. (1974) *Anarchy, State and Utopia.* New York: Basic Books.

Nyhan, W. L., and E. Edelson (1976) *The Heredity Factor: Genes, Chromosomes, and You.* New York: Grosset and Dunlap.

Office of Technology Assessment (1976) *Development of Medical Technology: Opportunities for Assessment.* Washington, D.C.: Government Printing Office.

———— (1978) *Assessing the Efficacy and Safety of Medical Technologies.* Washington, D.C.: Government Printing Office.

Olson, M. (1965) *The Logic of Collective Action: Public Goods and the Theory of Groups.* Cambridge, Mass.: Harvard University Press.

Ostheimer, J. M. (1979) "Euthanasia: Dimensions of a Growing Political Issue." Paper presented at the Western Political Science Association meeting, March 29–31, Portland, Oregon.

Ostheimer, J. M., and L. G. Ritt (1976) "Life and Death: Current Public Attitudes," in N. Ostheimer and J. M. Ostheimer, eds., *Life or Death — Who Controls?* New York: Springer.

Pancheri, L. U. (1978) "Genetic Technology: Policy Decisions and Democratic Principles," in J. J. Buckley, ed., *Genetics Now: Ethical Issues in Genetic Research.* Washington, D.C.: University Press of America.

Panel on Technology Assessment (1969) *Technology: Processes of Assessment and Choice.* Washington, D.C.: National Academy of Sciences.

Parfit, D. (1976) "Rights, Interests, and Possible People," in S. Gorovitz et al., eds., *Moral Problems in Medicine.* Englewood Cliffs, N.J.: Prentice-Hall.

Pauling, L. (1968) "Reflections on the New Biology." *UCLA Law Review* 15, 3: 267–272.

Peter, W. G. (1975) "Ethical Perspectives in the Use of Genetic Knowledge," in T. R. Mertens, ed., *Human Genetics: Readings on the Implications of Genetic Engineering.* New York: John Wiley & Sons.

Piattelli-Palmarini, M. (1973) "Biological Roots of the Human Individual," in CIBA Foundation Symposium No. 17, *Law and Ethics of A.I.D. and Embryo Transfer.* Amsterdam: Elsevier.

Pliskin, N., and A. K. Taylor (1977) "General Principles: Cost-Benefit and Decision Analysis," in J. P. Bunker, B. A. Barnes, and F. Mosteller, eds., *Costs, Risks, and Benefits of Surgery.* New York: Oxford University Press.

Pole, J. D. (1971) "The Cost-Effectiveness of Screening." *Procedures of the Royal Society of Medicine* 64: 1256.

Portnoy, B. (1970) "The Role of the Courts in Technology Assessment." *Cornell Law Review* 55: 861.

Powledge, T. M. (1974) "Genetic Screening as a Political and Social Development," in D. Bergsma, ed., *Ethical, Social, and Legal Dimensions of Screening for Human Genetic Disease.* New York: Stratton.

———— (1979) "Prenatal Diagnosis: New Techniques, New Questions." *Hastings Center Report* 9, 3: 16–17.

Powledge, T. M., and L. Dach, eds. (1977) *Biomedical Research and the Public.* Report prepared for the Senate Subcommittee on Health and Scientific Research. Washington, D.C.: Government Printing Office.

Powledge, T. M., and J. F. Fletcher (1979) "Guidelines for the Ethical, Social, and Legal Issues in Prenatal Diagnosis: A Report from the Genetics Research Group of the Hastings Center." *New England Journal of Medicine* 300: 168–172.

Purdy, L. M. (1978) "Genetic Diseases: Can Having Children Be Immoral?" in J. J. Buckley, ed., *Genetics Now: Ethical Issues in Genetic Research*. Washington, D. C.: University Press of America.

Pyeritz, R., et al. (1977) "The XYY Male: Making of a Myth," in *Biology as a Social Weapon*. Minneapolis: Burgess.

Ramsey, P. (1970) *Fabricated Man: The Ethics of Genetic Control*. New Haven: Yale University Press.

———— (1972) "Shall We 'Reproduce'? I. The Medical Ethics of In Vitro Fertilization." *Journal of the American Medical Association* 220, 10: 1346–1350.

———— (1975) *The Ethics of Fetal Research*. New Haven: Yale University Press.

———— (1978) *Ethics at the Edges of Life: Medical and Legal Intersections*. New Haven: Yale University Press.

Rawls, J. (1971) *A Theory of Justice*. Cambridge: Harvard University Press.

Ray, D. (1974) "Membership Stability in Three State Legislatures: 1893–1969." *American Political Science Review* 68, March: 106–112.

Reed, S. C., and V. E. Anderson (1973) "Effects of Changing Sexuality in the Gene Pool," in F. de la Cruz and G. Laveck, eds., *Human Sexuality and the Mentally Retarded*. New York: Brunner/Mazel.

Reilly, P. (1975) "Genetic Screening Legislation," in H. Harris and K. Hirschhorn, eds., *Advances in Human Genetics*. Vol. 5. New York: Plenum Press.

————(1977) *Genetics, Law and Social Policy*. Cambridge: Harvard University Press.

———— (1978) "Government Support of Genetic Services." *Social Biology* 25, 1: 23–32.

Restak, R. M. (1975) *Premeditated Man: Bioethics and the Control of Future Human Life*. New York: Penguin Books.

Reyzer, N. (1978) "Diagnosis: PKU." *American Journal of Nursing,* November: 1895–1898.

Riccardi, V. M. (1976) "Health Care and Disease Prevention Through Genetic Counseling: A Regional Approach." *American Journal of Public Health* 66, March: 268–272.

Rice, C. E. (1969) *The Vanishing Right to Live: An Appeal for a Renewed Reverence for Life*. Garden City, N.J.: Doubleday and Company.

Robbins, F. C. (1979) "Assessing the Consequences of Biomedical Research," in S. H. Altman and R. Blendon, eds., *Medical Technology: The Culprit Behind Health Care Costs?* Washington, D.C.: Department of Health, Education, and Welfare.

Robertson, J. A. (1975) "Involuntary Euthanasia of Defective Newborns: A Legal Analysis." *Stanford Law Review* 27, January: 213–267.

Rogers, E. (1962) *Diffusion of Innovation*. New York: Free Press.

Rorvik, D. (1978) *In His Image: The Cloning of a Man*. Philadelphia: Lippincott.

Rosenfeld, A. (1977) "An Early-Alert Task Force for the Public," in T. M. Powledge and L. Dach, eds., *Biomedical Research and the Public*. Washington: Government Printing Office.

_____ (1978) "The Case for Test-Tube Babies." *Saturday Review,* October 28: 10–14.

Rosenthal, A. (1974) "Turnover in State Legislatures." *American Journal of Political Science* 18, August: 609–616.

Rosenthal, G. (1977) "Anticipating the Costs and Benefits of New Technology: A Typology for Policy," in J. P. Bunker, B. A. Barnes, and F. Mosteller, eds., *Costs, Risks, and Benefits in Surgery.* New York: Oxford University Press.

Rothman, S. (1977) "Sterilizing the Poor." *Society* 14: 36–41.

Salisbury, R. H., ed. (1970) *Interest Group Politics in America.* New York: Harper & Row.

Scammon, R. M., and B. J. Wattenberg (1970) *The Real Majority.* New York: Coward-McCann.

Scheflin, A. W., and E. M. Upton (1978) *The Mind Manipulators.* New York: Paddington Press.

Schmandt, J. (1977) "Science Policy: One Step Forward, Two Steps Back," in J. Haberer, ed., *Science and Technology Policy.* Lexington, Mass.: Lexington Books.

Schoenberg, B. (1979) "Science and Anti-Science in Confrontation." *Man and Medicine* 4, 2: 79–102.

Schrag, P. (1978) *Mind Control.* New York: Pantheon Books.

Scriver, C. R., and C. L. Clow (1979) "On Caravans Passing and Dogs Barking in the Desert of Illiteracy in Human Genetics." *BSCS Journal* 2, 2: 9–10.

Selle, H. F.; D. W. Holmes; and M. L. Ingbar (1979) "The Growing Demand for Midtrimester Amniocentesis: A Systems Approach to Forecasting the Need for Facilities." *American Journal of Public Health* 69, 6: 574–580.

Severo, R. (1980) "The Genetic Barrier: Job Benefit or Job Bias?" *New York Times,* February 6.

Shaw, A. (1973) "Dilemmas of 'Informed Consent' in Children." *New England Journal of Medicine* 289, October: 885–890.

Sherman, J. K. (1973) "Synopsis of the Use of Frozen Human Semen Since 1964: State of the Art of Human Semen Banking." *Fertility and Sterility* 24: 397–412.

Shick, A. (1977) "Complex Policy Making in the United States Senate," in *Policy Analysis on Major Issues,* prepared for the Commission on the Operation of the Senate. Washington, D.C.: Government Printing Office.

Shinn, R. L. (1974) "Ethical Issues in Genetic Choices," in M. Lipkin and P. Rowley, eds., *Genetic Responsibility: On Choosing Our Children's Genes.* New York: Plenum Press.

Silber, S. (1977) "Vasectomy Reversal." *New England Journal of Medicine* 296, April: 886–887.

Singer, D. M. (1974) "Judicial Roles in Genetic Decision-Making," in M. Lipkin and P. Rowley, eds., *Genetic Responsibility: On Choosing Our Children's Genes.* New York: Plenum Press.

Sinsheimer, R. L. (1973) "Prospects for Future Scientific Development: Ambush or Opportunity," in B. Hilton et al., eds., *Ethical Issues in Human Genetics.* New York: Plenum Press.

_____ (1978) "The Presumptions of Science," *Daedalus* 107, Spring: 23–36.

Smith, G. F., and J. M. Berg (1976) *Down's Anomaly.* 2nd ed. London: Churchill-Livingstone.

Sonneborn, T. M. (1973) "Ethical Issues Arising from the Possible Uses of Genetic Knowledge," in B. Hilton and D. Callahan, eds., *Ethical Issues in Human Genetics.* New York: Plenum Press.

Sorenson, J. R. (1974) "Some Social and Psychologic Issues in Genetic Screening," in D. Bergsma, ed., *Ethical, Social and Legal Dimensions of Screening for Human Genetic Disease.* New York: Stratton.

———— (1975) "Social Aspects of Applied Genetics," in T. R. Mertens, ed., *Human Genetics: Readings on the Implications of Genetic Engineering.* New York: John Wiley & Sons.

Soskin, R. (1977) "Voluntary Sterilization: Safeguarding the Freedom of Choice." *Amicus* 2, February: 40–44.

Spilhaus, A. (1972) "Ecolibrium." *Science* 175: 711–715.

Spriggs, E. (1974) "Involuntary Sterilization: An Unconstitutional Menace to Minorities and the Poor." *New York University Review of Law and Sociological Change* 4, Spring: 127–151.

Stein, Z., and M. Susser (1978) "Epidemiologic and Genetic Issues in Mental Retardation," in N. Morton, ed., *Genetic Epidemiology.* New York: Academic Press.

Steiner, K. C., and H. A. Smith (1975) "Survey of Departments of Health About PKU Screening Programs." *Public Health Reports* 90, 1: 52–54.

Steinfels, P. (1974) "Individualism — No Exit." *Hastings Center Study* 2, 3: 1–10.

Stencel, S. (1977) "Abortion Politics," in *National Health Issues.* Washington, D.C.: Congressional Quarterly.

Stevenson, A. C., et al. (1977) *Genetic Counseling.* 2nd ed. Philadelphia: Lippincott.

Stine, G. J. (1977) *Biosocial Genetics: Human Heredity and Social Issues.* New York: Macmillan.

Strickland, S. P. (1972) *Politics, Science, and Dread Disease: A Short History of U.S. Medical Research Policy.* Cambridge: Harvard University Press.

Swanson, T. E. (1970) "Economics of Mongolism." *Annals of the New York Academy of Sciences* 171: 679–682.

Swazey, J. P. (1971) "Phenylketonuria: A Case Study in Biomedical Legislation." *Journal of Urban Law* 48: 883.

Swint, J. M., et al. (1979) "The Economic Returns to Community and Hospital Screening Programs for a Genetic Disease." *Preventive Medicine* 8: 463–470.

Task Force of the Presidential Advisory Group on Anticipated Advances in Science and Technology (1976) "The Science Court Experiment: An Interim Report." *Science* 193: 653–656.

Thomas, L. (1971) "The Technology of Medicine." *New England Journal of Medicine* 285: 1366–1368.

Thompson, M., and A. Milunsky (1979) "Policy Analysis for Prenatal Genetic Diagnosis." *Public Policy* 27, 1: 25–48.

Toffler, A. (1970) *Future Shock.* New York: Random House.

Tooley, M. (1972) "Abortion and Infanticide." *Philosophy and Public Affairs* 2, 1: 37–65.

Tribe, L. H. (1973) "Technology Assessment and the Fourth Discontinuity: The Limits of Instrumental Rationality." *Southern California Law Review* 46, June: 617–660.

_____ (1973a) *Channeling Technology Through Law.* Chicago: Bracton Press.

Truman, D. B. (1971) *The Governmental Process.* 2nd ed. New York: Alfred A. Knopf.

Tünte, N. (1975) "Sociogenetic Problems and Public Opinion," in C. Birch and P. Albrecht, eds., *Genetics and the Quality of Life.* Australia: Pergamon Press.

Twiss, S. B. (1974) "Ethical Issues in Genetic Screeing: Models of Genetic Responsibility," in D. Bergsma, ed., *Ethical, Social, and Legal Dimensions of Screening for Human Genetic Disease.* New York: Stratton.

_____ (1976) "Ethical Issues in Priority-Setting for Utilization of Genetic Technologies." *Annals of the New York Academy of Sciences* 265: 22–45 and 166–167.

Ulrich, L. P. (1976) "Reproductive Rights and Genetic Disease," in J. M. Humber and R. F. Almeder, eds., *Biomedical Ethics and the Law.* New York: Plenum Press.

Van, J. (1979) "Plug to Be Tested for Birth Control." *Chicago Tribune,* December 16, Section 1: 16.

Van Der Slik, J. R. (1977) *American Legislative Process.* New York: Thomas Y. Crowell.

Veatch, R. M. (1975) "Human Experimentation Committees." *Hastings Center Report* 5, 5: 31–40.

_____ (1976) *Death, Dying, and the Biological Revolution.* New Haven: Yale University Press.

Verba, S., and N. H. Nie (1972) *Participation in America.* New York: Harper & Row.

Verner, J. G., and T. Zins (1980) "Dimensions of Public Health Policy with Special Reference to Political Responsiveness to Public Health Care Conditions Among the American States." Paper presented to the annual meeting of the Midwest Political Science Association, Chicago, April 23–26.

Vukowich, W. T. (1971) "The Dawning of the Brave New World—Legal, Ethical, and Social Issues of Eugenics." *University of Illinois Law Forum* 1971: 189–231.

Wald, P. M. (1975) "Basic Personal and Civil Rights: Principal Paper," in President's Committee on Mental Retardation, *The Mentally Retarded Citizen and the Law.* New York: Free Press.

Walters, L. (1978) "Technology: Technology Assessment," in *Encyclopedia of Bioethics.* New York: Macmillan.

_____ (1978a) "Technology Assessment and Genetics," in H. H. Fudenberg and V. L. Melnik, eds., *Biomedical Scientists and the Public.* New York: Plenum Press.

_____ (1979) "Human InVitro Fertilization: A Review of the Ethical Literature." *Hastings Center Report* 9, 4: 23–43.

Watson, J. D. (1971) "Moving Toward Clonal Man: Is This What We Want?" *Atlantic* 227: 50–53.

_____ (1973) "Children from the Laboratory." *Prism,* May: 13ff.

Weinberg, A. M. (1972) "Can Technology Replace Social Engineering?" in A. H. Teich, ed., *Technology and Man's Future.* New York: St. Martin's Press.

Westoff, C. F. (1976) "Trends in Contraceptive Practices: 1965–1973." *Family Plan-*

ning Perspectives 8: 54–57.

Westoff, C. F., and R. R. Rindfuss (1974) "Sex Preselection in the United States: Some Implications." *Science* 184: 633–636.

White, E. (1972) "Genetic Diversity and Political Life: Toward a Populational-Interaction Paradigm." *Journal of Politics* 34: 1203–1242.

Williams, G. (1958) "'Mercy Killing' Legislation: A Rejoinder." *Minnesota Law Review* 43, 1: 1–12.

Williams, R. (1977) "The More Effective Political Control of Technical Change," in G. Boyle, D. Elliot, and R. Roy, eds., *The Politics of Technology*. London: Open University.

Williamson, F. (1969) "Population Pollution," *Bioscience* 19: 979–983.

Witkin, H. A., et al. (1976) "Criminality in XYY and XXY Men." *Science* 193: 547–555.

Wright, R. G. (1977) "The High Cost of Rawls' Inegalitarianism." *Western Political Quarterly* 30, 1: 73–79.

Index